Impact Standards

Designing District Systems That Power K12 Learning

By Jeffrey D. Bradbury

Impact Standards

Designing District Systems That Power K12 Learning

Published: March 2026

ISBN: 979-8-218-92746-2

Published by TeacherCast Educational Network Publishing

Bethel, Connecticut

www.TeacherCast.net

Scan to unlock your Impact Standards Toolkit. Access the templates, checklists, and resources designed to help you simplify your systems and amplify your impact.

Testimonials

Allison Petersen

Instructional Coach & Founder of the #NewtoCoaching Community

This book is a must-have for every Instructional Coach and EdTech Coach! It provides the tools and guidance to shape a clear vision for your coaching program and bring it to life, empowering you to make the meaningful impact you've always dreamed about!

Eric Sheninger

Best-Selling Author, Speaker, and Award-Winning Educator

"Impact Standards" is an invaluable resource for anyone leading the charge in digital learning. Jeffrey D. Bradbury expertly guides readers through creating a vision, designing a curriculum, and implementing effective instructional coaching. This book provides practical strategies and real-world insights to transform teaching and learning in the digital age. If you're passionate about leveraging technology to enhance education, this book is a must-read.

Diane E. Manser

Teacher and Author of "I Didn't Sign Up For This: One Classroom Teacher's Journey Through Emotional Fatigue to Personal Empowerment"

"A must-read for educators and instructional coaches committed to preparing students for the digital demands of our changing curricula and world. This book serves as an essential guide, offering actionable strategies and clear steps for teachers and instructional coaches to foster digital literacy and adaptability within their classrooms. Jeff Bradbury lives the processes he teaches in his text, helping teachers and instructional coaches navigate each step of implementing digital learning into their classrooms, while also providing sophisticated guidance on how to engage and support teachers who may feel hesitant about digital integration. As you read Bradbury's book, you will feel empowered and inspired to help students thrive in an ever-evolving digital landscape."

Suzanne K. Becking PhD

Professor, Fort Hays State University

This comprehensive guide is a must-read for administrators at all levels who are navigating the complex landscape of educational leadership and impacting the classroom and community. What sets this work apart is its masterful integration of big-picture strategic planning with practical, research-based implementation guidance. The author expertly demonstrates how to align coaching goals with education technology and district-wide vision and strategic planning - a critical connection often overlooked in educational leadership texts. As an academic who instructs present and future educators, I consider this resource invaluable for both current administrators and those aspiring to leadership roles as digital learning leaders. It bridges the crucial gap between traditional thoughts that say, "I don't have time to add technology to a lesson or process" and the specialized knowledge needed for effective integration of digital learning standards resulting in a culture of innovation in a school or district leading to higher student academic achievement.

Kathi Kersznowski

Educational Technology Specialist

Jeff Bradbury's Impact Standards is a fantastic resource for any school district or edtech coach looking to make real strides in digital learning. As someone who's been in this field for many years, I know how tricky it can be to create a clear vision and get everyone on board. Jeff really gets it—his book breaks down everything from building a digital learning plan to making coaching meaningful and effective. He offers a practical look at using standards like ISTE, aligning curriculum, and creating a culture that's focused on purposeful and relevant technology integration. Jeff's insight into relationship-building and focusing on people (not just the tech) is spot-on – the critical starting point for all great initiatives! I always say that edtech coaches are the #1 most critical edtech investment districts can make, and I love how Jeff highlights how this role is key to bridging technology and teaching. Impact Standards is packed with advice that every instructional leader or coach can put into action right away.

Greg Bagby

EdTech / AI Leadership Consultant

In Impact Standards, Jeff has craftily taken us through a progression from creation to implementing a Digital Learning curriculum inside a classroom. Like a tremendous four-part symphony leading in with an opening vision for digital learning, the piece adds movement to curriculum and skills and a transition to coaching and scaling. He closes the piece with a recap from learning leaders. This book is a staple for Instructional Technology Directors, Technology Coaches, and building-level technology directors. Jeff has done a great job helping us develop our programs to grow and be impactful.

Matt Miller

Educator, Speaker, Author: "Ditch That Textbook"

It's hard to guide digital learning for an entire school or district. If you've ever thought, "I'd love to sit down and pick the brain of someone who gets it — who has a plan," then you're in luck. In Impact Standards, Jeff Bradbury generously shares steps you can follow — and insight from his own experience. Read it, and you'll have a clear path forward.

Dr. Rachelle Dene' Poth

Educator, Consultant, Attorney, Author, Keynote Speaker

I have known Jeff Bradbury for many years and have continued to learn from his expertise in instructional technology. Jeff has put together a must-read book for instructional coaches or digital learning leaders who want to significantly impact their schools and school districts. Jeff provides educators with a clear and actionable roadmap for integrating technology effectively into the classroom. Full of practical strategies, comprehensive topics, and an emphasis on collaboration and relationship building, "Impact Standards" is a valuable resource for all educators. Jeff's knowledge and expertise will provide the guidance needed to help educators continue to grow professionally and positively impact all students.

ARE YOU READY TO AMPLIFY YOUR IMPACT?

Go beyond the book with powerful tools to support your work.
Get exclusive access to the Impact Standards resource library.

https://teachercast.net/impact-standards-website

The Instructional Coach's Workbook

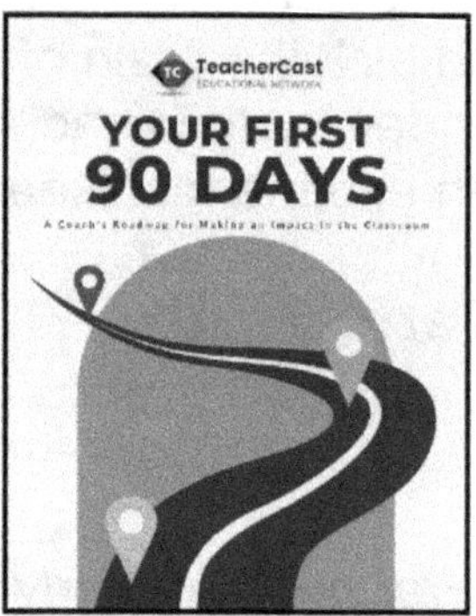

An Instructional Coaches First 90 Days

Private Online Instructional Coaching Community

The Impact Standards Podcast

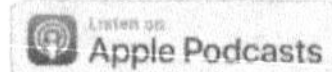

Table of Contents

Foreword

By Adam Bellow

CEO and Co-Founder of BreakoutEDU

I've often said that the education community - specifically the edtech community - is incredibly small. At least it has felt that way in the twenty years I have been studying, practicing, and living in that world. People you meet inspire you and provide both encouragement and healthy pushback decades later. It is a tight-knit group, largely driven by the ideals that everyone is doing the work they do for the right reasons. I first met Jeff Bradbury about 14 years ago. It was before the #eduTriplets and in the very first days of his expansive TeacherCast podcast empire. One thing was clear - this was an educator with ambition and drive. It has been clear in the many years since that the can-do, will-do attitude and drive to create and share are as strong in him today, if not stronger, than it was when our paths first intersected.

This book is a culmination of Jeff's work. It combines his tireless study of the education and edtech spaces with his passion for pushing and modeling positive change to help others.

In every generation of educators, there comes a moment - a defining shift - when the systems we've long relied on no longer match the needs of the students in front of us. That moment is now. Across classrooms, school districts, and communities, we face a rapidly evolving educational landscape, one where the traditional models are being reexamined, the pace of change is accelerating, and the demands on educators have never been greater.

And yet, amid the noise, confusion, and challenge, there is clarity to be found. Impact Standards is a push for that clarity - a roadmap not just for navigating the future of education, but for shaping it with intentionality, coherence, and heart.

Over the past two-plus decades, I've watched digital learning evolve from a fringe concept - an occasional PowerPoint, a computer lab visit - into a core pillar of classroom practice. But along the way, we've often conflated access with integration or confused novelty with innovation. Technology was added to the classroom like a garnish, rather than infused into the fabric of instruction as a tool for deeper thinking, collaboration, and creativity. Educators were told to "use tech," but rarely supported in the how, the why, or the what-for.

Jeffrey knows this challenge well - because he has lived it from every angle: as a classroom teacher, a coach, a district leader, a podcaster, and a national voice in educational technology. What he brings to this book is not theory from the sidelines, but experience from the trenches. He's sat beside the teacher feeling overwhelmed by device rollouts. He's helped leadership teams draft digital learning plans. He's hosted the voices of countless educators on his TeacherCast network, each one contributing to the collective understanding of what great instruction looks like in the digital age.

Impact Standards is not a quick fix or checklist. It is a thoughtful guide to culture change - something we all talk about, but few understand how to actually lead. Jeff breaks it down with clarity and conviction: before we can drive change, we must define what we mean by terms like "innovation," "technology integration," and "digital learning." Before we can demand adoption, we must design a shared vision. And before we can scale anything, we must support the people behind it - educators, coaches, families, and students - with intentional structures and ongoing, meaningful professional learning.

This book is more than a deep dive into educational leadership and instructional coaching, but it's also an invitation to reflect more deeply. What do we really want to see when we walk into a classroom? How can we align tools and standards to purpose, rather than treat them as ends in themselves? How do we flatten the Innovation Adoption Curve and bring everyone along - not just the early adopters?

Jeff's use of the ISTE Standards and Future Ready frameworks grounds this book in research and national best practices, but what truly makes this book powerful is how human it is. He knows that a district strategic plan means nothing without buy-in. That a tool, no matter how slick, won't work without purpose. That the real impact doesn't come from a dashboard - it comes from empowered educators, inspired students, and a community that sees learning as a shared mission.

There's also a beautiful metaphor that runs through this book, drawn from Jeff's background as a music educator. Like a great symphony, instructional design must be structured yet expressive. Like a conductor, a leader must draw out the best from each player - not by overpowering them, but by listening, aligning, and guiding with clarity. And like the audience of any great performance, students should leave a classroom experience moved, transformed, and wanting more.

This musical framing isn't just poetic - it's powerful. It reminds us that great teaching, like great music, requires both form and feeling. It demands both precision and passion. And it's not something that happens by accident. It's the result of practice, preparation, feedback, and continuous improvement.

In the chapters ahead, you'll walk through the steps of creating a district-wide digital learning vision that is grounded in standards and driven by strategy. You'll see how instructional coaching can be used as a lever for change - not as compliance officers, but as collaborators, facilitators, and champions of innovation. You'll explore how to design systems that scale - ones that recognize where staff members are on the curve, support them with tailored professional learning, and measure impact not by how much tech is used, but by how deeply students are engaged.

You'll also see how essential it is to bring families and communities into this work. As someone who has supported teachers and leaders in countless districts, I've seen how often we leave parents behind in the conversation about technology. Jeff offers strategies to make digital learning visible at home - to involve families not just as observers, but as partners. This kind of transparency builds trust, closes gaps, and ultimately improves outcomes.

But perhaps most importantly, this book aims to challenge us to move from reactive to proactive. To stop chasing trends and start building intentional systems. To stop relying on a few superstar teachers and start creating cultures where every educator feels confident and supported to try, iterate, and grow.

The message is clear: we cannot wait for change to happen. We must lead it. And to lead it well, we must do it together - with shared language, shared goals, and a relentless focus on what matters most: our students.

If you're picking up this book as a coach, a principal, a curriculum leader, or even a classroom teacher - know this: you have more power than you think. You don't need to be the superintendent to shape culture. You don't need a grant to start shifting practice. You simply need a plan, a purpose, and people who believe that the future of learning is worth designing with care.

Impact Standards gives you that plan. It gives you a language to build with, frameworks to align to, and stories to learn from. It gives you the "how" behind the "why." And it gives you permission to think bigger - not just about what you teach, but about how learning itself can be reimagined.

It's been said that the best leaders don't just light fires - they build lanterns so others can carry the light forward. This book aims to be one of those lanterns.

So as you turn the page, ask yourself: What does impact look like in my school? What would it take to define it, design for it, and drive it - together?

Dedication

This book is dedicated to the numerous Instructional Coaches, Teachers, School District Leaders, Public Relations Representatives, Educational Technology Vendors, Conference Promoters, listeners, subscribers, and students with whom I have had the privilege of collaborating since the inception of the TeacherCast Educational Network in 2011.

I extend my deepest gratitude to the many educators, coaches, and administrators who have supported my endeavors in the school districts where I have worked. To all who have engaged with my podcasts, participated in my workshops, subscribed to my social media channels, and allowed TeacherCast to assist them in their classrooms and school districts, your encouragement and engagement have been invaluable.

This book stands as a testament to your unwavering support and dedication to the field of education and to your staff and students.

Thank you for making TeacherCast, your home for professional development.

Most important, this book is dedicated to the amazing EduTriplets. I will never forget writing the beginnings of this book while sitting in the NICU holding all three of you while tethered to a million life saving machines. Thank you for the hugs, smiles, and support that you have and always do give me each and every day. I love being your daddy and I have strived every day to let the world know how proud I am of you all and your accomplishments. (and I never ever skip a day!)

Acknowledgements

Growing up as an only child for the first decade of my life, I embraced various roles in team sports. I played goalie for my soccer team, catcher for my baseball team, and enjoyed being part of the school bowling team. By the age of 13, I was the first in my group to earn the rank of Eagle Scout, achieving this milestone 3-4 years ahead of my peers.

Upon entering college, I ventured into orchestral conducting, which, in hindsight, was another pursuit that allowed me to work independently while supporting a large team. This journey ultimately led me to become a classroom teacher, Instructional Coach, District Administrator, Podcaster, Presenter, ISTE Certified Educator, and now, Author.

No matter how many activities I enjoy doing in the vacuum of my own internal creativity, the project has always remained the same. How can I put myself in the ultimate position to support others? How can I be in a position to be called upon when things need to be pointed in the right direction? Looking back, all these activities, while they may appear to be solo, have been my way of saying thank you.

No goalie stands alone. There is always a team in front supporting them. No Eagle Scout learns to fly alone. They all must learn how to camp, cook, swim, and clean on their way to earning 21 merit badges before they reach the pinnacle of Scouting. No conductor gets to wave their arms in front of an orchestra alone. Without the orchestra they are the only ones on stage waving their arms, looking in the wrong direction, and making no sound whatsoever.

The fact of the matter is that I could not have done any of these things or have any of these accomplishments if it were not for villages upon villages of friends, family, and professional learning communities pushing me, supporting me, and cheering me on.

To my parents: Thank you so much for pushing me at a young age to get up on the biggest stages possible. For sewing my uniforms together, cutting up orange slices, and making sure that I knew how to do a good turn daily.

To my extended Bradbury Bagel Group: Thank you for giving me the opportunity each summer to get up and sing, perform, act, and grow each summer in Ocean Park Maine. You are always there when I need you and I can never get enough hugs, rounds of Jenkins Up, or verses of “Oh Mona”.

To my musical family: One does not simply stand on a podium and conduct Beethoven 9. It takes a long walk in the woods and a trip to the lake before you learn what it is genuinely like to be vulnerable with others. If not for these experiences, I would not have the life I have now and I am forever grateful for the opportunities that allowed me to watch doves fly in the New England wind.

To my school district friends and colleagues: Thank you for allowing me to come into your classrooms, offices, and collaborate on lesson activities, school improvement plans, emergency preparedness websites, and library media centers. You may have already found that many of these conversations and experiences have found themselves in some way in this book.

To my EdTech and ISTE friends: You have been my extended family for more than a decade. No matter how crazy an idea I have, you have always been there pushing me as hard as I need to be pushed to make these crazy dreams come true. If not for you, I would not have crazy stories about TEDx Talks, EdTech Karaoke songs, wearing purple hats in Denver, broadcasting live from Atlantic City, or riding the Monorail at Disney World. You taught me how to take my octopus and turn it into a fish repeatedly. Thanks, Y'all!

To all those who supported the creation and publishing of this book. It took 14 years and several stops and starts to bring this book to its conclusion and I couldn't have done it without you.

To Adam Bellow, my older brother in the edtech world. I honestly lost track of all the times that I came to you with a crazy idea and a new direction for TeacherCast. You always welcomed the ideas with open arms and allowed me to pitch them to you with all the confidence in the world. With every new idea, you smiled and then gave me the older brother talk that more often than I wanted to admit was the right advice for the moment. It not only made me a better educator, but a better person.

To all of those who contributed to the Q&A section of this book, thank you for sharing your insights about your own experiences and coaching programs; McKenzie Fuller, Lisa Hockenberry, Cammie Kannekens, Sarah Kiefer, Steve Martinez, Adam Juarez, and Laura Thomas.

To all who have taken time to read sections or chapters of this book, thank you for all of the feedback and encouragement throughout this process: Ronda Blevins, Julie Christine, Tammy Dunbar, Heather Esposito, McKenzie Fuller, Jeff Gargas, Chrisstina Gupta, Jen Hall, Riina Hirsch, Lisa Hockenberry, Merry Hofmeister, Adam Jaurez, Erica Johnson, Cammie Kannekens, Tyler Keefe, Becky Keene, Lance Key, Sarah Kiefer, Dianne Krause, Brenny Kummer, Shira Leobowitz, Suzy Lolley, Michelle Manning, Steve Martinez, Ashley McBride, Scott McLeod, Matt Miller, Nancy Fischer Minicozzi, Tim Needles, Leah Obach, Bethany Petty, Lauren Pittman, Shana Ramin, Barbara Scully, Joshua Stamper, Sherry St Clair, Melissa Summerford, Debbie Tannenbaum, Wanda Terral, Becky Thal, Laura Thomas, Eric Verno, Sue Vincentz, Kim West, Krissy Venosdale, Nicole Zumpano.

To my many amazing cohosts, podcast guests, and co-presenters who have joined me on the microphone or on a stage: Thank you so much for joining me on this journey! To Nick Amaral, Jennifer Boulos, Josh Gauthier, Diane Manser, Jennifer Judkins, Jeff Herb, Sam Patterson, Wokka Patue, Toby Price, Grog the Zombie, Jon Samuelson, and Susan Vincent, and, thank you for all of the podcast episodes, week after week, where I kept promising that this book will be published "soon" .... Here we are! Thank you for sticking with me and taking the journey with me through hundreds of podcast episodes on every topic imaginable.

To my EduTriplets: If I have said it to you once, I have said it to you a thousand times, "If you think you can do something ... you can do it." Do not let anyone or anything tell you that you can't make your dreams become reality. Thank you for all the hugs and cuddles of encouragement. Thank you for helping me write, rewrite, and record all the chapters of this book. Because of your help with this book, we now have a wonderful LEGO Grand Piano in Daddy's office to play with. I love you more than you will ever know.

To my amazing wife, you always have my back no matter what. You always push me to take that extra crazy step, and you are always the one next to me showing me how to be the biggest advocate for what I want to accomplish. You will always be undefeated in my book baby! You gave me the world's greatest frogs and wolves and from the moment I woke up early on July 11, 2011, you never told me to stop reaching for the next chapter in our lives. Thank you for this great adventure that we are on together.

Part 1
Creating a Vision for Classroom Instruction

Chapter 1

What is Digital Learning?

"If I had six hours to chop down a tree, I'd spend the first four hours sharpening the axe."
Abraham Lincoln

You enter a school building, walk down the hall, and open a door to a classroom. You see a teacher. You see students. You see learning happening. At some point, the teacher asks the students to take out their devices and open to a Learning Management System (LMS), a website, or a project they have been assigned.

Is this Digital Learning?

You then continue your journey down the hall and enter another classroom. Students are working with paper, glue sticks, and scissors to create a project. The teacher has directions on a whiteboard for students to read and refer to. Everything you see happening in the room requires physical documents, physical objects, and group interactions. After a lesson is over, the teacher asks the students to hold up their projects and takes a photo of the work to be added to the front of their building's website and shares the experience on social media.

Is *this* Digital Learning?

The bell rings and you enter the music room. Students hurry to get their instruments ready; the way musicians have always done for hundreds of years. They place their sheet music on their music stands. Just before the teacher ascends the podium to start the class, you notice several of them take out their personal devices and open a tuning app to assist them in making sure their instruments were ready for the opening downbeat.

Is *this* Digital Learning?

Digital Learning is a frightening term for many teachers. Daily, teachers arrive at school facing the challenging task of meeting the needs of a diverse student population in a post-pandemic world. Their students come from diverse backgrounds, each presenting unique challenges. They carry both social-emotional, as well as mental-physical challenges that are often backed by legal contracts between the district and parents that must be met to the letter.

They're instructed to use technology to meet their students' needs, but receive only minimal training at the start of the school year with little ongoing support. These pressures are compounded by the fear that their peers are more adept with technology, adopting it at a faster pace. In essence, they're apprehensive about change and struggle to take the first step, even when assistance is offered.

Has Education Really Changed That Much Since We Were Students?

We recognize the challenges educators of all ages have faced with the digital learning shift since the early 1990s. However, we also understand the crucial importance of equipping students with skills for their futures through daily learning. This concept is often referred to as being "Future Ready."

How do we as educators ... do it?

How can we build a culture in our educational settings and communities that will support a huge change in how we teach not just "with", but "**through**" digital learning technologies that will help all staff members feel confident using digital learning strategies that will improve student achievement the most?

The solution to this question is the development of a digital learning method that follows standards and uses resources from not only within, but also beyond our classrooms and school districts. A method based on the input of educational stakeholders from every level of the school district and realized only through a coordinated and consistent approach to what the vision is for classroom instruction.

As Albert Einstein once said, "We cannot solve our problems with the same thinking we used when we created them." If this is true, let's look at what the thinking was then, and what it is now and how we can improve student achievement by adjusting this way of examining the problem.

Years ago, education embarked on a journey toward digital learning. The lone "computer in the back of the class" evolved into dedicated computer labs. These labs then gave way to mobile laptop carts, which were subsequently replaced by "Bring Your Own Device" (BYOD) initiatives. The progression culminated in districts adopting 1:1 programs, providing each student with their own device. During this evolution, a prevailing notion emerged: the mere acquisition of technology equated to practicing digital learning.

Classroom instruction then moved into a phase where learning was not just about how much technology was used, it was all about how many ways that technology could be leveraged to meet curricular goals. I remember when the second-generation iPad came out with its new back (only) facing camera. The fact that you could then have students working together on a project AND have another student taking photos and videos to act as a documentarian who would create a video diary of the experience was another major game changer.

More recently, education shifted from a model where one application or platform needed to be the end-all be-all into an environment of connections and collaboration. This shift seemed to happen overnight. I remember one year, during the annual ISTE (International Society for Technology in Education) Conference, vendors were showing off how many classroom activities could be supported by using their all-in-one solution. They each wanted to compete with the EdTech giants for market share. The next year, however, was drastically different as each company was touting the fact that it excelled in one or two areas of education but was excited about its connections to a Learning Management System, Student Information System, or was a one-click solution through a browser extension.

The influx of technologies that were entering the classroom environment compounded by the complexity and anxiety of learning multiple platforms was only agitated by the Pandemic. Teachers needed to be experts in their ever-changing curriculum and deliver their lessons with the added use of devices, applications, and job embedded expectations for using technology to support instruction.

This raises a crucial question: Are we merely expecting teachers to incorporate technology into their lessons, or are we asking them to infuse digital learning skills that help meet curricular needs and standards?

Taking the First Step ... Defining the Concept

Before we begin to create a concept for what technology infused learning might look like in the classroom, we must first step back and clearly define a few terms that often get tossed around without much thought.

- Technology Integration
- Innovation
- Digital Learning

These three terms often cause significant divisions in both pedagogy and philosophy among school districts. The first part of this book aims to help you and your district establish a unified, agreed-upon definition for each. This shared understanding will enable you to begin shifting the culture of standards-based classroom instruction, ultimately leading to improved student achievement.

Technology Integration

One commonly misused term in edtech is Technology Integration. For some people, this means using any type of technology in the classroom such as a digital board, a laptop or even an instrument tuner. In 2007, Edutopia, (www.edutopia.org) a popular educational website founded by the George Lucas Educational Foundation defined Technology Integration this way:

Technology integration is the use of technology resources -- computers, mobile devices like smartphones and tablets, digital cameras, social media platforms and networks, software applications, the Internet, etc. -- in daily classroom practices, and in the management of a school.

Two aspects of this definition, which was written nearly twenty years ago, are noteworthy. First, it covers a broad range of technologies and calls them "the use of" the devices. Second, it indicates that these technologies are under the control of the school.

This quote is used here because it is often widely adopted by educators and school districts. Meaning that schools provide hardware, and it is their job to manage it.

But does this definition still match Technology Integration in today's terms?

Innovation

According to Merriam-Webster, Innovation can be defined as “a new idea or method” or “the introduction of something new.” In the classroom, this could be using a new tool, teaching with a new slant on a topic, or even the inclusion of an original activity to support the learning of a standard.

If this is the definition then, can students be innovative?

Aren’t most ideas that come from students … *new*?

When thinking about the word Innovation, we often think of The Innovation-Adoption Curve that was created in 1962 by Ohio State professor Everett Rogers. This curve demonstrates a method of explaining the how, why, and rate at which innovation and adoption happens and spreads throughout a particular population or social group.

INNOVATION ADOPTION CURVE

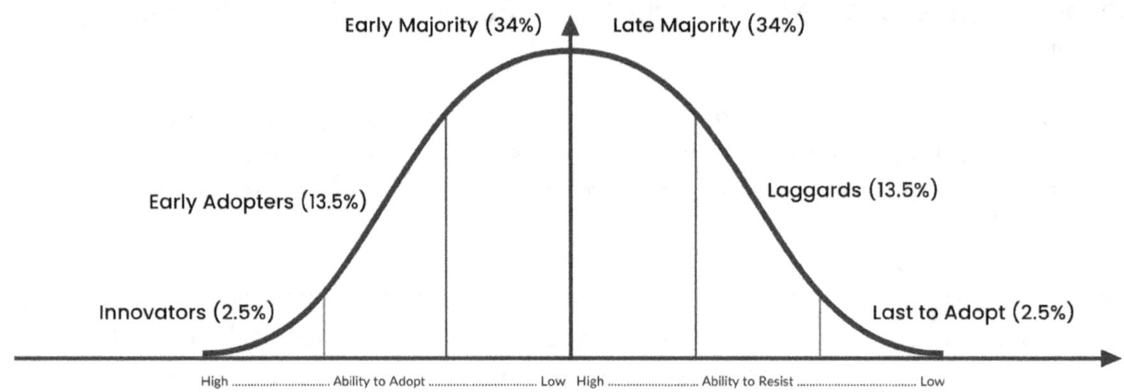

Figure 1: The Innovation Adoption Curve

The Innovation-Adoption curve is an invaluable tool for fostering and implementing standards-based Digital Learning strategies across school districts, buildings, classrooms, or communities. It offers insights into your population's current standing and provides a framework for developing a plan to shift people along the spectrum. We'll delve deeper into this curve and its strategic applications in subsequent chapters.

Digital Learning

Digital Learning is the term on this list that stumps just about everyone. What does it mean to say that you are experiencing "digital learning?" For some, this might mean that during a learning experience, some part of it requires a screen or computing device. This might mean the use of a computer, interactive board, or even a musical tuner.

The problem that many school districts are facing and the reason for at least a part of the backlash from teachers when it comes to fully embracing modern technologies and concepts in their classroom, is that these terms ARE subject to their own personal definition of the term.

For example, you might have a teacher sitting on the far left of the Innovation-Adoption Curve. Each day, their students come into class and open their Chromebooks, automatically open to Google Classroom, and watch the short intro video that the teacher created the night before to get the students prepped for today's lesson. Clearly, this is both an example of Digital Learning and Technology Integration.

Consider another scenario: a teacher's students enter the classroom and spend a few minutes struggling to locate the presentation slides prepared by the teaching team. The teacher then begins lecturing in front of an interactive board. This approach, while potentially representing the far right of the Innovation-Adoption Curve, might still be considered both Digital Learning and Technology Integration, depending on the teacher's comfort level with technology.

Meeting the Needs of All Staff Members ... and Pushing Forward

As district leaders, school leaders, and Instructional Coaches, the role we play in achieving this forward movement looks slightly different, but the one thing that is vitally important is that we all have the same goals, the same vision, and when asked, can clearly articulate the

> *"What do you want standards-based instruction to look like when you walk into the classroom?"*

answer to one single and important question.

To fully answer this question, we must first identify the curve and to the best of our abilities then make a plan to flatten it as much as possible so that every stake holder in the district from administrators to coaches, teachers, and even community members know and understand where the goal posts are and ultimately where we want our students to be.

So, how do we do it?

The answer to this question is easy ... but to fully embrace this question you must start by asking your district to answer that very question ... and then agree on the answer.

Chapter 2

Creating a District-wide Vision for Digital Learning

"Where there is no vision, there is no hope."
George Washington Carver

Imagine your ideal learning environment. If you could design the perfect classroom, with an exceptional teacher guiding you through your favorite subject, what would it look like?

If you gathered a group of educators in a room and posed this question to them, you'd likely receive varied responses. However, you might find that all the answers share common themes.

- Innovative and open learning environment
- Access to a wide variety of resources for learning
- Inspiring instructor

Now, consider your current district and ask yourself this question. Do you provide that for the students whom you serve?

How can we, even if we *can't* make every classroom into the ideal place for learning, design an educational space that inspires and supports students to do their best and succeed every day?

This chapter provides a brief overview of the key building blocks for facilitating a culture shift in your district. We will explore each of these topics in greater depth throughout the book.

These culture-shifting building blocks include:

- Finding the Pieces to Build the Puzzle.
- Developing a Shared Vision and Goals.
- Prioritizing Professional Learning in and out of your district.
- Creating a standards-based evaluation method that is flexible yet effective.
- Supplying constant support for students, teachers, and community members.
- Protecting students and promoting digital safety.
- Collaborating with parents and students to create community learning opportunities.
- Embracing and Celebrating the Impact Digital Learning has on students, teachers, and community.

Finding the Pieces to Build the Puzzle

When we think about creating a district-wide vision for what standards-based instruction looks like, we first must start at the top of the district ladder. By this, I mean the community, and community members who not only supply the students to fill the school, but also help select the district leaders who will be serving it.

When parents send their students to school, (public or private) they have expectations about the education their students will be receiving. They often wish for outstanding teachers, an inspiring curriculum, and for a safe and healthy classroom environment to learn in.

They want the best for their students, and they want to make sure that their students are going to be set up for their futures.

Let's look at this from a district and building administrator's lens. Each summer, district leadership comes together to plan for the school year. They set the calendar, the curriculum, and how each building will be managed throughout the school year. They leave their meetings with a sharp vision and expectations for what the school year will look like and how everyone can get to the end of the school year safely and with elevated levels of academic success.

When addressing classroom learning, specifically standards-based learning that will have a direct impact on the learning abilities and lives of each student, this same type of discussion and conversation should also be happening.

Members of this community might include:

- Community Members / Parents
- Business Owners
- District Cabinet Members
- Building Leadership
- Teachers
- Students

Once gathered in the same room, it's crucial to have an open dialogue about the district's current state and its desired future. We'll explore this process in greater depth later in this book.

Developing a Shared Vision and Goals

To understand the difference between setting a vision and creating attainable goals, let's first define these terms and explore how they support your school district and students.

Vision

- A vision is a statement of an organization's future aspirations. It's often broad to accommodate various subgroups' needs, yet should be achievable by all stakeholders.

Goals

- A goal is a specific, short-term target an organization pursues to realize its overall vision. Goals should be written to produce realistic results. They establish an accountability system, setting an achievable standard across the organization.

The first step in flattening the curve, as discussed in Chapter 1, is creating an attainable Vision for standards-based classroom instruction across all classrooms, along with a set of actionable Goals that define how to achieve this vision.

Many school districts accomplish this through a district-wide Strategic Plan. This plan, developed collaboratively by community and educational stakeholders, establishes the district's vision and roadmap for a 3-5 year period.

Typically, the Strategic Plan outlines a few broad goals based on major organizational divisions such as Curriculum, Finance, and Operations. Each of these pillars is then further divided into specific goals and action items.

When developing a standards-based vision for classroom instruction, a school district can use its own Strategic Plan as a blueprint to create a focused vision for classroom instruction.

Prioritizing Professional Learning in and out of your district

As mentioned earlier, the start of the school year is often welcomed with excitement, but also with anxiety. For district leadership, there are several items that need to be shared with staff and only a few short hours to do it before it's time to open the doors and welcome in students for the first time. For teachers, they are often found sitting in meetings where their only thought is about how they wished they had more time in their classrooms to get ready for day 1.

Professional development is an important part of the school year's beginning routine for teachers and district leaders. Making sure that needed information is meticulously organized and distributed is one of the leading items each year that causes stress for every staff member.

Because of its importance, one of the best ways to support a culture shift is by setting up professional development systems, both in and out of the district, that are supportive and continuous for staff members without being overwhelming. These new systems often begin by examining how your district currently shares news and information, as well as rethinking the distribution model. Instead of relying solely on administrative lectures, consider using a series of targeted emails rather than distributing lengthy packets that are often discarded after meetings. This might also be an opportune time to reassess the use of a staff portal for organizing both information and staff development resources.

Another way to support teachers through ongoing professional development is through your Instructional Coaches. These staff members are critical members of both the teaching community and educational leadership teams that can be used to share and spread new policy and procedures in a non-threatening and non-evaluative way. More on this in an upcoming chapter.

Once you have redesigned the way that staff members will be receiving and acting upon new information, district initiatives, and procedures, it is time to rethink the way that your new digital learning strategy can support district level evaluations.

Creating a standards-based evaluation method that is flexible yet effective.

A building leader walks down the hallway and enters a classroom. What do they see?

- Does it match with what the building and districts version of standards-based classroom instruction is?
- How do they track what they see?
- Who do they hold accountable for the events they may or may not be seeing in that classroom?

When setting up a system that supports the shifting of culture, it is not only the decisions that need to be created at the top, but the action items that go along with it. This comes in the form of a flexible standards-based evaluation system that helps all stakeholders but must be created both from the vision of the district and the expectation that all staff members are here to learn from each other.

Traditionally, staff members enter the school year and are told the vision and rules for the upcoming school year, and they are told what they will be evaluated on. However, what if during that meeting, staff members were asked what they were interested in learning throughout the year?

Setting goals and meeting them is a part of every employee's evaluation plan but, think about how often these goals are tied to professional development that is directly connected to supporting the districts standards-based approach to curricular instruction.

In a future chapter we will delve into this system in detail. You'll discover how to develop professional and personal evaluation frameworks that not only align with district requirements but also cater to individual learning goals. These goals will be identified by staff members through an instructional practices self-assessment survey.

This self-assessment allows an instructional coach to use that data to support staff members' needs. This self-assessment can then become an observable goal in the eyes of the supporting administrator. Involving your Instructional Coaches in the process of supporting district and building goals is a wonderful way to create a data-driven system of support for teachers but it isn't the only way they can be used to support the culture shift.

Providing Constant Support for Students, Teachers, & Community Members

One of this book's key themes is how your Instructional Coaching department can be the catalyst for culture change in the classroom and a major supporter of community programs.

When creating a culture shift that happens in the classrooms, a district must also be thinking about those times where their students are not actively engaged in traditional learning process. As we will discuss in a later chapter of this book, a school district's vision for standards-based learning in the classroom should also include activities that happen outside the classroom when students are being supported by parents and guardians.

This support could come in the form of adding curricular information in a teachers' home-based newsletters or through the inclusion of digital learning tips & tricks in building and district-based communications to help parents understand the technologies that students are being exposed to while in school. These slight additions to your communication channels can speak volumes at home during parent-student conversations.

Digital learning tips and tricks aside, the way that your building communicates with students, teachers, and community members is an important way of shifting a culture that supports your district's vision of what in-classroom learning should look like. It also is a terrific way of encouraging both at home and community conversations over issues of student safety that might be of interest when young students begin bringing devices home to complete curricular assignments.

Protecting Student Privacy and Promoting Digital Safety

One of the most important and challenging issues for me as a parent, an educator of digital tools, and someone who grew up with technology is how to protect student safety and information privacy. This is something that I always have on my mind with my three young triplets.

At home, the pandemic hit just as the triplets were in kindergarten. It was not long before we had to have three Chromebook's in three different rooms and I clearly remember running back and forth between all those rooms while at the same time trying to be a virtual teacher myself day after day, month after month.

Then came the time to get back into the classrooms and the education world felt a huge backlash from parents who were fed up with their students being glued to the screens. At home, we had the same issues. We wanted our students to learn how to be safe digital citizens but were concerned over how many minutes they were spending in work mode and passively watching TV.

While Digital Literacy is crucial and will be extensively covered in this book, Digital Citizenship (which is distinct) is equally important in supporting a culture shift. Every district should implement a multi-layered digital citizenship curriculum integrated into core subjects. Currently, many districts teach history in Social Studies and cyber safety in Technology classes separately. To fully embrace Digital Learning in the classroom, districts must develop a plan that merges these lessons. This integration allows students to learn both topics simultaneously through real-world, authentic projects aligned with standards-driven curricular goals. By combining the expertise of core subject teachers and technology instructors, students can develop a more comprehensive understanding of digital citizenship in context.

Working together with parents and students to create community learning opportunities.

As ambassadors for the culture change and vision that your district has, your Instructional Coaches can be looked at not just as leaders in the classroom, but also in the community. One of the best ways to do this is through community based professional learning programs on a small scale such as Parent Nights, or even on a larger scale in the form of a Parent University.

These types of events can start out as informational sessions about the school program and its student offerings and can morph into community learning nights that are fun for the whole family.

Leveraging Instructional Coaches as adult learning specialists, the Parent Night or Parent University concept offers an excellent opportunity for community engagement and direct learning from district staff. These events can focus on digital learning or highlight specific aspects of the school's curriculum, such as STEM (Science, Technology, Engineering, and Math) or Character Education. This approach helps parents better support their children's learning at home. Additionally, these activities provide a great platform for involving community members as instructors, further enriching the learning experience.

Embracing and Celebrating the Impact Digital Learning has on students, teachers, and community.

Culture shifts are challenging, but recognizing innovators in classrooms and communities is one of the most effective ways to foster widespread acceptance and enthusiasm for digital learning. Simple acknowledgments, such as a shout-out in a newsletter or a monthly certificate at a faculty meeting, can have a significant impact. Showcasing innovation can be even more powerful when student work is featured during Board of Education meetings or shared on social media platforms.

Where to Find Resources to Support Your Districts Vision

Creating a school district vision for classroom instruction is a weighty task that requires the backing of all stakeholders, including students. However, we must ask ourselves: Are students, teachers, district leaders, and community members the only essential components in crafting your digital learning vision?

In our next chapter, we'll explore Impact Standards, focusing specifically on the ISTE (International Society for Technology in Education) Standards for Digital Learning. We'll examine how your district can use these goals to "flatten the curve" and achieve its vision.

Chapter 3

Introducing and Infusing the ISTE Standards

"Education is not the filling of a pail, but the lighting of a fire."
William Butler Yeats

A teacher walks into a classroom and students enter. The lesson is about to begin. The teacher begins with a story, perhaps one that is designed to capture the student's attention and help them gather their thoughts about the learning adventure ahead. After a few minutes, a transition happens, and the story begins to relate to a curricular topic that quickly engages students in active participation. Within the first few minutes of class, students and their imaginations have been captured and in groups, they work on an activity they will share with the class once complete. To wrap up the activity, the teacher asks students to answer a series of questions about what they have learned. Just as the bell is about to ring, the teacher asks one last question to spark their curiosity and shares that this will be the question of the day during their next class period.

Teaching can be so simple sometimes. A visionary instructor meeting a wide-eyed group of learners. When the right combination of vision and imagination come together, magic will happen in the classroom.

To be honest, for the first 15 years as a public-school educator, and probably even throughout my high school and college careers, I never thought too much about instruction. Some of my teachers were amazing. They could light me up and inspire me to open books, create presentations, and even join the school newspaper club. Other teachers were fascinating but were a little on the bland side when it came to capturing my attention.

I think this is the reason I never thought about the structure of learning or the philosophies that go behind the creation of a lesson plan before I became an Instructional Coach. For the first 15 years of my teaching career, I was a Music Educator with only one goal each day. My goal was to harness the imaginations of as many students as possible and prepare them for the next public performance. Don't get me wrong, I loved putting together lessons in performance pedagogy, music history, musical theory, and performance etiquette but I never thought about the theory behind all that I was doing.

This all changed in 2012 when I attended my first ISTE Conference. I was introduced to ISTE when I first created TeacherCast and was told that it was the biggest conference in the country. Naturally, I wanted to attend. I packed my bags and flew to San Diego where my eyes lit up and I instantly had a brand-new philosophy of teaching and learning.

It was during these early TeacherCast years when I started transitioning from a music educator to a professional development provider and in doing so, began to question how effective teaching was structured and why some teaching strategies worked and why others did not. I realized that teaching has a lot in common with the music world, as both are undergoing rapid changes. To keep up with the latest developments in educational theory and practice, I created a series of podcasts that explore various topics in education. What I learned from these podcast recordings was that educational technology and music education were remarkably similar. Each has its own rules and roadmap to get you from one place to another. Both traditional teaching and classical music have a structure that can be rigid and flexible where it must be depending on the subject and the performer. Most importantly, the one entity that I was able to connect was that there are a set of guiding rules behind both teaching and classical music that provide a strong emotional connection between the learner and subject as well as the listener and the sound.

Let's explore what these structures are and how they help to maintain a high-quality teaching environment and how they are essential to enhance student learning in the classroom.

Understanding the Structure of Music

Why is music such a universal language? What makes it the one constant in just about every culture that both brings people together and helps them to tell their story to generation after generation?

Dating back hundreds and hundreds of years, people made sounds to communicate. Each sound was individual and unique to its possessor. Some people made soft sounds, and some made loud sounds. Some made sounds with their hands and others made it with their feet. Everyone was trying to share and communicate but they did not have a common way of doing this.

One day, a meeting of the minds happened and two people decided that they could get their point across by making the same sounds at the same time. This proved to be an improvement as their sounds were now combined to make one commanding sound. Soon others joined them, and the idea of back-and-forth communication or polyphony was born.

As people interacted more and more, questioning and responding became the dominant form of communication on the planet, and then a new voice joined the conversation. A voice that served as a contrasting voice to the back-and-forth antiphonal sounds that were happening at the time. Musical scholars call this counterpoint.

Time went on, and soon a musical structure started to form. Originally stories were told in an ABA format, in other words, one story was told, then a different story was told and then the first story was repeated. From there storytelling went to ABABA then ABCA where a third story was wedged into the conversation.

Soon, the traditional format for musical compositions begin to look like this:

- Theme A
- Theme B
- Development of A and B
- Theme A
- Closing

Sometime in the 1700-1800's, musical composers decided that it wasn't enough to add additional story blocks in the middle or the end of the music, they needed to add to the beginning of the musical composition. For this they created what is known as a "slow introduction."

It was during this time that it wasn't uncommon for a symphonic piece of music to have this simple yet heavily expanded structure:

- Slow Introduction
- Theme A
- Theme B
- Theme C
- Development of Theme A
- Development of Theme B
- Development of Theme C
- Closing
- Coda

This expansion then led to the creation of additional musical sections or "movements," giving rise to what is now known as "Symphonic Form."

This example illustrates how the need for communication and restructuring sound production and storytelling led to the creation of a musical standard. The development of the symphonic form made this possible. This form still guides composers today, providing boundaries for what can and cannot be done. It also offers a set of rules for what should and shouldn't be done when composers or performers want to take liberties during a performance to make it their own. The symphonic form thus acts as both a structure and a springboard for creativity.

Let's examine how this structure relates to the classroom environment.

Understanding the Structure of the Classroom

Since the dawn of time, learning has happened. Sometimes it happens through self-discovery. Other times it happens when someone shares knowledge with another. This cycle happens repeatedly every day. In its simplest forms, a classroom is where one person tells a story to another.

Sometimes the story is simple. Instructor speaks and students listen (AB). Other times the instructor speaks, and the students speak and then the instructor speaks (ABA).

When expanding this model in a lesson's structure, the form takes on a familiar format.

- Teacher Speaks
- Students Respond
- Activity Happens
- Teacher and Students come together to discuss the activity.
- Closing

Sometime in the last 50 years, the creation of classroom lessons and activities began to expand even more due to both the demands of parents and students and the raising of instructional standards.

Lessons no longer were simple conversations between teacher and student. They became increasingly more complicated to put together and now include strategies such as differentiation, inclusion, and needed to include educational technology devices as a core teaching tool to help educators immerse their students into the learning experience. They needed to have an opening anticipatory set and a closing exit ticket.

The modern classroom lesson today might look something like this:

- Opening / Anticipatory Set
- Introductory Conversation
- Student Activity / Responses
- Digital Learning Activity
- Conversation / Activity about the Introductory Conversation
- Conversation / Activity about the Student Responses
- Presentation of the Digital Learning Activity
- Final Wrap Up of the Topic
- Call to Action / Exit Ticket

You do not have to look too hard to see that the modern-day classroom looks extremely like the modern-day symphonic score. All of this is possible due to the creation of and use of educational standards. Rules that guide the teacher in the creation of their lessons and help educators across the world make sure that each student can perform the same tasks and learn the same skills.

To identify these guiding principles, let's explore four instructional frameworks designed to foster high-impact learning in the classroom and provide direction for effective instruction in both classroom and administrative settings.

The ISTE Standards

The ISTE Standards, created more than two decades ago, are a series of digital learning standards that, according to their website, “provide the competencies for learning, teaching, and leading in the digital age, providing a comprehensive roadmap for the effective use of technology in schools worldwide.” (Broken down into five distinct categories, (Students, Educators, Education Leaders, Coaches, ISTE Computational Thinking Competencies), they supply an essential structure for school districts seeking to put in place guidelines for supporting digital learning both in the classroom and in the community.

Within each set of ISTE Standards lie seven elements that ISTE refers to as “essential conditions” for how technology can be leveraged in a way to support digital learning backed by scientific research that will support all members of the school community.

Visit ISTE.org/standards to learn more

How can the ISTE Standards be Deployed in Your School District?

The ISTE Standards for Students, Educators, Educational Leaders, and Coaches provide school districts with a powerful set of tools, roadmaps, and guidelines for how to create a successful and impactful instructional practice in the classroom. Unfortunately, for the average educator, educational leader, or instructional coach, these standards may not be widely discussed when in planning sessions.

How can we start a culture shift in our school districts by including the ISTE Standards in common conversations?

One of the first things that an Instructional Coach or Educational Leader can do to put the ISTE Standards into practice is by having a conversation at the administration level. Ask your building leaders a single question that we will discuss multiple times in this book.

“When you walk into a classroom ... what do you want to see?”

Most often, educational leaders will answer by sharing that they wish to see high quality and high impact teaching that is student driven and engaging backed by data-driven practices. This is an exciting time to share how achieving these goals are documented inside of the ISTE Standards.

Another way of starting a culture shift towards ISTE Standards-based learning is by encouraging educational leaders to include both ISTE Standards for Educators and ISTE

Standards for Students in weekly lesson plans. School districts can use this data to track what skills are being addressed in each classroom and what they need support through coaching cycles or professional development.

Finally, when curriculum mapping and when working with teachers on their weekly lessons, take a moment to map out not just the curricular standards being addressed in each lesson, but map out what digital learning skills are being addressed and begin to chart what skills your students are learning for each grade level. The process of creating a vertical alignment for digital learning will be addressed later in this book and is a great way of building digital learning skills little by little as progress happens throughout the year and from grade level to grade level.

How Can Educators Leverage the ISTE Standards

Just as musical forms evolve, so do modern instructional practices. In today's classrooms, teachers must constantly adapt to student interests, content requirements, curricular standards, and evaluation methods. Administrators are tasked with creating a safe, robust learning environment that meets the needs of students, staff, and community members. Coaches face the challenge of supporting both leadership and learning, dividing their time between classrooms and conference rooms. What unites these diverse responsibilities?

When school districts create a vertically aligned, standards-driven, and data-driven curriculum, they empower their staff to design dynamic, student-centered lessons and their coaches to provide support using modern tools. However, this empowerment shouldn't stem solely from coaches. To foster a true culture shift at both classroom and school-wide levels, all stakeholders must come together to envision the future of teaching and learning. Collectively, they need to chart a course that propels their district forward, addressing identified instructional gaps and creating a blueprint to achieve the district and community-approved goals outlined in their Strategic Plan.

To transform the ISTE Standards into impactful guidelines, a district should develop a comprehensive EdTech Integration Plan or Digital Learning Strategic Plan.

Chapter 4

The Digital Learning Strategic Plan

"Learning is not attained by chance, it must be sought for with ardor and diligence."
Abigail Adams

In our initial chapters, we explored the critical importance of establishing universally agreed-upon definitions for key terms like Digital Learning, Innovation, and Technology Integration. We then delved into the significance of developing a clear, shared vision for classroom instruction across all grade levels.

Finally, we applied those definitions and shared visions to create a standards-based learning model rooted in the ISTE Standards and Future Ready framework.

In this chapter, we'll guide you through the process of developing your district's EdTech Integration Plan, also known as a Digital Learning Strategic Plan.

What are Strategic Plans?

As mentioned in Chapter 2, school districts create a Strategic Plan as a multi-layered document that sets the roadmap for where the district wishes to be over usually 3-5 years. It is a document designed over several months with the support of district leadership, board members, community members, teachers, and often students.

Once the districts' strategic plan is outlined, developed, and approved, these goals become the catalyst for every decision, action, and budget item. In other words, if something is going to happen in the district, or if there is an expense to be accounted for, it must meet the needs and be justified by the goals of the Strategic Plan.

Stemming from the Strategic Plan usually comes department plans that are created to help the district formulate a proposal for meeting the needs of each of the Strategic Goals. Traditionally, this is where school districts formulate a Technology Plan.

Technology Plans are usually created by the highest-ranking Technology Director and are often roadmaps for how the technology infrastructure is organized, purchased, and serviced. They discuss the number of devices available and being purchased, the location and shelf life of servers, and routers, and often are a blueprint for what happens in the case of a cybersecurity attack. For many schools, this is the only document that strategically supports the use of technology.

But should it be?

If a district has a clear vision for standards-based classroom instruction, shouldn't there be a guiding document that supports the school district's path to achieving its curricular and instructional goals?

This is where the EdTech Integration Plan—sometimes called the Digital Learning Strategic Plan—comes into play.

What is a Digital Learning Strategic Plan?

One of the important things that we will be learning about in this book are the terms "how," "and" and "with." These are important words that educators and school districts interchange and often stumble on. They are also words that can cause severe frustration if used incorrectly.

For example, a teacher might think they need to teach a lesson … "and" use technology to do it. A department might be looking to create a project, and they are told that they must complete that project "with" the aid of a certain piece of hardware. Both are examples where an extra item or burden is placed on the group. However, there is another term that we will be using throughout this book to help guide our missions of creating a standards-based culture shift in achieving the goal of shifting the culture of digital learning in the classroom. That term is "through." This is a term that is more of a helpful term than an additive term. The teacher is going to be successful in teaching a lesson "through" the use of technology. The department is going to be successful in completing a project "through" the use of their technology hardware.

When examining the concept of the EdTech Integration Plan, or Digital Learning Strategic Plan, we will explore how the school district can meet the needs of its Strategic Plan and Goals "through" the creation and use of this document. The school district must first declare "why" using instructional technology is important to student achievement. It must then explain how it will achieve its academic goals "through" this document. This process will set in motion a series of conversations and decisions that will support how a district establishes key aspects of learning and staff development. These include standards-based lesson planning and vertically aligned professional development. Additionally, it will provide all members of the district and community with a way to utilize instructional coaches. These coaches will support both staff and community learning experiences, ultimately having a direct impact on student achievement in the classroom.

To break down the creation of an EdTech Integration Plan or Digital Learning Strategic Plan, let's look at the steps that a district can take together in completing this document.

- Step 1: Create a District Snapshot
- Step 2: Define Your Endgame
- Step 3: Formulate an Essential Question
- Step 4: Conduct a Staff Needs Assessment
- Step 5: Create Individualized Professional Learning Plans
- Step 6: Build a Professional Learning Roadmap
- Step 7: Create an EdTech Menu of Professional Learning Opportunities
- Step 8: Develop Standards-Based Lesson Plans
- Step 9: Incentivize Professional Development
- Step 10: Clarify District Recommendations
- Step 11: Share Recommendations with District Leadership
- Step 12: Create and Present the Final Strategic Plan to BOE and Community

Once you and your district have taken these steps, you will have the tools and the blueprints for making your vision of standards-based classroom instruction a reality and will have the tools to do so.

Step 1: The District Snapshot

Congratulations! Your district is about to take a fantastic journey that, when complete, will help every single student and provide a professional roadmap for every single employee in your district for years to come.

But first, there is an important journey that your district must go on!

As Lewis Carroll wrote in Alice in Wonderland, “Begin at the beginning, and when you get to the end: then stop.”

For a district looking to rethink, reimagine, and recreate the learning activities that happen in the classroom, the first step is to look in the mirror and decide who they are at the beginning of this process. To do this properly, the district must create a holistic abstract of their district from both the internal and external viewpoints of what they want a classroom to look like in the form of a District Snapshot.

Keeping in mind that the journey that your district is about to embark on is the direct answer and response to its Strategic Goals, the purpose of the District Snapshot should be to begin to start to answer the question “How is my district going to meet the needs and challenges laid out and agreed upon in our Strategic Plan as well as our Vision and Mission ?”

What is a District Snapshot?

A school district snapshot is a document, report, or infographic that highlights where a district is at any time. A snapshot might be simple to put together or might take months to put together depending on the information requested by the district.

How Does a District Snapshot Work?

A district snapshot is a self-assessment tool that provides decision-makers the opportunity to look at and analyze data based on several criteria.

Where no two district snapshots are identical in how they are created or the data in them, best results from snapshots come in a combination of charts, graphics, and written statements that can be easily understood by a community-wide audience.

Creating a Single Focus Question

At the heart of any district, a snapshot is a single focus question that is trying to be answered.

Examples of a centralized focus question are:

- What is the overall makeup of our school district?
- How can we properly redistrict our students due to the increase of low-income housing?
- How do we want to effectively distribute next year's budget funds across all our school buildings to meet the needs of our Title I students?

No matter what the focus question is, once it is created and agreed upon a series of questions will help you create a story that helps you determine the answer to your focus question.

Formulating Your Instructional Technology Focus Question

When it comes to creating a snapshot of your district's instructional technology use, it is important not to drill too deep with your focus or supporting questions. At this point, the goal is to get a broad overview of how technology (both hardware and software) is being used in classrooms to support students.

Additionally, doing an instructional technology snapshot of a district provides an invaluable opportunity to poll your community to get a temperature of the district's comfort towards the instructional changes that are going to be affected by this process.

Examples of Instructional Technology and Digital Learning Focus Questions:

EdTech Integration District Snapshot Questions

When planning your survey questions, it's important to have a wide variety of topics. District surveys such as these will need to be completed by stakeholders of several expert levels and it's best to have questions that can be answered by those directly affected by the snapshot and the program that is being developed.

- What are some key motivators for your district's Technology Integration Plan?
- How is Professional Development set up in your school/district?
- How does teacher feedback play a role in Technology Integration decisions?
- What is going well for your school district's Professional Development program?
- What would you like to improve about your school district's Prof Dev program?

While the questions above are perfect for getting a general idea of instructional technology use and best practices in district-provided professional development, your district survey should also include data on topics such as:

- District Overview
- Vision, Mission & Beliefs
- Strategic Plan
- District Profile
- District History
- Demographics
- Equity
- Student Population
- Funding
- Free WIFI Coverage in the community
- Staff Wants/Interests
- Community Wants/Interests

Who should be asked these questions?

A District Snapshot has many qualities of a traditional community survey, but I do not recommend treating the two in the same way or ever confusing the two.

Where it is true that much of the data from your survey can be found easily in budget reports and by having conversations with department and community leaders, the best way to get a true snapshot of your community is to have simple conversations with as many people as possible.

As an instructional coach, I often find myself having meaningful conversations with teachers on many topics. During these conversations, I often slip in a few "snapshot questions" to get a feel of where the staff member is on the subject.

By doing this, you can get information and data that you are looking for without the need to conduct a formal survey of your staff. This also allows the staff members to be a part of the project and supply feedback without the need to do a formal survey that takes time out of their day.

When creating your District Snapshot, you should plan to include as many members of the community as possible to get a wide variety of answers.

Participants in the District Snapshot could be:

- Central Office
- Superintendent
- Office Workers
- Support Staff
- Central Office Staff
- Administrators
- Principals
- Department Leaders
- Certified Staff
- Teachers
- Coaches
- Non-School Personnel
- Community Leaders
- Leaders of Community Buildings
- Community Members
- Students
- Parents

How Can Your District Snapshot Support Instructional Coaching?

In creating your ideal Instructional Coaching program, your District Snapshot (District Profile) is the first tool needed to craft the ultimate role and function of your instructional coaches. It not only serves as an overview of how the district sees itself, but how those inside the district see themselves.

Before we can create an Instructional Coaching program to help the district go where it is going, it is vitally important to create the District Snapshot to first determine where it is.

Looking Beyond the District Snapshot

When creating a plan and pathway for creating a new way of delivering instruction in classrooms, the district snapshot is a vital tool in collecting and analyzing data about where the community would like to see instruction in years to come.

The next step in the process is to examine your data and choose how you would like to present your district's story through it. From here, your district can plan what it wants the final project to look like and what it wants to include in the final report.

Step 2: Defining Your Endgame

While Step 1 defines your district's starting point, Step 2 focuses on charting the path forward and envisioning your district's future state after completing the journey. This "endgame" often aligns closely with the goals outlined in the district's Strategic Plan.

As previously mentioned, every district creates some form of Technology Plan. However, the crucial question that should always be asked is, "What happens to all of this technology once it's in the district?" This is where the Educational Technology Plan comes into play.

The Educational Technology Plan shows not what but how technology will be used in a district. It is a roadmap for how to use educational technology and best practices in teaching through digital learning standards and for how staff members will be trained in it.

Is an Educational Technology Plan also known as a Professional Development Plan?

I would argue that these two things are not the same thing at all, however, it might be argued that there can be many overlapping components to the two plans and that they should absolutely be written in tandem with each other so that a school district has both its left hand and right hands speaking with each other.

How Should the Plan's Plan be Created?

At this point in the development process of creating an Educational Technology Integration Plan, a district is still in the planning stage. For this reason, the full district should be involved and included in the process of creating an outline for what the final document should look like and what will be included in it.

There are several steps that should be undertaken when planning an outline for the final document.

- Step 1: Review and discuss the district Strategic Plan and once again ask the question, "How do we want to respond to these goals and meet the needs of our students?"
- Step 2: Review and discuss the findings in the District Snapshot. Make a list of everything that someone says is great about the district and everything that has been identified as needing improvement.
- Step 3: Identify each key member of the district and assign them a task based on their areas of expertise and if possible, partner them up with another member of the district to collaborate on future tasks in this process.
- Step 4: Assign groups and committees to compose the remaining steps of the process.
- Step 5: Create an Outline of what the district would like to see in the final Educational Technology Integration Plan.
- Step 6: Set short term and long-term goals for planning, communicating, and create a meeting calendar to assist in project management.

What Does an Outline Look Like?

When a district is in the beginning stages of creating their Educational Technology Integration Plan, there are several variables facing them and it is possible that the outline will change over time.

Here is an example of what an Educational Technology Integration Plan Outline might look like as the process begins.

- **Presentation Overall Question to be Answered:**
    - Possible Question:
    - Possible Answer:
- **Materials Required for Project Completion:**
    - Hardware / Applications
    - Time Considerations
    - Material Considerations
    - Staffing Considerations
- **Possible Essential Questions:**
    - How Do You Want to Solve the Essential Question?
- **What is The Guiding Force Behind These Decisions?**
    - Strategic Plan
    - District Mission and Vision Statement
- **What do we want every staff member to know as district employees?**
    - How do we know that they know or do not know it?
- **What are the supporting Standards that we are trying to meet?**
- **Baseline of Knowledge:**
    - What do we think everyone currently knows?
- **What does the district want to have professional development look like?**
    - How will Professional Learning Work?
    - How will the district get buy-in and support for professional development?

Ready … Set …. Let's Get Started!

The hardest part of starting a journey is the moment that requires getting ready to begin the journey. This is where we are right now.

In our first section, we discussed the creation of a comprehensive District Snapshot that provides a baseline of data for where the district currently is. It supplies a clear picture for the district to look at its Strategic Plan and ask if the Plans goals are being met and begin the conversation to figure out what steps need to be taken to get to where it wants to be.

In this second step, a district creates an outline for what they would like their final document to ultimately look like. When completed, they will have a story of where they have been and what projects they will be working on for the months ahead.

The next step involves formulating an Essential Question. This question will serve as a guiding beacon, akin to the Bat Signal, unifying all district projects toward a single, focused goal. It's crucial that this focal point is not only endorsed by district leadership but also embraced by the entire community.

Step 3: Formulate an Essential Question

How can we create a Technology Integration Plan that excites teachers to want to bring new and innovative lessons and activities into their classrooms?

Throughout history, adventurers from all over the world embarked on voyages of discovery and wonder. Every one of these voyages had a common element: There was some kind of curiosity that needed to be satisfied. It might have been "Is there land over there?" or "What happens if we sail to the west instead of to the east?" Either way, these quests were first planned and designed to answer a single question, otherwise known as an "Essential Question."

In this part of the EdTech Integration Plan roadmap, you will learn how to work with your school district and your instructional coaches' leadership team to formulate an "essential question" that will help guide you through the EdTech Integration Plan process. Once identified, this "essential question" will be used to propel all other planning and action items in a school's journey to raise student achievement through the implementation of digital tools and an instructional technology framework.

**HOW CAN WE CREATE
A TECHNOLOGY INTEGRATION PLAN
THAT EXCITES TEACHERS
TO WANT TO BRING NEW AND INNOVATIVE LESSONS
AND ACTIVITIES INTO THEIR CLASSROOMS?**

Why is an EdTech Essential Question Important?

If every journey begins with a single step, and, if every quest is designed to answer one single question, the process of creating a roadmap and an EdTech Integration Plan must begin by asking one question.

- Which questions need to be asked?
- How should this question be chosen?
- Why is it important that this question be the right one?

Before we go any further, let us look back at the process we have gone through so far and remember why we are creating our EdTech Integration Plan. To begin the planning of an EdTech Integration Plan, a school district must first create and agree on a set of goals and values for itself called a Strategic Plan. The Strategic Plan shares with school and local community a vision for what it wants to be over a given amount of time (usually 3-5 years). This can be looked at as the "what statement."

The EdTech Integration Plan is the "how" in your school district. It is, in extremely broad terms, the vehicle from which we get from "Point A" to "Point B." Without it, there is no way of reaching the goals of your Strategic Plan.

What is an EdTech Essential Question?

Throughout the creation process of an EdTech Integration Plan, a district must complete a 12-step process that asks them to complete certain tasks. In the first few steps, the focus is mostly on preparing and planning. This is followed by several action items and finally the creation and presentation of several recommendations and a final report.

The most important of these steps is the formation of your Essential Question. Once it is formulated, it serves as the North Star for the entire project and should be always in the front of a districts mind when doing any type of planning by any type of staff member from central office administration to classroom teachers and support staff.

Ultimately, your Essential Question should be:

- Aligned with district goals and initiatives.
- Based on language found in the Strategic Plan.
- Focused on student achievement (not curriculum or technology).
- A vision for utopia.
- Easily understood by all community members.
- Achievable

What does an Essential Question Look Like When Complete?

When completed, the final Essential Question should be a single question which all your future work will hopefully answer.

HOW CAN WE CREATE INNOVATIVE AND ENGAGING LEARNING ENVIRONMENTS THAT FOCUS ON AUTHENTIC STUDENT ACTIVITIES AND ACHIEVEMENT?

In the example, the essential question is:

How can we create innovative and engaging learning environments that focus on authentic student activities and achievement?

Please notice that the essential question is not "how do we use more technology in the classroom?" or "how do we get more coaches in front of teachers?"

In breaking down the example above, this question is sharing that the district is trying to figure out how to first create "innovative and engaging learning environments." This is a clear reference to what the district wants to see in its physical classrooms. Yet, at the same time, it does not use the word classroom. This supplies the perception that a learning environment might be a library, an outdoor setting, a physical education space, or even an auditorium stage.

Next, the example Essential Question gives a vision for what it wants to see happen inside of those "innovative and engaging learning environments" when it says, "focuses on authentic student activities and achievement." This phrase specifically does not mention technology, rather, it mentions that the district wishes to see real-world experiences for students being offered by staff members that will engage the students in the learning process.

Both phrases ultimately come together to support and raise student achievement.

How is an Essential Question Created?

The process of creating a formal Essential Question is broken down into three distinct parts. Each of these parts is designed to help ground the school district both in its past, its present, and its future.

Step 1: Review the District Strategic Plan

If the Essential Question is an answer to the directions provided in the Strategic Plan, it is important to start the journey by reviewing the plan and asking it and its creators some fundamental questions.

- What were the goals and visions of the plan?
- What were some of the challenges in creating the plan?
- Where were the needs and areas of focus in the district when creating the plan?

Step 2: Brainstorm Action Words and Key Phrases

After taking the time to review the document and breaking it down into its essential pieces and individual goals, the next step is to brainstorm.

Much like how you would extract key terms and phrases from a job posting to include in your resume as buzz words, the brainstorming phase should begin by discussing your Strategic Plan to pull out any key terms or phrases that the district considers to be important.

Step 3: Ask Yourself These Two Questions

In my work with several school districts over the last decade on this process the first steps in creating an Essential Question usually begin by coming together to answer these two questions:

Activity Suggestion: Time to Think-Pair-Share

One uncomplicated way of completing the steps above is through a series of what I often call “brain dumps.” This is a simple exercise where you read the Strategic Plan, The Mission Statement, and Vision Statement and write down important terms and phrases on a Post-it Note to be stuck on a wall or whiteboard.

Pretty soon, you will see a pattern form on the wall as multiple participants begin to share and post the same or similar words. The words that get posted the most often are the ones that the district holds dear to its values and should be included in the creation of the Essential Question.

Who should make up the Essential Question Committee?

As with the earlier steps in this process, the Essential Question should be created by a cross section in the district. Because it will be the guiding statement that will lead to many months of work, it is important that all levels of the school district know and understand what it is, why it was created, and what purpose it serves.

No matter how big or small your committee is in choosing your Essential Question, the one person who should have a vote in its definitive version and who should champion this project is your Superintendent. The Superintendent, having recently completed the Strategic Plan, will be a vital resource in formulating the Essential Question.

Can it be changed once created?

While it is completely possible to adjust your Essential Question midway through the process of creating your EdTech Integration Plan, it is important that your Essential Question stay grounded as much as possible. This is simply because it is grounded so much in the Strategic Plan (which will not change).

Who needs to approve it?

Once your committee has taken the steps of analyzing your Strategic Plan and created the Essential Question, it should be agreed upon by the district senior leadership team. This does not mean that it should be something discussed at a Board of Education meeting, but it should be a table topic that the Superintendent is involved in. This one question and guiding statement will be the beacon that starts a long quest that will take many resources involving both time and money from all parts of the district. For this reason, it is important to get everyone on board. It is equally important for the Superintendent to champion this quest.

How does the Essential Question guide the process of creating an EdTech integration plan?

During the process of creating an EdTech Integration Plan, a district must take many steps forward using a variety of tools, methods, and resources so that they can meet the goals created in the Strategic Plan.

In the next phase of the EdTech Integration Plan, we will learn how to create a Staff Needs Assessment.

Step 4: Conduct a Staff Needs Assessment

The Staff Needs Assessment is by far one of the most important and, at the same time, most stressful part of the process in creating an EdTech Integration Plan for your school district. When created properly and rolled out with the support of district leadership, it can be used to springboard instructional coaches into the classroom. However, if created improperly and without proper support, it has the power of not only crumbling a coach's relationship with their staff but turning a teacher's union against a school district.

In this section, we are going to learn what a Staff Needs Assessment is, how it should be created, and how it should be shared with your staff.

What is a Needs Assessment?

A Needs Assessment is a powerful self-reflection tool that allows educators to evaluate their current classroom practices while identifying skills they wish to develop through collaboration with an Instructional Coach. This process enables teachers to share their professional growth aspirations with the assessor, fostering a targeted approach to future learning opportunities.

Needs Assessments can be given verbally or in written/digital format and, when properly supported, can massively support teachers by meeting their needs rather than just supporting larger district-provided goals.

Why is a Needs Assessment Important?

Just as teachers spend the first few weeks of the school year working with their students to figure out strengths, weaknesses, and needs, Instructional Coaches find themselves doing the same with their teachers. One of the things that both teachers and Instructional Coaches have in common is that they need to figure out where their "students" are at the beginning of the year so that they know how to formulate their goals and strategies throughout the school year.

For teachers, this is easy because they work with their students each day. When a unit starts, they might ask some pre-chapter questions or even give them a pre-test. These non-evaluative classroom assessments are types of self-evaluations. They allow both the teacher and student the opportunity to acknowledge where they are when guiding the planning and instruction of the material for the year. The same can be said for an Instructional Coaches self-evaluation. The students in this case, however, are the teachers.

How does your Needs Assessment fit into your EdTech Integration Plan Roadmap?

The first three steps of this process primarily involve "planning" and "preparing" for the school district. However, the Needs Assessment step marks a significant shift towards active creation of the EdTech Integration Plan.

Only after collecting, analyzing, and sharing the Staff Self-Assessment data with stakeholders can the remainder of the process unfold, paving the way for a clear path forward.

Who should be included in creating and distributing a Needs Assessment?

The creation of a Staff Needs Assessment should not be taken lightly. It is the first time that teachers and other staff members are learning about the EdTech Integration Plan. It also will come as a small shock to them when they are asked to take a "quiz" that "evaluates" their skills. I use quotes for these two terms because it is important to help everyone understand that the Needs Assessment is a tool to determine where a particular person feels they are at any given point in the year and is NOT an evaluative process or procedure.

For these reasons, the final Staff Needs Assessment should be created with, and have the buy-in, from both the Instructional Coaching department and supporting administrators. This is because you are openly asking staff members to take a formal assessment of their skills that will be analyzed and developed into your action plan.

What does a Needs Assessment need to include?

As with any survey, a Needs Assessment should be created in a way to get not only quick and easy to read charts and graphs, but also to provide the teacher with the opportunity to share their own thoughts about their own personal needs.

Pro-Tip: A Needs Assessment should cover the skills a teacher knows, NOT the skills you wish your teachers know.

For example, let's say that your district is currently a Google based school, and your district is transitioning to a more Microsoft focused learning environment. It would not make sense for you to ask questions about PowerPoint in the survey. It would make much more sense to ask questions about Google Slides and then, when combing the data, use previous knowledge to support the planning for future professional development session on the new tool.

When creating your Needs Assessment, it is highly recommended NOT to make it all about the tool. In the world of digital learning, it is never about the tool. It is always about the skill and/or learning outcomes for our students.

An example would be:

- Do you know how to use text wrapping in Google Docs?
- Would you like your students to be able to create infographics to support classroom projects?

In this example, the first statement focuses on the tool where the second example focuses on student learning outcomes and goals that a teacher might have about an upcoming project.

One of these might make a teacher feel embarrassed and negative about their current skillset while the other option might open the door for a future conversation between the coach and the teacher.

Additionally, one of these answers is specifically about only one application that a teacher may or may not be completely familiar with. The second example naturally leads itself to allowing the coach and teacher to select from any number of solutions to a project concept.

Tool Based vs Skill Based

It is also important that your Needs Assessment not only be multiple choice based but created in a way to give your teachers the opportunity for short or long form personal reflection.

The reasoning behind the text-based questions is so that they can elaborate on their own personal needs as a teacher or to share their thoughts on a subject after being presented with single option questions in earlier sections of the survey.

An example of open-ended questions might be:

- What would you like to do with your students this year that you are looking for help with? OR What would you like to learn more about this year?
- Moving forward, what format of professional learning do you prefer?
- What personal goals would you like our Instructional Coaches to work with you on this year?

Meeting Your Staff Where They Are … Not Any Higher

There is always this moment in the relationship between a coach and a staff member where one-party questions why the coach is standing there trying to help them. They might feel inadequate or inferior because of the lack of digital learning skills. They might think that the coach is there to “tell on” them to the principal if they do not know how to do things. It is extremely easy for a coach, no matter how experienced they are, to accidentally send an unspoken vibe to another staff member. This gets worse when the staff member is asked to take a test that they feel or think judges their skills. For this reason, it is important to set up carefully the event in which the Needs Assessment will be given and do it in a way that does not put them in an uneasy position before the survey is distributed.

Let us look at how a coach can successfully create and distribute the staff Needs Assessment to their buildings.

3 Steps for Creating and Conducting a Successful Needs Assessment

Step 1: Clearly Define Your Needs Assessment Objectives

Before sitting down to create your Needs Assessments, you must first produce your goals for the data that you will be collecting. This will help you formulate the correct questions to ask and not allow you to ask too many questions.

Before creating your Needs Assessment, ask yourself:

- Why are you conducting the Needs Assessment?
- In what way would you like to see the data when the assessment is finished?
- What do you plan to do with the findings?

Step 2: Secure Buy-in from Building and District Administrators

A Needs Assessment given to staff without an administrator's backing holds no water. (Please read this sentence again, and again, and again) At the moment that the survey is distributed to the staff members, your administrator MUST be standing next to you giving the directions for the activity or at the very least, up in the front of the room showing support for you. Staff members will notice where the administrator is very quickly, and the coach will completely lose all credibility for the survey if they feel that there is no "need" to take things seriously. (Please read this paragraph again … aloud.)

Before distributing your Needs Assessment, ask yourself:

- Is your building principal on board with your Needs Assessment?
- Is the Needs Assessment meeting their needs and building goals?
- Is the Needs Assessment supporting district needs and their long-term vision?

Step 3: Identify Your Target Audience and Data Sources

The reason this chapter refers to the survey assessment as a "Staff Needs Assessment" is because when collecting data, you want to know where every member of your building or district is in their ability to put digital learning skills into action. In later sections of the EdTech Integration Plan process, we will address the importance of this and break down professional development by staff member positions.

Before analyzing your Needs Assessment, ask yourself if your data can be used to break down:

- Teachers
- Non-Certified Staff
- Support Staff and Office Workers

What Could Your Needs Assessment Look Like?

In this section, we'll examine a Needs Assessment recently administered to an elementary school faculty. The survey was conducted during a staff meeting, following a brief presentation by the coach on classroom digital tool usage. The presentation concluded by highlighting the various ways the coach could support teachers in their classrooms.

The Needs Assessment was designed based on the skills required for Google Level 1 and 2 certifications, utilizing a combination of Likert scale and open-ended questions.

Needs Assessment Directions

In the directions, it was clearly written that this was a non-evaluative survey designed to create a customized professional learning plan for each teacher.

Provide simple directions and your reasons "why" your needs assessment is being given.

How would you rate your comfort level in the following?

	1	2	3	4	5
Creating, Editing, Sharing a Google Doc	○	○	○	○	○
Formatting Text, Working with Images	○	○	○	○	○
Table of Contents, Revision History, Tables, Hyperlinks	○	○	○	○	○
Commenting, Suggested Edits, Citation Tools, Equation Tools,	○	○	○	○	○
Google Docs Add-ons	○	○	○	○	○

Setting Up Your Survey Questions for Success

This staff Needs Assessment survey was created in 6 application-based sections followed by a demographic section and an open-ended section.

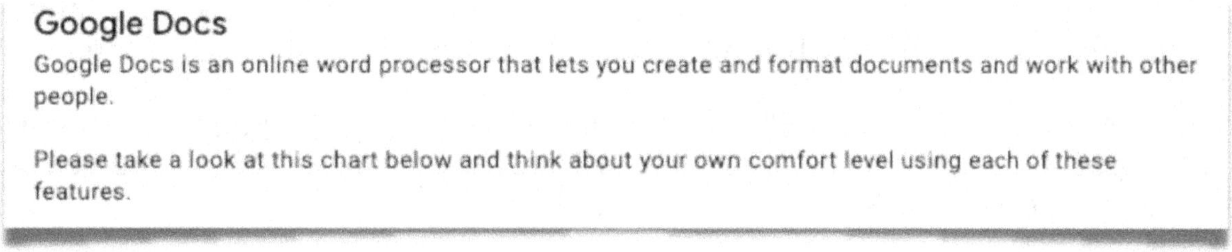

Google Docs

Google Docs is an online word processor that lets you create and format documents and work with other people.

Please take a look at this chart below and think about your own comfort level using each of these features.

For each application-based section, there were brief directions that explained what the application was. For this survey, Google Docs, Slides, Forms, Sites, Classroom, and Microsoft Teams were included.

For each section, there were 5 multiple choice questions that were written from easy to more complicated. These skills-based questions were written as "how much do you know" but, if you look closely at them, they also outline a SAMR type of structure.

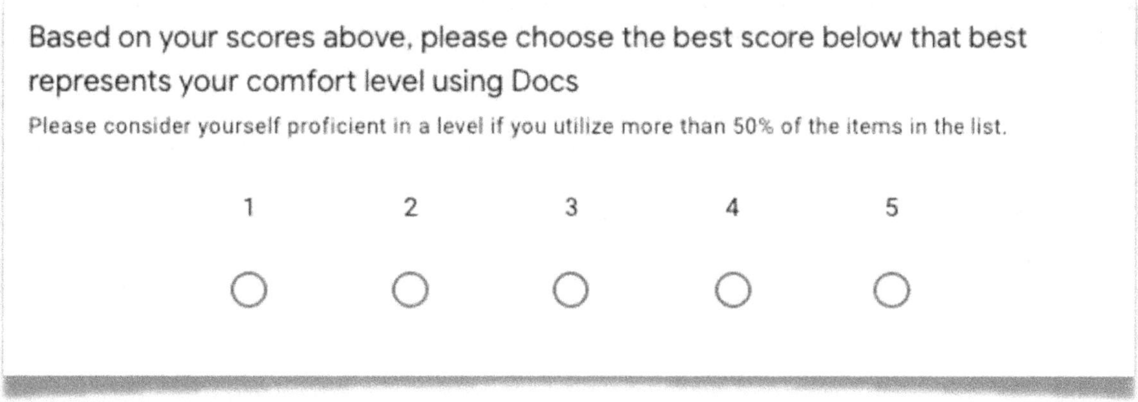

Based on your scores above, please choose the best score below that best represents your comfort level using Docs

Please consider yourself proficient in a level if you utilize more than 50% of the items in the list.

1	2	3	4	5
○	○	○	○	○

When you look at the chart:

- The first question is a “Substitute” question.
- The second question is an “Augmentation” question.
- The third and fourth are “Modification” questions.
- The 5th question might be able to be thought of as an “Augmentation” question.
- The last question is designed to have people really think about how much they know about the application AFTER they are asked a series of qualifying questions.

These questions were not just questions about a staff members' skill set, they were also designed to get someone to think about what skills really go into “knowing” a particular application. This sets up the last question in this section.

Have you ever asked someone “Do you know Google Docs?” That person might say … “oh yeah, I use it every day!” By presenting the Likert questions first and providing them with several skills that they may or may not know about, it then gives them an opportunity to step back and ask themselves, “How much do I really know about using Google Docs?”

What Happens at The End of the Survey?

The staff Needs Assessment is not only a tool that can be used to collect valuable self-reflective data about your staff, but also the first section of a two-part survey.

No matter if you are using Google Forms or Microsoft Forms for this, each platform gives you the opportunity to add a customized thank you note. But the crafty coach uses this section to their advantage.

As mentioned earlier, the survey above was delivered to building staff members during a PD (Professional Development) session to get them pumped up about what is possible in the classroom and to share how the coach could be used in the classroom. Then a survey was given. Once the survey was distributed and as they were being submitted, the “thank you” screen shared one additional form for the staff members to click on. The link went directly to the coaches booking form.

How do you Analyze the Data Collected in the Needs Assessment?

No matter if you are using a Google or Microsoft Form, data from the survey gets transferred into a spreadsheet. The spreadsheet above had a few dozen columns of data because the Likert charts had multiple questions in each section.

One of the things that was able to be created from the data in this survey was a "heat map" that showed visually where each staff member was based on their own self-assessments.

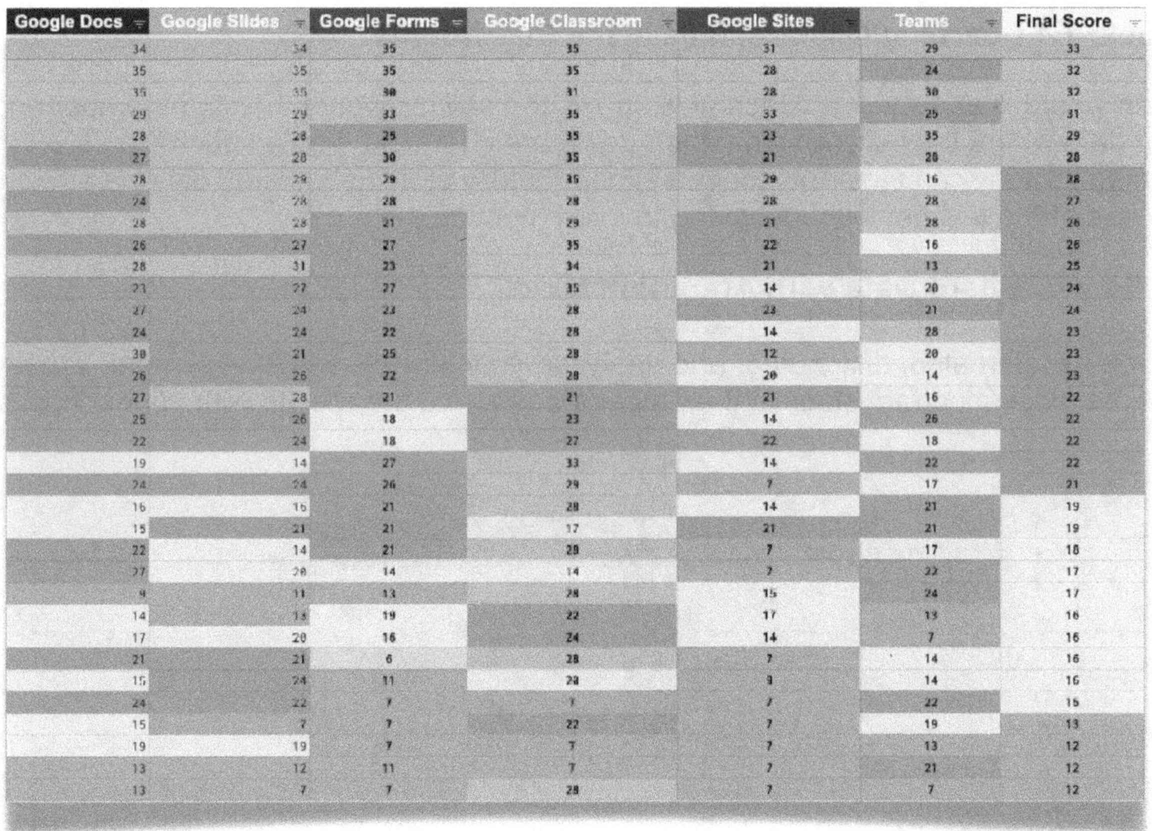

Google Docs	Google Slides	Google Forms	Google Classroom	Google Sites	Teams	Final Score
34	34	35	35	31	29	33
35	35	35	35	28	24	32
35	35	30	31	28	30	32
29	29	33	35	33	25	31
28	28	25	35	23	35	29
27	28	30	35	21	20	28
28	29	29	35	29	16	28
24	28	28	28	28	28	27
28	28	21	29	21	28	26
26	27	27	35	22	16	26
28	31	23	34	21	13	25
23	27	27	35	14	20	24
27	24	23	28	23	21	24
24	24	22	28	14	28	23
30	21	25	28	12	20	23
26	26	22	28	20	14	23
27	28	21	21	21	16	22
25	26	18	23	14	26	22
22	24	18	27	22	18	22
19	14	27	33	14	22	22
24	24	26	29	7	17	21
16	16	21	28	14	21	19
15	21	21	17	21	21	19
22	14	21	28	7	17	18
27	20	14	14	7	22	17
9	11	13	28	15	24	17
14	13	19	22	17	13	16
17	20	16	24	14	7	16
21	21	6	28	7	14	16
15	24	11	28	3	14	16
24	22	7	7	7	22	15
15	7	7	22	7	19	13
19	19	7	7	7	13	12
13	12	11	7	7	21	12
13	7	7	28	7	7	12

In the screenshot above, data from each of the sections has been organized and given a number that is then averaged on the right column into a final score. By using this process, we can then use Conditional Formatting to color code the scores visually.

What can you do with this data after it is analyzed?

From this point in the process, you and your administrators can create a plan to support teachers.

Option 1: Ability Level Based PD

During the next PD opportunity, teachers can be broken into groups based on their scores so that PD is given based on self-perceived ability levels. This way the more advanced teachers are not learning with those who are not as tech centered.

Option 2: 1:1 Coaching Opportunities in the Classroom

Once this data is analyzed, a coach now knows the ability level of the staff member and the written data where they shared what their goals are. The next time a coach works with that staff member they can steer the conversation or future projects towards either a strength or weakness of the teacher without having to even mention the survey.

How do you Share Data with Administration?

After you have created, distributed, and analyzed your staff Needs Assessment, you are at one of the most important steps in the process ... sharing the results with your administrative team.

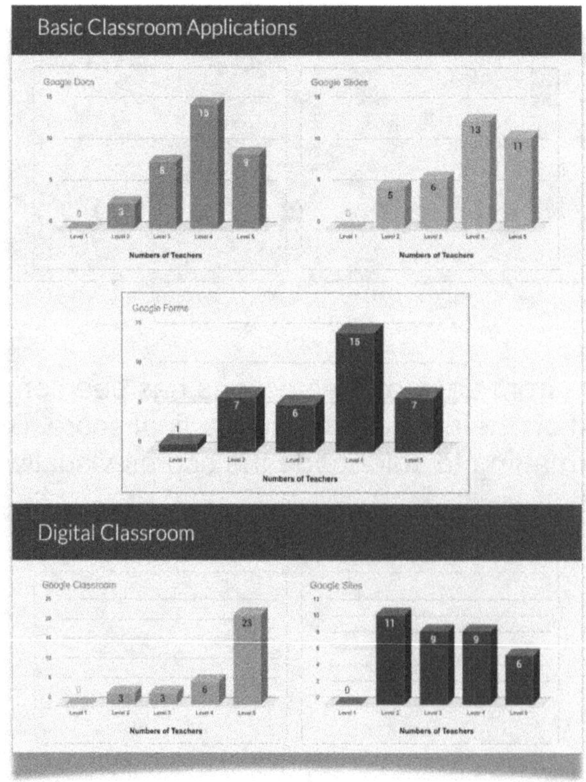

The sharing of information in the example above was created using Google Sites by embedding Charts created in Google Sheets. Each application question was color-coded for easy viewing and the charts were altered so that you can see the data labels clearly.

Who Should See the Data?

When it comes to the topic of sharing data, there are three basic thoughts:

1. Only share with administration
2. Plan for both coach and administrator to share the data with the staff.
3. Only the administrator shares the data with the staff.

Unfortunately for too many coaches, the data never gets seen. The administrator looks at it and that is the end of the story. Even worse, the coach is asked to share the data with the staff members, and they are told that they must present it alone. When this happens, it is traditionally a negative experience for the coach.

The best situation when sharing the data is for the administrator to stand up and give a motivational speech about goals and objectives and how we are "here" and how we need to be "there" and the only way for us to do this is by working with the coach.

In other words, this is an opportunity to either empower, or completely crush the coach and their chances of being successful during the rest of the school year.

What Happens Next?

In this section, we have covered every angle of the creation, distribution, analyzing, and sharing of staff Needs Assessment surveys and data. This is the part in the race where the flag goes down and the race begins.

Now that we have created our outline, formed our essential question, and collected baseline data, the next step in the EdTech Integration Plan is to begin the process of identifying how to support each staff member based on the needs of their position and role within the building or school district.

Final Thoughts

The Staff Needs Assessment is an essential tool in creating an EdTech Integration Plan. When done properly, the survey supplies a baseline of data from which major decisions about the coaching program can flow from. It can also provide the coach with the information needed to plan and collaborate with teachers in the classroom.

Step 5: Create Individualized Professional Learning Plans

Have you ever walked into your school's main office and asked the secretary for help with a task like printing labels or doing a mail merge, only to find they couldn't assist you? You might have left wondering, "Why don't they know how to do these basic tasks?"

When it comes to finding support getting some of the more basic aspects of digital life it all comes down to making sure that the staff members who need to do specific tasks know how to do those specific tasks. To make sure this happens, we need to first identify each of the key members of our educational family and determine what skills they need to know to effectively do their job.

Providing Individual PD (Professional Development) for Each Staff Member

To make sure that all our staff members are not only fully prepared to do the tasks assigned to them, but to also have the support of the Instructional Coaching Department, it is important to break down each member of your organization and determine what they need to learn and what skills from each application need to be taught.

Traditionally, a school district can be thought of as having 3-4 subsections of employees.

- Administration
- Certified Staff
- Non-Certified Staff
- Other

Unfortunately, it is too often the case that, during professional development days, the certified staff are in some type of professional development, the administrators are overseeing that professional development, and the non-certified staff are in their offices or at their desks doing whatever their normal day-to-day tasks are.

Is this effective planning? Does this get the job done? Does this type of professional development plan support the growth of all staff members?

Instead of breaking down professional development into “those who need it” and “those who don’t think they need it,” it is far more effective to break down every member of the team and assess what they need.

Your district could then be broken down into the following:

- Superintendent
- Business Office
- Central Office Executive Assistants (Confidential & Non-Confidential)
- Principals & AP's
- Building Administrators (Department Chairs)
- Building Secretaries
- School Councilors
- Special Services
- Support Staff
- Aides
- Teachers
- Coaches
- Long Term Substitutes

Notice that at the top of this list is the Superintendent. It is essential that the Superintendent have a Growth Mindset and be the first one to share with the team the importance of being a constant learner. I have had many amazing meetings with my upper administrators which were basically "show and tell" sessions that involved sharing the latest and greatest features of applications being used in the classrooms. This is a fantastic way to get your Coaches in front of Central Office leadership.

Building a Professional Development Platform for ALL Staff Members

During this step of the EdTech Integration Plan process, it is important to sit down with your district and not just clearly identify everyone who is in your district but exactly what applications, tools, and equipment they need to know and then, identify what it is that they need to know about each of those items.

Let us take Microsoft Word or Google Docs for example. Would you put a secretary and a middle school teacher in the same professional development session and teach them the same way with the same curriculum? Of course not. You would want to teach your office worker how to do things such as paragraph styles, mail merge, and find & replace. The middle school teacher, however, might be taught paragraph styles but would also want to be taught how to use Microsoft Word or Google Docs to create a dynamic lesson with their students.

Same application … two completely different PD sessions.

Going Beyond the Major Applications

While it's straightforward to compare professional development approaches for word processors, this concept extends far beyond computer applications. For instance, how frequently does your district allocate time to properly train office staff on merging and holding phone calls, sending complex print jobs to the copy machine, or translating documents into multiple languages?

How Should You Break Down Your District to support Job-Based Professional Development?

The first step in this process is to lay out all the applications and equipment used in the district. In this example the school district is running a Google-based platform and additionally supports a Student Information System.

The school district would have these items to organize:

- Google Workspace Applications
- District Website
- Chromebooks
- Digital Learning Platforms
- Safety & Security Protocols
- Frontline
- IEP Direct
- PowerSchool
- Telephone System
- Copy Machine System
- Windows OS
- Chrome OS

As you can see, there are plenty of major topics that a district needs to think about in its quest to support every staff member.

How Do You Break Down Individual PD Sessions for each Staff Member?

Let us take the first topic, for example, Google Workspace. Inside of the Google system, you have a series of major applications (Docs, Sheets, Slides). Each of these has its own set of skills that staff members need to be aware of based on their role in the district.

When using a large brush stroke, a teacher may need PD on:

- Google Docs
- Google Slides
- Google Forms
- Google Drive

However, an office staff member might need to PD on:

- Google Docs
- Google Slides
- Google Forms
- Google Drive
- Google Sheets
- Google Calendar

You can see in the example above that the office worker needs added professional development time to learn additional applications within the Google Suite to be able to completely do their job effectively.

How Do You Provide Professional Development to Every Staff Member Effectively?

In this section, we have looked at the 5th step in the journey towards creating an effective EdTech Integration Plan for your school district. If you are at this point in the progress, you are now in the "building" phase meaning, your district has already produced a District Snapshot, you have Identified your Essential Question, and you have surveyed your staff to learn what type of skills they think they have.

The 6th step in the EdTech Integration Plan process is to create your Professional Learning Roadmap. This is where we take all the research and information that we have compiled and along with the knowledge of what each staff member needs to know based on their role in the district, create a plan of action that will demonstrate how the professional development will be given.

Step 6: Build a Professional Learning Roadmap

Picture this: It's midway through the school year, and a professional development day is looming on the horizon. Suddenly, someone turns to you and asks, "So, what's your plan for this PD day?"

Does this sound familiar?

Professional Development days are magical opportunities built into the school calendar that allow staff members to come together and learn without the stress of the average school day. These days, staff development can take many forms from active physical large group sessions to passive virtual sessions behind a screen and they are always meant to propel staff learning forward.

There are many ways to create a successful professional development day. Some of these would be to use guest speakers, the creation or formation of a group project, and simply to provide teachers a "free afternoon" to get caught up on schoolwork. No matter what type of professional development is provided or how it is set up, there should always be a goal in mind for each session and a curricular activity that follows it up to directly support and impact learning in the classroom.

In this section, we will look at the creation of a Professional Development Roadmap.

Three Things Every PD Session Needs

One of the most important things about your Professional Development Roadmap is the ability to not only provide your staff member what they need, but to also provide the district with a reason or rationale for why they are being asked to attend each and every session. PD, no matter if it ties into district, curricular, building, or department goals should always have three things to be considered successful:

- A reason for being.
- A call to action
- A follow up action that leads to classroom instruction

Meeting Staff Members where they Need It

In an earlier section, we learned about the importance of creating a staff needs assessment (Or self-assessment). In this brief survey, one of the questions that should be asked is "in what ways do prefer to learn." Usually created as a drop-down list, options for this question might include:

- 1:1 Learning with a Coach
- Small Group Learning
- Large Group Instruction
- Virtual Learning

By asking your staff this important question and knowing how interested most of them are in learning, you will have an idea of the best way to create your professional development roadmap.

Let us look at all these types of learning and dig into the pros and cons of each.

1:1 Learning

One to One learning (1:1) can be considered many things. Mostly this refers to a session where you have one coach and one staff member. One-to-One learning serves both the coach and staff members greatly because they are given the opportunity to ask direct questions and dig into topics that would not be able to be tackled in a larger group for a variety of reasons.

Where 1:1 learning is ideal for certain situations and even for certain types of individuals it is not always the best way to plan professional development due to the amount of time it takes to have your coach meet with each member of the group. I do, however, think that it has some advantages in professional development planning. For example, when providing large group training, for example, to office workers, I like to schedule a final session with each member of the group 1:1 at their desks to make sure that we cover individual questions about individual projects or tasks that only they must work on each day.

Small Group

For the sake of discussion in this post, Small Group Professional Development refers to a handful of staff members getting together for a learning session. Generally, this is where a coach sits down with a grade level of less than 10 in a room.

One of the nice things about working with small groups of like-topic staff members, a coach, can be more dressed-down and more relaxed in their coaching sessions. Conversations often surrounding a common topic and questions are often on point for the group's needs.

Medium Group

Growing in numbers, Medium Group Professional Development is defined as a coach working with several departments (or grade levels) at the same time to even a crowd the size of a full building staff. Generally, these are what faculty meeting style PD sessions.

One of the great ways to use Medium Group Professional Development is to introduce a common topic in a short amount of time and then build a commercial around an added opportunity where coaches can work with smaller groups of teachers.

When building faculty meeting sessions, it is best to keep things short. Remembering that most faculty meetings are after school, a shorter session is far better than a longer session due to the fatigue of staff members after a long day of teaching.

Large Group

Every so often, an opportunity comes in front of an instructional coach where they need to address an entire school district on a particular topic. Sessions such as these are usually online (these days) and are designed to cover extremely broad topics.

Much like building level faculty meetings and even smaller group sessions, anytime a coach is in front of a large number of people, the goal should always be to show an overview of the topic and provide a call to action for the coach to get into classrooms to work more intimately with teachers on specific skills or applications.

Virtual Learning

When thinking about all the items that a staff member needs to learn throughout the course of a school year, there are times where physical or live professional development is not the best way to transfer knowledge.

For this reason, there is always the opportunity to create a virtual learning program to quickly teach many staff members the same thing at the same time.

A good example of this type of professional development comes at the beginning of the school year. Many school districts ask their staff to read several policies and take a standard survey to check their compliance with any new rules and regulations. This is often provided in the form of a short series of videos and an online quiz to show attendance and completion of the project.

Creating a Professional Development Calendar ... Before the School Year

Your district professional development calendar should be conceived and outlined over the summer months when everyone is together planning out their building and department goals and objectives. I always found that the summertime is the best time to meet with district leadership 1:1 and discuss their upcoming goals for their buildings. This is an exciting time to bring up the inclusion of the Instructional Coach into the schedule.

Where it is true that the building and district leadership create the overarching professional development calendar and roadmap, the Instructional Coach should have an opportunity to support any district initiatives that come up so that they are ready weeks if not months before an actual event that was placed on the calendar during the hotter days of the year.

Building a Calendar for All Staff Members

When a new staff member is welcomed into the district, they are often provided with an opportunity to attend a New Employee Orientation (NEO). However, what happens once NEO is over, and staff members need to learn how to survive in their classrooms? One of the best ways to support new employees and especially brand-new teachers is through the creation of a Teacher Learning Academy.

Example of a Teacher Learning Academy:

- New Teacher Orientation (All New Staff Members)
- General Information
- Human Resources
- Finance Department
- Technology Department
- Account Setup
- Help Desk Ticket
- Safety and Security
- Digital Learning Department
- Curricular Applications
- Google/Microsoft Applications
- Classroom Hardware
- Email / Calendar
- First Year Teachers ... (Every other month)
- Google Classroom
- Google Sites
- Second Year Teachers (Every other month)
- Supporting Curricular Activities
- Example: Using Audio/Video in the classroom
- Third Year Teachers (Every other month)
- Some type of project that helps the district.
- Fourth Year Teachers (Every other month)

Certified Staff Members

Professional Development for Certified Staff Members usually comes in a variety of shapes and sizes. Although there are scheduled times for certified staff members to have meaningful professional development, one of the best opportunities to work with staff members in a non-stressful matter is during the summer months.

Although the opportunity to create what is commonly referred to as “Summer Academies” or “Bootcamps” due to contractual, financial, and philosophical reasons, I have extremely fond memories of working with teachers from all grades and subject areas during summer sessions.

Office Workers

When planning professional development for office workers, you need to keep a few things in mind. The first thing is that these staff members are not used to attending professional development. For this reason, I always make sure that I have everything set up for them in the room before they show up. This includes both a laptop (plugged in) and a wired mouse. (Word of advice … NEVER try to do office worker PD with only a tiny track pad … you will thank me later)

When planning professional development for administrative assistants, I tend to have a basic outline that is similar, yet completely different than what I schedule for certified staff members.

Example of Administrative Assistants Training:

- Session 1: Intro to Drive and Docs
- Session 2: Intro to Sheets and Forms
- Session 3: Intro to (something more specific for their position)
- Session 4: 1:1 session at their desk

By creating a 4 session (or 3+1) format, generally in 90-minute segments, you can support all office workers no matter where they are on the digital learning ability scale.

Administrators

How many years have you been teaching and how often have you had an administrator ask YOU to teach THEM something new?

When it comes to creating a meaningful and long-lasting professional development program, learning does not just stop where the hallway begins. There are so many things that can be done to support your administrators.

No matter if your administrators are veterans or relative newbies, there is always something that can be discussed when it comes to the extremely important topic of "what do they want to see when they walk into the classroom?"

In the past, I have led some awesome Administrator PD sessions where instead of teaching directly at them, the sessions were designed more towards helping them create a clear vision of what classroom instruction should look like through the lens of digital learning tools. We covered topics such as the SAMR model, and I shared with them some of the more popular projects that I do with their teachers to help them understand my role as an Instructional Coach.

Professional Development when set up to be aligned with the strategic vision of the school district is a wonderful thing. It can build staff morale and bring a group of teachers together focused on a common goal. When planning your professional development, it is best to start in the summertime by discussing a district/building/department goals and objectives for the school year and mapping out various times during the school year to make the best use of your Instructional Coaches.

No matter what type of PD session is offered (large, medium, small) it is important to remember that everything should in some way propel the use of 1:1 conversation in the classroom between the Instructional Coach and the staff member.

In our next section, we will look at the creation of your "EdTech Menu," a series of professional development offerings that are provided to staff during the school year to support personalized professional learning throughout your district.

Step 7: Create an EdTech Menu

Is all professional development created equal?

In a small school district or a single school, there's typically one Instructional Coach. This individual develops and delivers a single set of lessons for staff. But what if a district has multiple Instructional Coaches?

Let us say that your school district has two or more coaches. Each of them is asked to provide a specific professional development session on a specific topic or application. Each coach takes it upon themselves to create a dynamic professional development session for their staff members. At the end of the day, each group of teachers is tested on their knowledge of the app and scores differently.

In the instructional classroom, we use a standardized curriculum to ensure that all students of a grade level learn the same topics and skills and are instructed using the same materials so that students get the same education. If this is the case for our students, the question comes up "Why can't this be the same for professional development?"

Because of the growing need for larger school districts to have a standardized professional learning pathway, it is important for digital learning departments and Instructional Coaches to create and adopt an EdTech Menu.

What is an EdTech Menu

Consider a typical chain restaurant. You order a cheeseburger, confident that it will be identical to the one you'd get at any other location of that chain. The consistency—not necessarily the burger itself—is what keeps you coming back. It's made with the same ingredients and follows the same procedures every time.

This concept applies equally well to professional development. When a principal requests an Instructional Coach to lead a session on "Intro to Google Drive," several questions arise: What should the coach teach? What are the administrator's goals for this session? What if two coaches accept this request and develop completely different agendas?

At its core, an EdTech Menu could resemble a restaurant menu or be as straightforward as a basic spreadsheet. The fundamental idea is that the Coach or Digital Learning Department has carefully analyzed an application or concept, determined the most effective teaching method, and created a standardized approach.

How to Create an EdTech Menu

Do all applications need an EdTech Menu style approach? Of course not! Coaches should be free to teach as they need and adjust lessons and conversations for any situation. However, when looking at broad concepts and PD (Professional Development) sessions that need to reach a wide audience, it is important to have a common set of skills and activities.

Step 1: Identify Key Applications

The first thing to do when creating an EdTech Menu is to identify what applications you think will need to be taught to a large group of staff members. These would be considered your core applications.

An example of core applications is:

- Google Classroom
- Microsoft Teams
- Device Monitoring Systems
- College Recommendation Systems

Applications like those listed above should be thought of as “menu-based PD” that a coach has in their back pocket and is ready to go for whenever a district or building leader asks for their staff to be trained. By having a set menu of these items, it’s easy to create a learning session once and then update year after year as needed.

Step 2: Identify Key Concepts

Once you have your core applications, the next step is to identify the key concepts that are needed to be successful in getting started with the application.

From this point, you are looking at what might be referred to as your “101” and your “201” type of skills.

Step 3: Collect Materials Needed to Plan Lessons & Activities

Once you have your applications broken down into key concepts, the next step is to decide how to create unified and standardized presentations.

The biggest reason for creating an EdTech Menu is twofold:

- You have a pre-made bank of PD session that you know you will be teaching during the school year.
- Multiple coaches can teach the same applications the same way without the need for duplicating the prep work.
- Everyone in the department gets to work together.

What Does an EdTech Menu Look Like?

Below is an example of an EdTech Menu that might be used within a Digital Learning Department. In this menu, each application is broken down into both beginner and advanced topics.

Google Docs

101	201	Admin Assistants
Introduction	Working with Text Formatting	Mail Merge
Toolbar	Modifying Header Styles	Form Letters
Seetting up a Page	Word Art	Mailing Labels
Page Color	Hyperlinks & Bookmarks	Suggestions and Tracking Changes
Entering Text	Find and Replace	
Saving & Opening Files	Tables	
Formatting Paragraphs	Inserting Audio Files	
Paragraph Headers	Inserting Video Files	
Bullet Points & Numbering	Table of Contents	
Working with Graphics	Footnotes & Endnotes	
Margins	Editing PDF Files	
Section Breaks	Embedding into Google Sites	
Headers & Footers		
Commenting / Suggesting		
Sharing Documents		
Printing Documents		
Downloading as PDF		
Downloading as Word		

What Happens Next?

Over the course of an EdTech Integration Plan process, a school district goes through several steps of identifying its goals and recommendations for the future. In this step, the creation of an EdTech Menu is meant to support those goals by supplying both school districts and Instructional Coaches with the opportunity to create a series of preplanned and prepackaged sessions to address many staff members.

In our next section, we will take this step further through the creation of ISTE (International Society for Technology in Education) Standards based lesson plans that address both the needs of the students and the needs of all staff members that are aligned with both district and digital learning goals.

Step 8: Develop Standards-Based Lesson Plans

What is the difference between having a plan for something, and simply making it up on the spot?

For many Instructional Coaches, a daily routine is to support teachers through the creation of daily lesson plans and activities. Coaches meet with teachers, discuss the content of a lesson, and do their best to build up the lesson through a series of digital learning activities. At the end of the day, the teacher has an amazing lesson that they can perform in front of their students and if needed, turn into their principals at the beginning of the week.

When planning out a years' worth of professional development and creating a roadmap for success amongst multiple Instructional Coaches, there comes a time where a standard needs to be set for what is taught, when it is taught, how it is taught, and (most important) why it is taught.

In our last section, we learned the importance of creating an EdTech Menu. An EdTech Menu is a crucial step in the EdTech Integration Planning process where applications and concepts are broken down into a variety of categories and mapped. This allows multiple coaches to teach the same topic simultaneously to separate groups of staff members.

In this section, we are going to take the EdTech Menu concept one step further and discuss the creation and importance of having ISTE Standards based lesson plans that support not only the instructional aspects of professional learning, but also fill the needs and goals of a school districts Strategic Plan and align directly with curricular, as well as digital learning goals.

What are Standards Based Lesson Plans?

In the world of Instructional Coaching, rarely do you find an actual written and formal lesson plan for professional development sessions. For years, I planned all my sessions using a simple slide deck (Google Slides or PowerPoint) and I had a basic outline that I would present from.

This type of planning might work for some, but what happens if you have multiple Coaches in one department all doing the same presentation? It is logical that two coaches might be interested in using one single slide deck or they may also be interested in creating their own presentation materials. But what is important is that they all walk into their respective professional development sessions teaching the same skills with the same (or similar) activities so that everyone learning the skills is getting the same learning outcomes.

Understanding the ISTE Standards

For the last 10 years, I have looked towards the ISTE Standards for Teachers as a guide for all my professional learning sessions. The Standards provided by ISTE are designed to serve as a roadmap for helping teachers infuse digital learning skills into their lessons and their daily teaching habits. It is from these Standards that Instructional Coaches should plan their professional development.

The ISTE Standards for Teachers are broken down into seven unique categories.

- **Learner:**
    - Educators continually improve their practice by learning from and with others and exploring proven and promising practices that leverage technology to improve student learning.
- **Leader:**
    - Educators seek out opportunities for leadership to support student empowerment and success and to improve teaching and learning.
- **Citizen:**
    - Educators inspire students to positively contribute to and responsibly participate in the digital world.
- **Collaborators:**
    - Educators dedicate time to collaborate with both colleagues and students to improve practice, discover and share resources and ideas, and solve problems.
- **Designer:**
    - Educators design authentic, learner-driven activities and environments that recognize and accommodate learner variability.
- **Facilitator:**
    - Educators facilitate learning with technology to support student achievement of the ISTE Standards for Students.
- **Analyst:**
    - Educators understand and use data to drive their instruction and support students in achieving their learning goals.

How To Use the ISTE Standards for Professional Lesson Planning

In looking over the ISTE Standards, it is recommended for teachers to be learners, collaborators, designers, and analysts. For many teachers, these are foreign concepts. But when an Instructional Coach unpacks what the ISTE Standards are calling for teachers to be and develops professional learning sessions that include activities that allow teachers to dive deeper into these learning styles.

Let's look at a typical professional development lesson that an Instructional Coach might provide at a department or building level. For conversation, let's say that a coach will teach about how to use Google Forms to create self-graded quizzes.

A Coach might use the following as guidelines in developing a meaningful and dynamic lesson.

Learner

- Teachers would begin the lesson by engaging in dialogue with each other about some of the positives and challenges they are having in their classrooms. The discussion then might lead to naming things they would like to “fix” which would lead into a transition to the topic of the day.

Collaborators

- Instructional Coaches are always looking to drive conversations from small talk into the creation of a collaborative session that helps the coach work side by side with the teacher in the classroom.

Facilitator

- Once in the classroom, the Instructional Coach and the Teacher work together to infuse digital learning skills and technologies into their lesson planning.

Analyst

- After the lesson, the Coach and Teacher work together to reflect on the lesson and decide what went well and determine how to adjust and create future projects together.

What do Standard Based Lesson Plans Look Like?

Below is a sample lesson plan that I use to create my workshops and professional development sessions.

The lesson plan is broken down into these sections:

Strategic Goals

- How does this professional development session relate and reflect the strategic goals of the district?

State Technology Standards

- Many states have their own technology standards that address digital learning skills.

ISTE Standards

- List the ISTE Standards addressed by the professional development session.

Course Goals

- What are the goals for the professional development session?

Course Description

- Probably one of the most important parts of the Lesson Plan, the course description is what your users might read if you are listing this session on a professional learning course menu.

SLO – WALT

- SLO = Student Learning Objective
- WALT = We Are Learning Today

Materials and Procedures

- What do you need to have with you or prepared (or bookmarked) to run the course?

Reflection

The reflection section of the lesson plan is generally where I write notes after the session to remind myself of the following:

- What worked well or not well?
- What tips or tricks work well for this part of the lesson?

Follow up Activities for Staff Members

- What would the homework be for staff members?
- Is there a Call to Action?

Links and Resources

- What else needs to be included in this lesson or activity that perhaps others have shared with you during a session?
- What are examples of student or teacher work that might be able to be shared in the next session you give on this topic?

Where it might be obvious that a formal lesson plan might not be something that gets put together each and every time that a Coach does a Professional Development session, it is an extremely valuable tool for highlighting the professionalism in the position and providing a guide for coaches who may be teaching a particular course multiple times.

When you create standards-based lessons using the ISTE standards for both Teachers and Students as a guide, you are going to be able to create a standard for what everyone in the district will learn and how they will learn it. This is extremely useful when working across multiple school buildings through multiple Instructional Coaches

While creating standards-based personalized professional development is a crucial step in shifting culture, it's only half the puzzle. In our next section, we'll explore another piece: the incentivization of professional development, often referred to as micro-credentialing.

Step 9: Incentivize Professional Development

I am the proud father of an amazing set of triplets. They are the light of my life, and I revolve everything I do around them. Usually, they are pretty good at doing what they are told to do. In the afternoon they come home from school, put their coats away, and take out their homework. Things work (nearly) perfectly every day.

There are, however, some days there they need to be reminded to do their homework. Other things in their busy lives get in the way and their mother and I need to focus them on their studies so that they can (hopefully) one day grow up to be big and strong members of society. When times like this creep up, we must resort to a tactic that incentivizes their learning by offering them treats, or (in my house) bribes to get them to be diligent students both in school and at home.

Incentivizing learning works wonders for small children. Often at home, you can hear me say “you can watch TV if you get your homework done” or “if you read for another 20 minutes, you can play Minecraft.” Let’s face it, these motivational tricks also work well in the classroom to motivate students to learn. How many times have you heard of teachers who try to trade good behavior for extra time at recess?

If extra recess or added time playing Minecraft work well for students, would it make sense that there is merit in incentivizing professional development for adult learners?

How do you Incentivize Professional Development?

I was recently speaking with an Instructional Coach who has created a unique incentivized learning program for teachers in her school district. She said to me something that was remarkable but at the same time, it was a simple concept that should be adopted by any school district wishing to put a value on the professional well-being of their staff members.

Step 1: Define What Professional Development Truly Is

The first step in incentivizing professional learning is to define exactly what professional development is. For many school districts, professional development is only counted if the staff member is doing it on one of only a handful of days during the school year where PD (Professional Development) is offered by the school district.

This discourages staff from looking outside of school for professional learning opportunities and punishes them for the times they look to improve themselves.

What is professional development? Using broad brush strokes, professional development could be an online course, Edcamp Conference, graduate course or by simply working with an Instructional Coach on a lesson.

Step 2: Recognize that Staff Members are Constantly Engaged in Professional Learning

Once it has been set up that opportunities for professional learning are abundant, the second step is to recognize your staff members for taking advantage of these opportunities and praising them for doing so. Recognition could take the form of online badges, comp time, or even a certificate of recognition from your school district.

In the example that my Instructional Coach friend mentioned about her school district. Teachers take part in a variety of professional learning opportunities and when finished, submit hours, certificates, or other tokens of completion through a Google Form and it is collected and organized in a central location in the district.

This is a notable example of how one school district values the time that staff members spend on professional learning opportunities. Let us look at another.

Step 3: Formulate A Plan That Compliments the Strategic Plan

Above all, your professional development program needs to be designed to meet the needs of the district Strategic Plan. This is a great example of how one school district values the time that staff members spend on professional learning opportunities. Let us look at another.

Professional Development Example Through Badging #1

In this example, a school district created a badging program based around the 4C's of Instructional Technology Integration. Each marking period was given a "C-Theme" and inside each of the themes, teachers were encouraged to earn up to 4 badges to demonstrate proficiency over each of the C's.

Here is an example of this school district's planning document.

Soaring Through the 4C's of Technology Integration

- Egg - Hatchling - Fledgling - High Flyer-

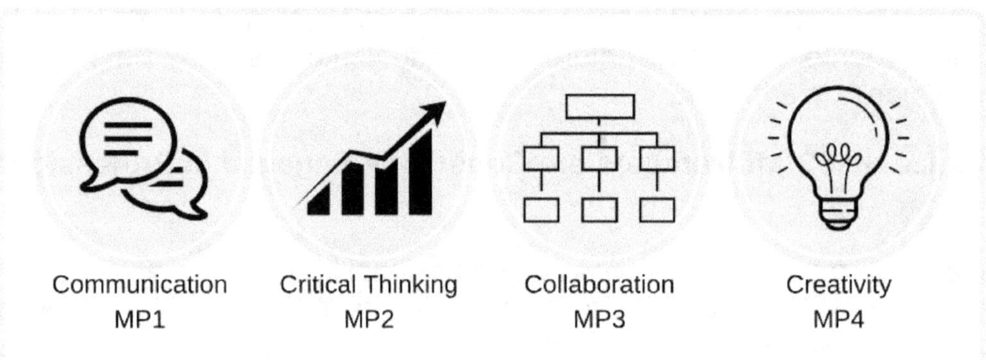

The School District has adopted the "4C's" technology framework to promote Critical Thinking, Creativity, Collaboration, and Communication in our classroom lessons. To implement a comprehensive and learner-centered approach to technology that engages and empowers students, we have created four pathways of learning for our staff.

High-Flying through your Curriculum

Professional Development will be focused on one of the 4C's (Communication, Critical Thinking, Collaboration, Creativity) during each semester of the school year. Staff members will be encouraged to earn their "Highflyer" badge in each of the C's during those semesters. It will take two (2) complete school years to earn all four Highflyer badges.

To become a "Highflyer," teachers will have to earn at least 4 badges by demonstrating their knowledge of that particular "C" by using and implementing certain tools in their classroom and by demonstrating student learning in their respective subject(s)

What are digital badges?

Badges are a way to recognize staff members for gaining skills and experiences they can use with their students. They allow teachers to create their own pathway of learning and customize their individual professional development pathway. By offering badges, as part of the incentive for professional development, teachers can highlight what they are working on in their classrooms and be quickly identified as experts in the classroom. Badges can be earned by a staff member at their convenience or after a training session takes place. Training could be a 1:1 session, group meeting, or online learning module.

What types of badges could be offered?

- Essential Skills: Training activities that do not require a learner to demonstrate knowledge of a particular skill or topic. (Example: Gmail / Calendar / Keep)
- Classroom Tech: These badges are awarded to staff members who take part in a training session and after using it in the classroom with their student's present evidence of proficiency in the form of a link to a project or artifact. (Example: Kahoot)

How Do I Earn a Badge?

To earn badges, teachers can visit our Staff Portal and choose the menu option to visit "Cardinal University." This website will provide teachers with both online and 1:1 learning options to help them learn how best to integrate educational technology to benefit their students.

To earn a badge, a teacher will find a tool or application of interest and enter the online learning portal for that tool. To earn the badge, a teacher must first demonstrate knowledge of the online tool and then provide evidence of using that tool in the classroom with their students. Evidence could include a link to a finalized project or a file inside of their Google Drive.

After completing the online learning course, the teacher will be emailed a badge for that skill. Four tools in the appropriate category will qualify the teacher to receive their "Highflyer" badge for that particular "C." Teachers can learn about and take any course at any time; however, they may only qualify for the "C" that we are focusing on during that particular semester.

What can teachers do with their badges?

Badges can be added to a staff members' website and could be used to link to specific projects.

Can badges count for professional development credit?

5 Badges might equal 10 PD hours.

A Word of Warning for Badging Programs

So far, we have looked at how Micro credentials and Badging Programs can support professional development and enhance digital learning skills both in staff members and students. But one question often comes up when discussing micro credentials. Do they work for every school district?

One of the first things that you need when planning a badging program is support from the administration. The concept of giving out a token for attending a PD session or signaling out one staff member over another is also a concept and discussion that might need to have support from your local teacher's union. I have seen, unfortunately, Instructional Coaches get excited about creating badges for completing PD courses, only to have something backfire due to union issues.

Is it possible to have a staff member attend a PD session and then at the end get a "thank you" token? Absolutely, but the moment that a coach introduces a leader board or some type of tracking statistics that are shown publicly, things often go south (and quickly).

A Word of Advice for Incentivizing Professional Learning

In speaking to several Instructional Coaches about their professional development plans, the size of the school district does have a direct correlation on the success of staff recognition programs. Where there are many exceptions to this, it appears that the smaller the school district, the easier it is to create such a program where staff recognition is part of the culture. If you are in a school with a successful staff recognition program, I would love to invite you to reach out and share your story with me.

The question often arises: "If it works for students, why can't it work for teachers?" When developing staff development and incentive programs, it's crucial to create a bottom-up approach that still has full top-down support. The key to a successful program—whether it involves micro-credentials or staff certificates—is providing professional support that treats your staff as the professionals they are.

Step 10: Defining Your District Recommendations

At this point in the process, your Digital Learning team has met several times and formulated a solid plan to define, develop, and support a standards-aligned digital learning transformation across all levels of the school district. The last few steps of this process require some added thought about how to present the groups findings and conclusions to a group of individuals who might not have been along for the ride and might be preparing to learn about this vision for the first time.

To truly define your districts recommendations so that you can easily present your information to others, you must first make sure that your vision can be presented as quickly and as succinctly as possible so that your audience, whomever it may be, can easily understand what your group is trying to accomplish.

One way your group can clearly define and describe your vision is by creating a series of presentations on the topic that might be given over several weeks at board of education meetings. Because your final Strategic Plan has the potential to be big and bulky, having the opportunity to discuss its various components in smaller segments over the course of several meetings might be something that is appealing so that you can create an environment that allows your audience (or Board of Education) the chance to digest where you are and where you are hoping to be in the future.

Another way to present your plan to a large group is through an infographic. Creating a smaller vision, or series of images can help walk your audience through the concept and process that has taken place over several months. Because you are supporting your findings and recommendations with a graphic, your audience will have the opportunity to spend their time listening to you rather than reading several hundred words while you are in the middle of our presentation.

A third way that has become popular in recent times is to create an online portfolio or website for your strategic plans. This is a great way to chunk your roadmap into smaller pieces and display it in an online presentation that could be no more than 4-7 pages in total. These pages could be used to share the entire plan in great detail or be developed as question starters for audience members to formulate verbal questions during a more detailed presentation.

No matter how you ultimately choose to package and promote your final strategic plan, it's important that you create it clearly to understand, easily digestible, and backed by resources, strategies, and curricular standards.

Step 11: Sharing Recommendations with District Leadership

Congratulations! You and your school district have made it all the way through the journey of creating your EdTech Integration Plan. At this point, you should have a good idea of who your district is, what its needs are, and where you want to see yourself in the future. Most importantly, you have a clear answer to the question "What do you want to see when you walk into a classroom?"

In this section, we will discuss the last steps in creating an EdTech Integration Plan.

- Making recommendations by creating an Action Plan
- Sharing your plan with administration
- Creating and presenting the final EdTech Integration Plan

Each of these steps should be completed with not just one, but with your entire planning group to make sure that all research you have done up to this point is included in the final document and that every part of your district is represented and accounted for.

Let us look at the first step: Creating a Recommendations List.

Putting Your EdTech Integration Puzzle Together

Throughout the process of creating an EdTech Integration Plan, a school district goes through several steps that we have covered in an earlier chapter:

- Create a District Snapshot
- Define Your Endgame
- Formulate an Essential Question
- Create a Staff Needs Assessment
- Identify Staff Member Needs Based on Title and Position
- Build a Professional Learning Roadmap
- Create an EdTech Menu
- Develop Standards-Based Lesson Plans
- Incentivizing Professional Development
- Develop Recommendations
- Share Your Plan with Administrators
- Create and Approve your Final EdTech Integration Plan

What Goals are you Trying to Meet with your Recommendations?

It is important to always remember that your EdTech Integration Plan is the "answer" to your district's Strategic Plan. It is the document that supports the question "How do we meet the goals of our district in the classroom?" For that reason, each of the recommendations made by the committee must be aligned with the Strategic Plan.

What are you Aligning your Recommendations To?

In addition to meeting the needs of your district's Strategic Plan, your recommendations must also be aligned to agree upon standards. In your EdTech Integration Plan, you might use the ISTE Standards as a guide and roadmap to ensure you are meeting the needs of students and (all) staff members in your district.

Who is Supported by your Recommendations?

When creating your recommendations list, it is important to include all stakeholders in the plan. As we have discussed throughout the planning process, an EdTech Integration Plan is not just about supporting students and not just to support your teachers, but it is an essential roadmap that will help meet the needs of administrators, office workers, support staff, teachers, students, and your community.

How will Professional Development be Presented?

One of the most important parts of your recommendation list is an agreeable format for how professional development and professional learning should be both created and implemented. In an earlier section, we discussed how to lay out a roadmap of professional learning when collaborating with your staff that included 1:1 Learning, Small Group Learning, Medium Group Learning, Large Group Learning, and Virtual Learning.

When will Professional Development be Presented?

Creating meaningful professional development is not only essential to teacher development but also to developing critical digital learning skills for our students. But when should it be done? When creating your recommendations for professional development, it is important to lay out a full year calendar that sets up time for both large and individualized professional development opportunities that flow directly in and out of each other so that there is a clear understanding of why teachers are being asked to do what they want to do every time they are together.

How will Digital Learning Skills be incorporated within the Curriculum?

Months of planning, hours of discussion, and hundreds of amazing applications are wonderful, but they do not hold any water in the classroom unless they are effectively used to enhance what the curriculum demands of it. When creating your final recommendations of what digital learning should look like in your district, it is vital that it all supports curricular activities and that lesson plans are not only standards aligned for instructional technology, but also for individual curricular goals.

Step 12: Sharing Recommendations with Administrators

The penultimate step in the EdTech Integration Plan process is sharing your plan with your administration. For many administrators, the presentation of the contents of your EdTech Integration Plan step shouldn't be a surprise because they would be members of your planning committee. However, this step requires you and your committee to prepare your presentation and essentially "sell" the concepts and data that has been collected over the course of the last few months.

As you prepare to present your findings to district administration, remember the following things:

- Make sure your plan is supported by standards and is achievable.
- Include Curriculum, Technology, and District Initiatives throughout the entire document.
- Make sure you can defend your recommendations by backing them up with research.
- Include various artifacts including Staff Surveys, Roadmaps, and Instructional Standards.

One of the things that your group should be prepared for when it comes to your presentations to administration is the inclusion of innovative ideas for your recommendations.

For example, you might recommend to the group that you can present (for example) 3-4 times during a semester at a large group faculty meeting where in reality, principals might not have that much time to allot for this topic due to other items on the schedule that need time and attention.

Creating and Presenting your Final EdTech Integration Plan

Once you have made your recommendations and presented them to your building and district administration, it is time to complete the process by creating your final and district approved EdTech Integration Plan.

Your final EdTech Integration Plan should include:

- A brief one-sheet that can be read quickly.
- A brief history of why the document was created.
- A recap of the Strategic Plan, Curricular Goals, and Tech Plan and description of how each drives the creation of this document.
- A roadmap of how the plan was formulated with links to research.
- A detailed and comprehensive document that includes links to all-important documents, websites, and resources.
- A comprehensive calendar roadmap both micro and macro.
- A list of deliverables and goal markers.
- A plan for professional development.
- Recommendations for success.

How to Present Your Plan

To help keep things organized and able for everyone to read and understand, I recommend that your EdTech Integration Plan come in two formats, a single page "one-sheet" and the full, multi-page document.

Your EdTech "One-Sheet"

Your EdTech "One-Sheet" is an outline of your full EdTech Integration Plan. Essentially, your One-Sheet can be thought of as a single page document that links out to each of the items that is presented in your full plan. The difference is your full plan has all the details agreed upon throughout the year.

The reason for creating a One-Sheet is to make what might be a 20+ page document easy to understand and read.

The Full EdTech Integration Plan

Your final EdTech Integration Plan is your full, multi-page document that includes every detail about how you want to see digital learning presented in your district. In addition to the summary of your district, your committee's findings about how your district sees itself and wishes to have professional development developed, it also includes a list of deliverables from which you will be sharing with your district including several key action items for putting your plan into place.

Conclusion

During my time as both an Instructional Coach and Digital Learning Leader, I have had the opportunity to share the journey of the EdTech Integration Plan creation process with many school districts. I have had the chance to present this at many conferences over the years and even to work closely with school districts as they took the journey themselves.

As mentioned above in this chapter, every school district creates a Strategic Plan that declares to the district and community what it believes in and where it would like to see itself in the future. The answer to this document is the EdTech Integration Plan. Only by having this document and plan in mind that discusses exactly what learning should look like in the classrooms can you then create a meaningful Instructional Coaching Department that supports the integration of digital learning skills both in the classroom and in the community.

If you have any thoughts about this series or would like to discuss how to bring an EdTech Integration Plan or Instructional Coaching program into your school district, I would love to hear from you and work with you.

Part 1 Summary

To create a culture shift in your classroom, you must often start at the end of the journey. In education, the journey always ends in the classroom, and it is always focused on student achievement. By starting with the question, "What would you like instruction to look like in the classroom?" You can then formulate a plan to make that vision become a reality.

For over a decade, I have worked with Instructional Coaches and Digital Learning leaders on this topic. I usually start my conversations with them by asking this question. Often, there is a clear and exact answer for what their vision is. Sometimes, there is no clear answer. This becomes the Chicken and Egg routine. What comes first, the vision or the endgame? In this section, I argue that they both should start in the beginning and become the blueprint and catalyst for the culture shift rather than a result of it.

There are three key steps that a school district must take when putting together a plan for meeting the needs and goals set forth in their Strategic Plan.

1. Create a vision for what instruction should look like in the classroom.
2. Align the vision with a framework and standards.
3. Create a roadmap to support the creation of a digital learning strategic plan.

In my conversations with Instructional Coaches and Digital Learning Leaders, there's always one topic I approach with trepidation—the commitments and visions of their Superintendent and upper district leadership. I often anticipate the answers before asking the questions. This aspect is crucial because these top-level leaders must spearhead the culture shift. Such a transformation cannot be effectively initiated from the bottom up.

What can we learn from the "Guy on the Hill?"

There is an incredibly famous video online. It is a video that I have seen several motivational speakers use and has tens of millions of views on YouTube. The video is usually called "Guy Dancing on the Hill" In this video, a large group of people have amassed outside during a concert. Everyone is sitting down on blankets enjoying the lovely day and the music.

In the video, a single person starts to get up and dance to the music. He is alone and, to be honest, he looks quite silly dancing all by himself. What happens next, however, is remarkable.

How does this Relate to Education?

I often show this video during workshops and presentations to demonstrate the concept of how to shift the culture of a school district. We watch the video once, discuss it, and then show it again. I then ask the group to identify who in a school district is the first guy dancing and who is the second in the district?

Quite often, I get answers such as, "the first guy is the principal" or "The first guy is the coach." These answers are thoughtful, but ultimately not the best answer. When starting a culture shift, a movement, a push forward, the first person to start waving their arms ultimately, must be the Superintendent. Without the Superintendent believing in a concept or leading the team, all other thoughts, ideas, or perceptions about what classroom instruction should look like are simply that … thoughts, ideas, and perceptions.

So, who represents the others on the hill?

When thinking about the video example, we should look at each part of this movement from a standpoint of rank and influence in the school district.

The Lone Nut

The Superintendent is identified as the first one on the hill dancing. We often refer to this position as "The Lone Nut." When everyone is sitting down, enjoying their day with their family, the Superintendent is the one to stand up and set a vision for how the music should be enjoyed. They have the guts to stand up and look ridiculous in the face of the surrounding crowd.

In this example, the Superintendent is the one to say proudly, "I think we should be dancing." And so, they do. But there is a catch. The dance routine can't be difficult to do. It must be precise and simple for others to understand or else they risk the possibility of nobody else following them into the future.

The First Follower

Whenever a Lone Nut has the courage to get up and set a new vision for the future, the vision and direction must be validated by at least one more for the Nut to feel secure and continue pointing in that direction. This position is called "The First Follower." The First Follower is simply there to do exactly what The Lone Nut is doing and share in the experiences. Their job is to publicly show everyone how to follow the directions of The Lone Nut. If The First Follower decides to walk up and go against The Lone Nut, the movement will never happen. When this happens, it is critical for The Lone Nut to recognize that they are a team and together are moving in the same direction, flawlessly and succinctly. It is the First Follower that turns The Lone Nut into a leader and shows the world that the vision is worth following.

Transferred into your school district, The First Follower is your building principal. The principal must take the vision of what learning looks like from the Superintendent and the Strategic Vision of the school and share it with their staff. The First Follower has a much harder job than the Superintendent. It is often an underappreciated form of leadership. All the Superintendent must do is get their building leaders to buy into their vision. The principal, however, needs to push that vision further and for that, there is often another staff member that they turn to support this building level culture change.

The Second Follower

You now have two people dancing on the hill and it is time to turn things up a notch by forming a crowd. The second follower's role is not just to validate the first two dancers but also to show others how to do so. Think about the game Whisper Down the Lane, or perhaps the game Telephone. There is traditionally a message that gets passed on from person to person. This activity or display of leadership is no different.

In an educational system, the second follower, or the person who plays the role of validating both district and building goals and visions is the Instructional Coach. They play a critical role in the learning environment, not only as a leader but also as an instructor and mentor for others. Instructional Coaches are the ones who are both in the planning meetings where critical decisions are made, and they are also the ones in the classroom supporting those decisions to make sure that classroom instruction is meeting the vision set forth by both district and building leadership. For this reason, it's important that the Instructional Coach be seen as “one of us” (meaning teachers) rather than “one of them” (meaning administrators).

Momentum Builders

Once the three dancers are really rocking it, it's time to grab a few additional dancers. These are the people who generally go with a movement and are willing to take the journey if it means they get in on the ground floor. These often are referred to as “generals” or “lead teachers.” They are the ones that an Instructional Coach or building leader can turn to when launching new initiatives. Their job is to learn the new skill quickly and share it with others in their grade levels or departments. If you can get 5-7 teachers involved in something new and innovative, you have a great chance of starting a movement in your school.

Once you have 3-5 teachers doing an action, using a new digital application, or building standards-based lesson plans through innovative strategies, backed with the support and recognition from their peers and leaders, more teachers will see this and want to do the same so they and their students can in turn become recognized for their accomplishments.

Developing a Culture within a Community

In Chapter 2 of this book, we looked at the Innovation–Adoption curve. This curve stands for not just how adoption of an idea happens; it also clearly demonstrates how to shift the culture of a community. This is also clearly backed by the video of the people dancing on the hill.

The Innovation Adoption Curve

Take a moment and think about who your early adopters are. How do they react to innovative ideas and offerings from the district?

Now think about what it will take for those early adopters to become leaders themselves in the movement and be supporters of the culture shift that will be taking place in your district.

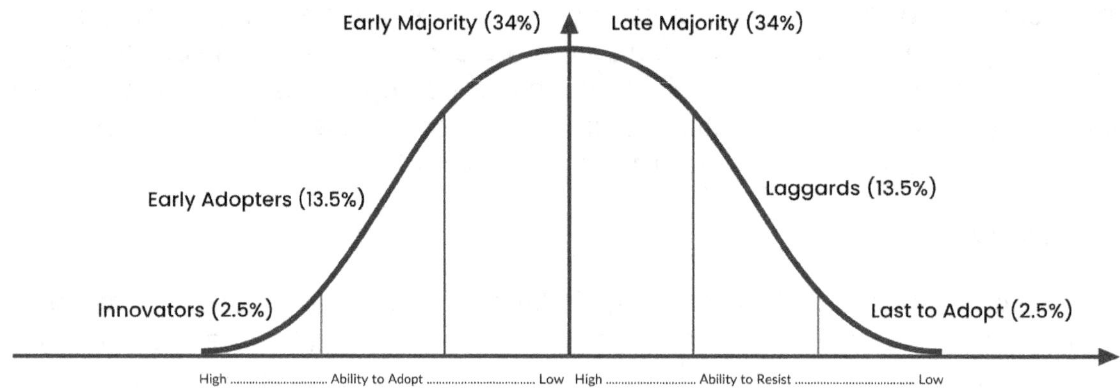

At the beginning of this section, we asked the question, "How do you flatten the curve?" I hope you can see that it isn't easy, and it can't happen from the level of the Instructional Coach. It is a process that happens over time, perhaps many years and is one that can only happen when district leadership gets up and becomes the vision they wish to see.

In Part 2 of this book, we will look deeper into what you wish to see innovative classroom instruction look like for both teachers and students. We will learn about creating a standards-based curriculum that harnesses both curricular and digital learning standards. Standards that are not only robust, but vertically align the competency and proficiency skills that are required of students as they move from elementary to high school level grades.

Part 2

Designing a Curriculum to Support Digital Learning in the Classroom

Chapter 5

What is Digital Learning?

Scenario #1

It is the middle of the summer. A teacher receives their teaching assignment for the upcoming school year. They are about to teach a section of Pre-Algebra, a section of Algebra 1 and a few sections of Geometry. Even though these courses run independently of each other, the teacher understands that each of these courses are designed to be building blocks to ultimately have a student enter courses such as Statistics and Calculus. Each of these courses contains material that is course specific but the concepts inside are also prerequisites for the next class in the sequence. The teacher works through the curriculum throughout the year knowing that if a student doesn't meet the required skills or master certain topics, they will not be successful in future courses. To put it another way, the teacher understands that for her Algebra students to be successful the following year in her class, she needs them to be fully competent in the skills taught in Pre-Algebra.

Scenario #2

A fourth-grade teacher is excited to once again be returning to fourth-grade for the upcoming school year. They are already experts at teaching the fourth-grade curriculum because they have taught fourth grade for the previous four years. The teacher knows this year's job is to have students master the fourth-grade curriculum which consists of topics like animal adaptations, US Geography, and local government. These are topics important for students to know about but do not impact their performance or ability to enter fifth grade the following year. To put it another way, the teacher is solely responsible for working with this particular group of students and the job is to teach them as much as possible and move them to the next grade.

When we think about creating a digital learning curriculum, educational leaders should consider both of scenarios … constantly. Having a clear concept of what digital learning skills should be introduced in each grade level and how they relate to each other is a critical step in creating a unified and standards-based K12 Digital Learning Curriculum.

In the previous chapter, we explained the process a school district could follow to develop their Digital Learning Strategic Plan. One of the steps involved making a digital learning roadmap to assist with the plan's formation, as well as to help a school district decompose each digital learning skill into its parts and determine which grade level should teach those skills.

In this chapter, we will look deeper into this concept and help you and your school district formulate not only a plan of action in completing this task, but help you clearly identify several reasons why it is important to create your Digital Learning Curriculum alongside of your Core Curricular activities. When doing this, you will be able to create a complete K12 Program of Studies where each skill builds on top of each other, just as each subject and grade level builds on top of each other.

Before we take this journey, we must first ask ourselves, "*What is a Digital Learning Curriculum?*"

Understanding the concept of a Digital Learning Curriculum

What *is* a Digital Learning Curriculum? If you asked a dozen educators and educational leaders, you'd likely receive at least a dozen different definitions. To help frame this chapter and clarify the concept, let's first examine what a Digital Learning Curriculum *isn't*.

What is NOT a Digital Learning Curriculum

A teacher uses their iPad to capture images of student work and adds them to an online slide deck for presenting to the class. The teacher then shares the slide deck online with administrators and parents.

- Is this a Digital Learning Curriculum? **(No)**

A teacher accesses curricular materials from an online source such as Google Drive, OneDrive, or directly from a curriculum company to instruct students and build dynamic lessons.

- Is this a Digital Learning Curriculum? **(No)**

You walk into a classroom and observe a teacher instructing students. They are using Chromebooks, and students are engaged in a Google Classroom assignment.

- Is this a Digital Learning Curriculum? **(No)**

You might be scratching your head. Aren't all these examples ways that a teacher is demonstrating the use of Digital Learning in their curriculum?

The answer to that question is ... **yes**. Each of these examples shows a teacher's ability to infuse digital tools—such as iPads, online slide decks, Google Drive, and Chromebooks—into their learning environments. However, for this chapter's sake, we won't consider this a Digital Learning Curriculum.

If these examples don't qualify as a Digital Learning Curriculum … *what does*? How **should** we define the creation of a K12 Digital Learning Curriculum?

What IS a Digital Learning Curriculum?

To provide clarity and support the creation of a K12 standards-based Digital Learning Curriculum, let's define the term:

A Digital Learning Curriculum is a blueprint designed to support the scaffolded inclusion of skills and technologies that foster a student's growth and development. It's based on several factors agreed upon by your school district, including—but not limited to—the district's Strategic Plan, Digital Learning Integration Plan, ISTE Standards, and Core Curriculum Standards. With this blueprint, your district can map out its entire Program of Studies to create a comprehensive educational system.

When considering the creation of a Digital Learning Curriculum, I often think of it in two similar yet distinct paths:

- **Students as Learners**
    - When creating your roadmap, consider what skills your students should acquire throughout their K12 career.
    - How can students not only excel in topics such as animal adaptations, U.S. Geography, and local government, but also demonstrate their knowledge using digital learning skills like audio production, video creation, or building online website presentations?
- **Teachers as Learners**
    - When designing your roadmap, reflect on what skills your teachers should be teaching throughout the school year in their core subject areas.
    - How can we create a learning environment where teachers learn to incorporate ISTE Standards-based lessons alongside traditional subject standards?

When we consider Instructional Coaches as the ultimate professional development providers and key factors in successfully shifting a school district's culture, we begin to recognize the importance of viewing curriculum not just in micro terms (day by day / chapter by chapter) but in the broadest macro terms (year by year / course by course / elementary into secondary).

As we step back and begin to analyze the term "Digital Learning Curriculum" as a K12 curriculum, we broaden our definition. However, in doing so, we often start to confuse this term with others. Let's examine how some might claim they are meeting the digital competency needs of their staff and students.

Three Often Confused Digital Competency Terms

Imagine you're at a conference or meeting, conversing with educators from various school districts. You mention "Digital Learning." Do you think everyone shares the same definition? What about "Digital Literacy"?

And then there's "Digital Citizenship"—a term often tossed around more frequently than the first two.

Are these terms all relevant?

Do they mean the same thing?

When examining a program and a Digital Learning Curriculum, these three terms all play crucial roles in the conversation.

Digital Learning

Digital Learning is a term that can be used to describe the way a student is being educated. It is a way of teaching. For example: are students learning by reading a book or are they learning by reading PDFs on a Chromebook?

When we think of the SAMR Model, we first look at the letter “S” which stands for “Substitution.” This usually means that the activity is being done on a digital device rather than a paper one. The teacher essentially “substitutes” a technology tool for a physical tool.

If content is being taught through some type of digital learning method, the student must possess some type of digital learning skills to show competency of the materials. These skills belong to our next term.

Digital Literacy

Digital Literacy encompasses the skills students need to effectively navigate and utilize digital learning environments. These skills range from basic competencies, such as using a mouse to drag and drop objects on a screen, to more advanced abilities like conducting sophisticated research using search engines and databases.

Regrettably, educators often overlook Digital Literacy skills. Many teachers, lacking confidence in their own digital abilities, fall into the trap of assuming that students "know more about this stuff than I do." This misconception can hinder students' digital skill development.

To clarify the distinction between these terms:

- Digital Learning is the "what"—the content and method of instruction
- Digital Literacy is the "how"—the skills needed to engage with digital learning

Having identified the "what" and the "how," we must now address the "why." This brings us to our final—and often most misunderstood—term: Digital Citizenship.

Digital Citizenship

Digital Citizenship is the study of ethics. It is what we teach our students to provide them with a moral code when they are online. We teach our students that just because they can do something does not mean that they should do something.

It is through the teaching of Digital Citizenship skills that we can help our students become digitally literate and complete the trinity of Digital Competence.

Can Digital Learning Skills and Core Curriculum Skills Coexist?

When planning a K12 curricular roadmap, school districts assign specific outcomes to each grade level. This ensures that by the time students transition from elementary to middle school, they have acquired a solid knowledge base. These foundational skills then enable students to succeed in middle school and beyond.

The same principle should apply to digital learning concepts. This raises an important question: "When and how should we teach these digital learning concepts and skills, and in which core subjects can we integrate them?"

To address this effectively, schools should create a comprehensive K12 Digital Learning Curriculum that incorporates both curricular and digital learning standards. All teachers, from kindergarten through 12th grade, should implement this curriculum. Lesson plans should logically integrate both core curriculum and digital learning skills, allowing students to build their abilities progressively—chapter by chapter and year by year. By the time students reach each major educational milestone, they should possess both the necessary curricular knowledge and digital competencies for the next grade level.

To achieve this, teachers must master not only their core subjects but also the art of teaching their curriculum through digital learning skills. In Part 3 of this book, we'll explore how to equip teachers with these tools and how Instructional Coaches can support this process both in and out of the classroom.

The next chapter will delve into the creation of a complete K12 Digital Learning Curriculum, providing you with the foundation and templates needed to initiate this process in your own school district.

Chapter 6

Building Digital Learning into the Curriculum

How do you build Standards-Based Digital Learning Skills into Core Curriculum Subjects?

A school district finalizes its Strategic Plan and prepares to present it to the public. At the same time, they also have a brand-new program of studies to highlight that aligns to the strategic plan and provides a complete curricular standards-based roadmap from Kindergarten through Grade 12. It is now time to begin the process of reimagining each course to break it down into units and lesson plans.

At some point teachers are called into central office to meet and discuss how each course will be broken down and what topics will be taught. They write or revise curriculum, upload approved documentation to the district website and start teaching.

If this process sounds familiar, it should. This is a generalized, yet customary practice for many school districts. But let us look at this process and ask ourselves if there is something missing from this sequence of steps.

By going through this process, the school district has the “what” outlined and organized. They know the subjects, courses, and content. But they didn’t yet hit the “how.” Sure, they create a list of procedures and action steps in their lesson plans, but this is now the “how” we are looking for. For this new program of studies and its various components to be complete, there needs to be some thought into “how” these topics will be taught. Additionally, it is not just the “how” that needs to be addressed, but the “through” as well. This is where standards-aligned digital learning skills come into the conversation.

The merging of both curricular lesson plans with a series of digital learning tools and materials is not easy. It takes a completely new set of eyes on each curriculum to ask not only what the teachers should be teaching but “how” the teacher should be teaching and “through” what tools and actions should the teacher be teaching it.

This chapter will explore several key reasons why every course, curriculum, unit plan, and lesson plan should be developed with both curricular and digital learning perspectives in mind. We'll examine how this integrated approach supports both core subject and digital learning standards.

Can Digital Learning and Subject Area Content Standards Coexist?

As a coach, one of the hardest things I ever did was try to convince teachers that they are allowed to stray away from what was written down in district provided lesson plans. When preparing to work with a teacher, or a group of teachers, I always went into meetings knowing not only what their curriculum was, but what the district-provided instructions were for the curriculum. Together, we would sit down and go over the materials. There would always be a single turning point in the meeting where it was my turn to suggest a method of teaching the lesson. I might suggest teaching it through video, or by using a digital tool that was recommended and approved by the district. Then I would wait.

Sometimes teachers would embrace the concept, and we'd embark on a collaborative journey in a traditional coaching role. More often, however, I'd encounter resistance from teachers at the mere suggestion of something new and innovative.

"It's not in the lesson plan. I don't have to do what you're asking."
"The principal told me to stick to the lesson plan and not deviate from it."
"Nobody else is doing things this way... why are you asking me to?"

Let's be honest—this was, at its core, both frustrating and heartbreaking for a digital learning coach.

Question: How can an Instructional Coach (and school district) successfully support the implementation of standards-based real-world authentic learning when the one goal they are given by the district to accomplish is not directly in curricular documents?

Adding digital learning benchmarks and standards to paper lesson plans is only the beginning of the conversation. To truly create lesson plans and curricular activities that generate teacher buy-in and motivate educators to begin the transition from the right side of the innovation curve to the left side, the district must look at two other terms, "and" and "through." One of these terms is a stress maker and the other, in contrast, is a stress reliever.

Creating "Through" Experiences out of "And" Experiences

Let's jump back into my example above of my experiences working with teachers. In this example, there was a single conversation, yet each party involved interpreted the words being spoken in a completely unique way.

My teachers were stressed about a new lesson they were being asked to dissect and teach. They met with me for help, and they heard me say that I would help them out "and" I would be asking them to learn and use a new digital learning tool that they were also not comfortable with.

They, in their minds heard “and” a word that brings added stress and a burden of adding even more work to their already busy plates.

However, what I was actually saying was that we were going to be putting this lesson plan together and that they would be able to teach this lesson in a more streamlined way “through” the use of digital learning tools and activities. The “through” was implied, but it was an intentional way of helping the teachers actually do less, accomplish more, and provide students with an opportunity to meet both curricular and digital learning standards in an innovative way.

Over the years, I began adjusting the words that I was using during coach/teacher meetings and adjusted my approach so that I would begin sharing the ways to destress the teacher before I would introduce the method in which I introduced the “through” activities.

This adjustment brought more teachers on board with accepting a digital learning curriculum, but significant challenges remained. To address these, it's crucial for school districts to develop a Digital Learning Scope and Sequence. This tool helps map out the digital learning skills and activities teachers should incorporate into their lessons. Additionally, it creates a flow chart showing where students should learn foundational skills *before* they need to apply them in core subject areas.

What is a Scope and Sequence?

Imagine that you wanted to teach your students how to cook a wonderful home cooked meal. The final product would involve the students, at home, preparing a three-course meal plus dessert and capturing the process through images and video to create a short video for a final project.

This is not an assignment that can be created all in one day. To have the students be able to complete this project they must first learn about basic food groups, how to select and purchase their ingredients, and how to successfully transport them home. Next, they need to be able to wash and prepare them so that they are ready for cooking and assembling on the table.

Each step requires a detailed lesson that over several years the students have been building their talents on skill by skill.

In addition to the culinary skills needed to carry out this task, there are also technical skills involving the use of cameras and audio equipment, as well as the skills of editing and producing.

To properly expect students to be able to create this, a scope and sequence must be created. A Scope and Sequence might be thought of as a grid. One side of the grid has the action items to be taught. The right side has either grade levels, or dates outlining when each skill or action will be taught.

Once all skills are taught and mastered, then the teacher can feel confident in giving out the assignment of creating a fully produced and published home cooked meal.

To do this, the student needs to go through three phases of the learning process, Learn – Explore – Use. First the student learns the fundamentals. Next, they explore many ways of using those skills, and then finally, they put those skills into use to display their mastery of the curricular expectation.

How To Create a Scope and Sequence?

A Program of Studies can be loosely defined as a series of grade levels or courses that build on top of each other year after year. In the early grades, a student simply moves from one level to the next. Once a student reaches middle school, they may be added to specific courses that build on each other based on merit and competency (example: Pre-Algebra, Algebra, Geometry).

When creating the Program of Studies and organizing what topics are introduced in each subject there is often careful consideration to what curricular topics are being built upon each other. When plotting out your Digital Learning Curriculum, it's important to work with your Program of Studies team to include a scaffolded series of digital learning skills that identify both where they will be first introduced and in what lesson plan they will be explored so that they can be put to good use in core curricular subjects.

Step 1: Identify Major Digital Learning Topics to be Taught into Categories.

It's easy to imagine a world where your students enter their high school years with a large amount of fundamental technical knowledge of both skills and topics. Many teachers have the opinion that students "know everything about computers" and because they possess that concept, they do not feel the need to plan to teach those skills formally. Unfortunately, this is not the case for all students and there must be a plan for getting all students the skills needed to be able to accomplish real world tasks once they graduate and are in the real world.

When planning your Digital Learning Scope & Sequence, the first thing to do is to decide what types of activities and projects you would like to see students engaged in while learning core curricular subjects. Do you want your high school students to be working with and creating morning announcements in the form of daily live streaming video? What about asking your science department to document each experiment through video to then be produced and added to lab report?

To have your upper grade students be able to have these experiences, you first need to break down the skills needed to complete these tasks (much like the example of producing a video of a student creating a home cooked meal) into smaller chunks.

Some of the skills categories that need to be planned out are:

- Technology
- Digital Literacy
- Device Management
- Research
- Digital Citizenship
- Social & Emotional
- People and Personal
- Presentation and Self Reflection

Once you have created a list and identified all the traits that you hope make up your graduating class, it's time to create a K12 roadmap that teaches those skills and where in the core curriculum the students will demonstrate competency of those skills.

Step 2: Identify a Core Curricular Lesson for each Category.

Imagine that you are going to ask your Chemistry and Biology students to participate in dynamic experiments and during the process, you will ask each lab group to document their process and procedures so that they can demonstrate their knowledge of a subject by submitting a formal video presentation. Where do they learn the skills to perform all these curricular and technical requirements?

In Step 2, each category listed above should be broken down and assigned either a unit of study, or a grade level where they will be introduced and taught. By doing this, your Program of Studies not only could provide a curricular topic but also a standards-aligned technical topic as well that students will be demonstrating competency in. It is common at this stage that a category might cover multiple grade levels or courses.

Step 3: Break Down Digital Learning Categories into individual Skills.

Now that you have broken down each category into smaller chunks and paired those categories with curricular lessons, it is time to break down the categories into individual skills. In step 3 each skill will be broken down by major grade level grouping.

For example,

- Technology Skills
    - K-2:
        - Identifying computer components such as the keyboard, mouse, monitor, and printer.
        - Using a mouse to select, drag and click objects on the screen.
    - 3-5th:
        - Understanding how to save objects both locally and in a cloud storage drive.
        - Understanding basic concepts surrounding data privacy and how to protect yourself online.
    - 6-8th:
        - Using a mobile device as an educational tool for learning.
        - Mastering online safety and citizenship when working on a team or on social media.

- Digital Literacy Skills

    - Basic computer skills
    - Basic information research skills:

- Digital Citizenship Skills:

    - Media Balance
    - Online Privacy
    - Relationships & Communication

- Social & Emotional Learning:

    - Self-Awareness:

        - Identifying emotions, accurate self-perception, recognizing strengths, self-confidence, and self-efficacy.
        - Understanding online cues.
        - Identifying Red flag feelings when using technology.
        - Reflecting on how social media affects personal identity.

    - Self-Management:

        - Impulse control, stress management, self-discipline, self-motivation, goal-setting, and organizational skills.

        - Exhibiting media balance/self-discipline.
        - Managing one's emotions around media.
        - Setting goals to achieve a healthy media balance.

- Social Awareness:
    - Perspective-taking, empathy, appreciating diversity, respect for others.
    - Taking others' perspectives
    - Showing concern about others
    - Identifying the norms of their online communities, including unjust ones

- Relationship Skills:
    - Communication, social engagement, relationship-building, teamwork.
    - Maintaining healthy relationships when communicating online
    - De-escalating digital drama
    - Supporting their peers if they experience cyberbullying.

- Responsible Decision-Making:
    - Identifying problems, analyzing solutions, solving problems, evaluating, reflecting, and ethical responsibility.
    - Developing curiosity and open-mindedness
    - Evaluating the positive and negative impacts of being online
    - Using technology responsibly to promote personal, family, and community well-being.

Step 4: Determine What Skills should be Taught in each Grade.

Once you have concepts broken down into subgroups you can then determine what grade each skill is taught in. You do not necessarily have to have a skill taught in the same grade where it will be applied in a curricular context. Many of these primal skills should be taught in the early grade levels and then built upon year after year so that they can be unleashed in the upper grade levels.

Step 5: Assign each Skill to a Staff Member.

Next, your scope and sequence should have a plan for who in the building will be teaching these skills. For example, if a research skill is being developed and used a 5th grade classroom, it might be best to have that skill introduced by the Library Media Specialist either a few weeks before the classroom activity, or it could be a skill that is practiced routinely over the course of a full year before it gets utilized by the core area teacher.

Step 6: Update Curricular Lessons to include Digital Learning Skills and Standards

Finally, once your scope and sequence is completed and everyone in the district has had a chance to look it over, the last step is to add the information directly into lesson plans. By doing so, it eliminates the awkward conversations as discussed earlier in this chapter between the coach and a teacher not interested in moving away from the central office provided written directions.

The lesson plan should even include where students should have prior knowledge of a topic. For example, if a lesson plan is asking student to research a particular topic, it should mention that the teacher reach out to the library media specialist a few weeks ahead to engage them in teaching specific research topics on specific topics that students will soon be learning in the core subject.

How Do You Support the Inclusion of Digital Learning Skills in the Core Curriculum?

Creating a unified Program of Studies that combines curricular and digital learning skills—and gives teachers multiple ways to teach each lesson based on their technological comfort level—is not easy. It requires time, planning, and resources to get it right. To achieve the goals of the Strategic Plan, a district must do significant work in advance. However, it's only after completing this process that a district will see results in years 2, 3, 4, and 5, as the curriculum shifts to a maintenance schedule rather than a revision schedule.

So, who should be responsible for supporting this work?

The straightforward answer is a collaboration between your Curricular and Digital Learning teams. This process shouldn't be done in isolation by either digital learning or curricular-themed coaches, as the strength of this method lies in the combined knowledge of both departments. Once your district has clearly defined this process, it's crucial to allocate time for professional development and training on the philosophy behind the system.

From Horizontal Planning to Vertical Alignment

Core curricular standards and digital learning standards are as inseparable as peanut butter and jelly. Neither should be sandwiched between two pieces of bread without the other.

In this chapter, we explored several reasons why school districts should consider incorporating ISTE Standards and digital learning components into district-provided lesson plans:

1. By integrating digital learning standards and activities into core curricular lesson plans, instructional coaches have a better chance of supporting reluctant teachers and introducing new activities that provide students with real-world and authentic learning experiences.

2. The process of breaking down digital learning skills and aligning them with core subjects within the Program of Studies fosters professional collaboration between curricular and digital learning departments. This creates a unified message and vision for teachers to understand and follow when planning daily lessons and activities.

3. Assigning specific parts of a digital learning scope and sequence to certain staff members, such as the Library Media Specialist, clarifies everyone's role in K12 education. This approach allows the Instructional Coach to support both the introduction and inclusion of these individual skills, regardless of where students are asked to demonstrate them.

In our next chapter, we'll pivot our scope and sequence vertically to create a standards-aligned, multi-level approach to infusing both curricular and digital learning standards. You'll learn the importance of planning not just horizontally (K through 12) but also vertically (lower, middle, upper) to chunk the key skills and standards you want your students and teachers to know and interact with in the classroom. To achieve this, we must first create vertical alignment within our digital learning curriculum.

Chapter 7

Creating Vertical Alignment for Digital Learning Skills

How do you create a K12 Digital Learning Curriculum that is standards aligned and based on your Digital Learning Strategic Plan?

The year was 1987 and I was in third grade. I remember the day our music teacher called all students in our grade level into the cafeteria to show us the orchestra's string instruments. Looking back, this was probably one of the most defining moments of my life. For whatever reason that day, I walked out of the assembly and went home to tell my parents that I wanted to play the viola.

I played the viola all through elementary, middle school, and high school. I remember going on trips, playing symphonies, musicals, and auditioning for district orchestra. Orchestra class was the one class that I looked forward to each day. When the time came to choose a college major, I decided that the viola would be my ticket to getting an advanced education. I graduated four years later as a Music Education major.

I sometimes look back at my life and ask, *"How did this happen?"*

Building Vertical Alignment in Core Subject Areas to Build a Solid K12 Program

The reason this happened was because the school district I attended had created a solid music program that was designed to attract participants at an early age and featured activities that challenged each student to become the best musician they could be. The elementary program featured individual learning groups in grades 3, 4, and 5. The middle school program offered the chance to participate in string orchestra with students from other schools. The high school program allowed us the opportunity to perform in pit bands, string quartets, and local adjudications to help us all have a sense of pride in ourselves and our school district. It was pretty awesome.

When I was officially able to become a music teacher, I brought all these memories and experiences. I first taught strings for a school district in grades 3-8 at the elementary and middle school levels. I then transferred to a district where I taught the entire program, grades 3-12, all by myself. I then served two additional school districts teaching high school for more than a decade combined. No matter what grade level I was teaching, the one thing that I took with me from those experiences was the need and desire to produce student musicians who were able to perform at a high level, had a deep understanding of musical pedagogy, and who loved supporting one another both on and off the stage.

This was the time where I first realized just how important vertical alignment is when developing a complete program of studies. To have quality musicians coming out of your program, you must first break down each level of the school district and decide exactly what skills each student needs to know to be able to perform their best at any given time. This is not easy. If you ever find yourself teaching an entire K12 program of studies like I did, it's pretty easy to do. You know what resources you have, and you know what the students need to know before they hit the next level. However, if you are teaching one single grade, or in only level of the district, it's often difficult because you might not have the opportunity to study what happens with the overall curriculum before or after your particular program.

It was in the middle of my career as a music educator where I came up with a simple concept. One that I use today when supporting coaches and school districts in building their own Program of Studies and Digital Learning Curriculum. To create a successful program that guarantees student retention and success at the time of graduation, each faculty member must know and understand their role in the student's development. For this example, let's break down a school district program, specifically the music department in three levels, elementary, middle, and high school.

The goal for this example is to have the best sounding high school musical possible. To be able to have the community come out each year to the high school to watch students perform Broadway level shows, they need to be able to have a pit orchestra of self-motivated, competent, and energetic student musicians accompanying them that are able to play professional level compositions with very little rehearsal. What most people do not realize is that to reach this goal, the musical rehearsals for the high school actually started back in third grade when the students (like me) were first pitched the idea of joining the orchestra and learning how to play an instrument like the viola.

Elementary School

If a school district is going to have a goal of creating an outstanding high school music program, the elementary music staff needs to understand that they have one job to do. It's an extremely simple job, but one that is often most overlooked. It's a job that doesn't have anything to do with pedagogy or scheduling, or musicianship. The job of the elementary music teacher is to recruit as many students as possible to be in the group and then, (most importantly), encourage them to be members of the program as they pass on to the middle school level. That's it. Nothing more, nothing less. The job is to get a hundred students to sign up and pass on as close to a hundred students as possible.

Middle School

The middle school program has a similar job of bringing students in from the elementary and passing them on to the high school, but there is an added degree of difficulty to their position. The job of the middle school music teacher is to be the orchestrator. They need to welcome in dozens of flute players, trumpet players, and drummers and turn them into piccolo players, a full low brass section, and mallet percussionists. Their function in the process is to get students excited to play multiple instruments and build a blended ensemble that will then be passed on to the high school program for performance and competition.

High School

Finally, we have the high school program. The high school program is the group of students that is the most visible part of the entire department. They are the ones marching on Friday nights during football games, seen on weekends at parades on chilly days, and are backing up the theater department during musicals. They are the face of the program and the reason it's important to have a strong feeder program. If the high school program doesn't receive a high number of students from middle school who are musically competent and able to perform at a prominent level, they have a harder time putting on a quality performance in front of the tax paying community. But visible performances are not the only function of the high school music program. The true task of the high school program is to work with the middle school and elementary school programs to inspire young musicians to not only sign up for the music department programs but to stick with it throughout those long elementary and middle school years.

In many ways, this could be seen as the circle of life. But how does this relate to creating standards-based vertical alignment in our digital learning departments?

Creating Vertical Alignment for Digital Learning Skills

Just as the musical example demonstrates, each program level must connect to its predecessor to ensure success and help students meet district goals. This same principle applies effectively to a standards-based digital learning curriculum.

What is Vertical Alignment?

As students progress toward high school and college, they need to demonstrate specific digital learning skills. But where and how do they develop these abilities? The answer lies in our Scope and Sequence document from the previous chapter, which helps us align digital learning standards with core subjects.

Through Vertical Alignment, we develop a comprehensive scope and sequence that shows how elementary, middle, and high school levels work together to build these skills, supporting student learning both inside and outside the classroom.

Why is Vertical Alignment Used?

Similar to how elementary teachers recruit students and pass them on to middle school, where middle school teachers then orchestrate those students into specialized roles, we can apply this same concept to digital learning.

Elementary School

In elementary school, students are generally located in the same room all day with few exceptions. They have one teacher responsible for teaching them all the core subjects. Because of this, the core subjects, and the core standards themselves are the primary focus of elementary school. Students must learn these basic educational rudiments to be successful in middle school. For digital learning standards to fit into this model, the technology or digital tools must serve as a compliment to what the students are being taught in English, Math, Science, and Social Studies.

For this reason, it's important for teachers and Instructional Coaches to understand that it is the digital learning application that is the supporter of the core subject. It is the digital learning application that is being set up as a supplement to help the student understand and master the content standard.

Just as the musical example discussed, it is important for the elementary program to provide students with as many digital learning skills and tools as possible and pass them on to middle school with as much rudimentary knowledge of how to create with video, build a basic slide deck, and add formatting to a document. What happens next in middle school is where the transformation truly takes place.

Middle School

Like the musical example showed, middle school is where the magic happens as students flow through the program. In the digital learning context, this is when students dive deeper into core skills like video production, presentations, and digital writing, transforming from learners into creators. During these years, students often discover their strengths in particular types of media creation and apply these skills to their assignments and projects.

As students develop this self-awareness about how digital tools can benefit both them and their teachers, we can nurture these emerging interests as they progress into high school.

High School

There comes a point in the path of a young musician where they stop learning new skills that are helping them master their instrument and they start using what they have already mastered on their instrument to become motivated to learn new skills. This also applies to our digital learning curriculum.

In the elementary classroom, we mentioned that students are focused on learning their core curriculum skills. They are in the same room each and every day learning what their teacher is teaching them, and it's being backed up by an elementary knowledge of digital skills and applications. In high school, it is the complete opposite that is true.

In high school, because students have the opportunity to select their own educational courses and pathways, they soon find that the subjects are secondary to the actual skills that they are interested in. They might find that they are in a humanities class, but they ask to complete each assignment using their favorite digital medium or technology application. The years they spent in middle school finding out for themselves where their passions are will allow them to bloom academically. They become writers, videographers, and public speakers because of their courses. Not the other way around.

This is not just another version of the circle of life, but the reason why it's important to understand how to create vertical alignment in both your core curriculum and digital learning curriculum so that you are being led by the standards that seek students to be Empowered Learners, Digital Citizens, Knowledge Constructors, Innovative Designers, Computational Thinkers, Creative Communicators, and global Collaborators.

It is through Vertical Alignment where you truly see how impactful the Digital Learning Standards are when properly implemented across the entire K12 curriculum.

How do you Vertically Align your Digital Learning Curriculum?

In this chapter, you learned why Vertical Alignment is important and what happens when educational levels don't consider this concept. Now for the key question: "*how do you do it?*"

Just as our musical example began with a school district's vision of students performing in pit orchestras and on football fields, we need similar clear goals for both core subjects and digital learning standards.

Start by asking yourself: "What should your graduates excel at when they leave your school district?"

Consider skills like:

- Presenters
- Audio / Video Creators
- Graphic Designers
- Writers
- Musicians

In order to have your students meet those expectations, the first thing to do is to sit back and develop a full K12 plan that supports students being introduced to as many skills and tools as can be available in elementary school, then having the opportunity to put those skills into action in middle school. By establishing this continuous link from elementary to high school, you will understand how your high school program and annual graduating class relate directly to the lessons and skills first taught in grades K-3.

In other words, the Scope and Sequences should be built on top of each other year after year so that each core teacher understands where they fit in in the larger circle of life. Once this is mapped out then you can move onto the last step in this process that truly brings together your core curricular standards with digital learning standards … Curriculum Mapping!

Chapter 8

Digital Learning Curriculum Mapping

When sitting down with your team to write your K12, Standards-based digital learning curriculum, it is important not just to have a vertical roadmap as we have discussed in Chapter 7, but also to have a horizontal roadmap as well. In an earlier chapter, we learned the importance of lining up your full program of studies end to end and chunking down each of the skills that you plan to introduce to your students so they can ultimately become whatever it is your district's mission and vision says they will become. But what happens after you complete your vertical roadmap? How do we ensure that our students meet the macro goals of our vertical alignment and our scope and sequences?

To support the reaching of both our curricular and digital goals, objectives, and standards, we must first do an exercise in Curriculum Mapping. A process which requires not just curriculum leaders but teachers from every level to really think about how individual units of study, chapters, and each lesson will be designed to fit into the bigger puzzle and compliment not just each other but the entire K12 curriculum. This work is not easy. It is tedious and minute but when done correctly, each and every week of the calendar year can be planned out to provide not just the blueprint and roadmap, but the entire script for how to get students from the first day of kindergarten through graduation on the last day of their senior year.

What is Curriculum Mapping?

Curriculum mapping is a method of organizing classroom instruction based on various criteria, including curricular standards, digital learning standards, units of study, and chapter topics. It creates a calendar-based outline that shows when specific topics and curricular milestones should be taught throughout the school year. A curriculum map helps identify gaps in curricular planning and determines the optimal timing for introducing skills and standards within each subject area.

What does a Curricular Map Include?

Curricular Maps vary from school district to school district depending on how the district wishes to set them up and how much information is designed to be showcased in any particular area of study. Usually a Curriculum Map consists of:

- Standards – Both Core Curricular and Digital Learning.
- Scope and Sequences - For individual Courses.
- Content Highlights – Including Chapters, Topics, and Units of Study.

- Skills – Target areas for students to reach by a certain time in the school year.
- Assessments – These could be or linked to specific documents.
- Course Resources – This could be linked to specific examples and documents.
- Lesson Plans – A district could have one general lesson plan, or this could show multiple links that are created by many teachers.
- Pacing Guides – Created to help teachers stay on track of when to teach subjects and how long to stay on a subject.

Are Curriculum Maps Essential Tools?

When faced with creating curriculum maps only for the courses you may be teaching, it is easy to ask why this procedure is necessary. It is only when a teacher takes a step back and sees their particular course in the larger scope of the overall curriculum or perhaps sees their curricular roadmap in the context of a student who is also taking 4-5 additional classes when they can see how their subject fits into the entire picture. They can then see why it is important, for example, that they teach something in September and how it is going to be backed up and reinforced in a different class in October and beyond.

For this reason, it is important that school districts aim to support teachers in this process by including them in curricular teams not just in their own department, but across multiple departments so that they think of their curriculum as a single piece in a much larger educational puzzle. They can then see how each lesson assists students in mastering the curriculum standard by standard rather than simply lesson by lesson or assessment by assessment. The important part of this journey is that teachers are learning why they are an important part if the educational roadmap not just a pawn in a larger game played by someone at a higher level than they are in the district. Ultimately helping them to understand just how much of an impact they can have on students and their K12 journey.

Is it Challenging to Create Curriculum Maps for an Entire School District?

Creating a comprehensive curriculum map involves breaking down individual subjects and plotting out chapters or units based on various educational criteria. While this may seem straightforward at first glance, the reality is far more complex. Here's why:

Time and Resource Management

The process requires careful coordination of instructional time, teaching resources, and learning objectives across multiple subjects and grade levels. Each component must be strategically placed to build upon previous knowledge while preparing for future learning.

Cross-Curricular Integration

Effective curriculum mapping demands thoughtful integration of skills and concepts across different subject areas. This ensures students can make meaningful connections between various disciplines and apply their learning in diverse contexts.

Assessment Planning

The mapping process must incorporate well-timed assessments that accurately measure student progress and understanding. These assessments need to align with both immediate learning objectives and long-term educational goals.

Adaptability Requirements

A successful curriculum map must be flexible enough to accommodate different learning paces, teaching styles, and student needs while maintaining consistent educational standards. This balance between structure and adaptability presents a significant challenge for many school districts.

Scheduling, Scheduling, Scheduling

One of the difficulties of starting this process is knowing where to start. When thinking about vertical alignment, it is easy to document when students will be learning certain skills and meeting standards. It is also easy to list in what grades these skills and standards will be addressed in the overarching K12 journey. However, when looking at things on a more micro level such as a grade level or even in the bigger bands of Middle School and High School, it is easy to see one big challenge presented.

This challenge is that not every student will be taking every course offered in the program of studies. Because of this, when plotting out a Curriculum Map, it must be taken into consideration that certain skills and certain standards (both core-curricular and digital learning) must be introduced as if it was the first time being introduced, in multiple classes. For example, if a certain class is to assume that students already have a fundamental knowledge of how to do or perform something, they school needs to make sure that it is introduced in at least 2-3 classes so that every student has exposure and doesn't miss learning the skill because they are not in a particular class.

Supporting Multiple Instructors

Another challenge of Curriculum Mapping appears when you have a course led by multiple instructors. It is even more challenging when those instructors have different views on how a course should be run, in what order they should be run, and with what resources they should be run. Imagine that you have a teacher who enjoys teaching a certain topic using video demonstrations and asks their students to create a series of video tutorials to highlight how much they have learned about a topic. Now, imagine that same class being run at the same time. However, the teacher isn't asking technology savvy questions and instead, asks their students to showcase their learning through a series of multiple-choice question tests using paper-based assessments.

Same course, same concepts, but different experiences. One group of students is mastering a completely different set of digital learning standards than another.

Courses Based on Student Achievement or Ability Level

Finally, some courses are designed around students' ability levels in a given subject, such as music, art, or digital media. A teacher might teach multiple sections of the same course but needs to adapt their teaching approach for each class based on the students' abilities and mastery of performance skills. In these types of classes, students must demonstrate mastery of foundational concepts before moving to the next unit. As a result, one class might progress through more curriculum material than another, simply due to differences in student ability levels.

Part 2 Summary

A Digital Learning Curriculum, when implemented effectively, impacts not just students but the entire educational community—teachers, administrators, coaches, and parents alike. The curriculum is uniquely powerful because it addresses the "what," "how," and "through" of education, serving as the driving force behind classroom activities and shaping each graduating class.

Consider your school district's most recent graduating class. These students, having spent years progressing through the district's educational system, now step forward to declare their life aspirations. Their choices stem primarily from their classroom experiences—the activities their teachers designed for them. Through these experiences, they've developed essential skills in collaboration, critical thinking, communication, and creation.

Given this significance, school district leaders must carefully examine our digital learning standards—our impact standards. These standards do more than develop empowered learners, digital citizens, knowledge constructors, innovative designers, computational thinkers, creative communicators, and global collaborators. They transform our students into true impactors. That's why this book is dedicated to helping school districts and you, as a member of the school leadership team, become ambassadors for these impact standards.

In the next section, we will explore a critical role in implementing these impact standards effectively: the Instructional Coach. This pivotal position serves as the cornerstone of successful digital learning implementation, bringing expertise and guidance to the educational environment. As we transition from understanding the curriculum's importance to its practical implementation, we must recognize these dedicated professionals who help bridge the gap between theory and practice, ensuring that educational innovations translate into meaningful classroom experiences. These educational leaders work tirelessly alongside teachers, providing support, resources, and mentorship to transform abstract standards into engaging, dynamic classroom experiences that resonate with students. Through their guidance and collaboration, Instructional Coaches serve as catalysts for meaningful change in our digital learning environments, fostering innovation and growth throughout the school community.

The journey from classroom teacher to Instructional Coach is unique for each educator, shaped by their individual experiences, professional passions, and unwavering dedication to supporting fellow teachers. This transformation often involves years of classroom expertise, continuous professional development, and a deep understanding of both pedagogical principles and technological integration.

Part 3

Supporting your Digital Learning Curriculum through Instructional Coaching

Chapter 9

What is an Instructional Coach?

When I was growing up in the Philadelphia suburbs, music was my life. I began playing the viola in third grade and never put it down throughout my K12 years. I was always the student who would rather be in the orchestra room than in class and often did anything that I could to get out of class just so I could play with orchestra classes that I was not officially scheduled for. It was a wonderful experience for me as I grew up.

Because of this love for music, I never actually asked myself what I wanted to do in college. The choice was always music. Back then, you had two options in the music department at most colleges, Music Performance, and Music Education. Back then, I knew that having a Music Performance Degree would mean that my abilities on the instrument would be my only source of qualified income, so I chose to go into Music Education. To be honest, I really didn't think much of it. I basically just checked a box on the application and with that, I was an education major.

I graduated from West Chester University with a B.S. in Music Education in December of 2001, and I was one of the lucky ones in that graduating class. I ready had a full-time teaching job lined up and waiting for me. From 2002 through 2012 I was a music teacher. I taught string orchestra from grades 3-12 in several wonderful school districts and had a blast working with students of all ability levels. In addition to working in public education, I also had the opportunity to earn my M.M in Music Performance for Orchestral Conducting and was named either Assistant Conductor, Guest Conductor, or Music Director of several symphony orchestra, musical, or opera companies between Philadelphia and New York City.

While my background is in music, my true passion lies in performance art. I love getting up in front of people—regardless of the audience size—and putting on a show. I love the entire process: assembling the performance, running rehearsals, and most of all, experiencing the audience's reactions after a great show.

It was around 2010 when I was working as a Director of Orchestras for a New Jersey High School when I was first approached with the idea of teaching a professional development class for my teachers. With a little hesitation and a little imposter syndrome, I agreed to teach an afternoon session on how to use technology and show them some of the ways they could integrate student devices in their classrooms. Keep in mind that in 2010, this was a novel concept—teachers were very hesitant to try new approaches for fear of supervisory criticism.

One PD session turned into two sessions and then it became part of my weekly schedule. It was fun to work with teachers and help them widen their pedagogical playbooks. It was in the fall of 2010 when a total stranger came into my world and little did I know it, my world was about to change forever.

It all started with a Podcast.

My wife, a professional bass player, was scheduled to take a trip to Long Island, New York to get her Double Bass tuned up. I agreed to go with her, and we headed up the New Jersey Turnpike. I had been searching for ways to learn more about educational technology so I could turn my passions for learning about tech into curricular lessons in my professional development sessions. I came across a podcast hosted by a guy from California that was all about teaching people how to use their iMacs and iPhones.

On the way up the New Jersey Turnpike, we put on one episode and then binge listened to a few more. I fell in love with the concept of the show. Here was a “regular guy” sharing his passion for teaching and here I was learning from him on the other side of the country. (I was new to podcasts at the time.)

I remember my wife and I arriving at the bass shop where we had some time to kill. I sat in the waiting area, put on my headphones, and listened to the latest episode. During that episode, the host offered a $50 iTunes Gift Card for the first person to respond and email him the correct answer. For whatever reason, probably because I had time on my hands, I sent him an email and gave him my best guess on the answer. It was not more than a few hours later during the drive home, that he had emailed me back and told me that I was the winner of the gift card.

Over the next 6-8 months, the host and I went from being email friends to starting a podcast of our own together. This was my first attempt at creating content for an audience greater than my high school. Podcasting quickly became another vehicle for me to be a performer, however it wasn't just 2-3 of my high school teachers I was performing too, it was the entire planet. I fell in love with it then, and I am still in love with it now.

From Music Director to Educational Broadcaster

It was in June 2011 when he and I had a conversation after one of our recording sessions and I gave him this idea for a show that I wanted to create where instead of talking about the latest apps and features of the iPad, I would speak directly to teachers about how they could use technology in their classrooms. It was at that point when he challenged me to go and do it and with that, my world changed forever.

It was on July 11, 2011, when I first came up with the concept for TeacherCast. It happened in the middle of the night. I couldn't sleep and around 2:00 AM, I went downstairs and after learning that the .com was taken, I registered TeacherCast.net. In the next few hours, I had a name, the concept for a logo, and a first website up and running with a complete outline for what this podcast could look like. TeacherCast would go on to be more than just a podcast, it would eventually become the vehicle from which I would shift my career from music to Instructional Technology.

It all started because of a podcast on the New Jersey Turnpike.

Through TeacherCast, I began creating both audio and video content as well as writing blog posts for both my own website and other globally known brands. I began speaking at local conferences and had the opportunity to co-create Edcamp New Jersey with a team of outstanding educators.

Because of TeacherCast, I had the opportunity to attend the Google Teacher Academy and become connected with several high-profile educational brands and conferences.

This was when I decided that it was time to change careers and follow my passions.

The Many Hats Instructional Coaches Wear

In this third section of the book, we will be looking at the Instructional Coaching position and figure out how your school district can clearly define that role and what the function of that role will be to anyone that they encounter. This isn't an easy topic to present in written format because if every school district with a coach or coaching program can define the role and position anyway, they wish.

The coaching position is not at all similar to one of a classroom teacher. Some school districts have part-time coaches where staff members serve as classroom instructors and then are given mentorship roles to support others. In other districts, the role of a coach is more of a support role where the job is all about professional learning rather than inside the classroom support. For other districts, an Instructional Coach is a full-time role without a set schedule with both classroom and leadership duties combined into one set of responsibilities.

I have often said that if you put 10 Instructional Coaches in a room, you will soon find that you have 25 job descriptions. No matter what the official job description or role is on paper, each Instructional Coach must be a master in wearing many hats within the school community to be successful in their positions.

To create as robust of a list as I could, I asked the members of my Instructional Coaches Network to share with me what they do each week. Here is the brief list:

- Artifact Creator
- Bulletin Board Creator
- Cafeteria Monitor
- Co-Teacher
- Copy Maker

- Curriculum and EdTech Evaluator/Reviewer
- Data Analyst
- Data Coordinator
- Digital Signage Creator and Manager
- Idea Generator
- Initiative Cheerleader
- Instructional Designer
- Interventionist
- Leader
- Lesson Plan Resource Creator
- Member of building and district leadership teams
- Mentor
- Multitasker
- On-Call Substitute Teacher
- Photographer
- Planner
- PLC Facilitator
- Printer and Projector Fixer
- Professional Development Planner and Provider
- Program Coordinator
- Project Manager
- Projector Bulb Replacer
- Social Media Manager
- Standards Researcher and Aligner
- State Test Coordinator
- Strategic Planner
- Technician
- Technology Integration Specialist
- Therapist / Friendly Confidant
- Translator of directions between leadership and the classroom
- Videographer

This brings up what should be a simple question, *"What is an Instructional Coach?"*

What is an Instructional Coach?

Simply put, an Instructional Coach is a staff member who is in the position of supporting another staff member in the creation and execution of curricular lessons inside of a learning environment.

Instructional Coaches come in a variety of specialties including:

- *Character Education Coaches*
- *Digital Learning Coaches*
- *ELA Coaches*
- *Math Coaches*
- *Performing Arts Coaches*
- *STEM Coaches*
- *Technology Coaches*

Traditionally, it is the role of the coach to work with staff members through what is often called a Coaching Cycle to plan, create, and execute lessons and activities in the classroom to help teachers become more comfortable and confident using a particular application, system, or tool.

Instructional Coaches need to be multi-dimensional. They can be rolling on the floor in Pre-K for one minute and then walk down the hallway to have a strategic meeting with district administration another only to then enter a classroom and be able to fix an interactive board during a co-teaching session.

How Do You Become an Instructional Coach?

I often think back to my first Instructional Coaching position and wonder how I ever earned the position. The year was 2015 and I had been presenting at ISTE for a few years and had already become a Google Certified Educator and Google for Education Trainer. I remember hearing about a district in North Jersey that had a Technology Coach position open. Due to the distance from my home to the school district, it was offered to have the interview through a virtual platform.

The day of the interview came, and I was all dressed up in my studio and ready to go. The video meeting started, and it was a group interview where the Superintendent had assembled about a dozen district leaders. Then it happened. The Superintendent told me to share a bit of information about myself. After a few minutes of speaking, I waited for the next question to come in. Instead of a second question, members of the administration team and interview panel spoke up and shared their experiences of working with me to the Superintendent. One member spoke up and shared that they had been a subscriber to the podcast for a few years. Another mentioned that they were in a recent PD session that I led at a local conference. It was amazing to sit there and have the entire room speak on your behalf. I accepted the job, and the rest was history.

This is my story. The one that I began creating the moment I turned on my first microphone. But this story isn't for everyone. Quite often, while working with teachers, I have been asked the question about how they might be able to take their first steps towards a career change and become an Instructional Coach.

Let's look at three things every coaching candidate should have or should be pursuing if they wish to be considered for an Instructional Coaching position.

Credentials and Professional Associations

When I applied for my first Instructional Coaching position, I was a Music Educator. I had been teaching orchestra for my full career. Although I had taught a few "non-ensemble" style classes such as Music Theory and Music History, I did not have any experience on my resume that showed that I was competent at supporting K12 curriculum in general subject teachers. But what I did have was a series of micro credentials that showed that I had the professional qualifications to have my name be considered for technology integration positions.

Do you need to badge up to become a Coach?

One of the more often asked questions that come up when speaking with teachers about a new career path is on micro credentials and professional associations in the edtech world. When faced with this topic, I often have two answers.

No, you do not need badges to become a Coach.

For many Coaches, they first were "discovered" in their own buildings where they had been a teacher. For some, they were teaching in a building, and a part-time coaching position came up and it was either recommended for them to apply, or they applied and were offered the position. The need for having professional micro credentials was not needed because district leadership already knew them and knew their skills. In many cases, the coaching position was created ***for*** them due to their outgoing personalities and ability to be a mentor to others in the building.

Yes, you do need badges to become a Coach.

Let's say that you aren't looking for advancement in your current position. Your goal is to leave your district and seek employment in a different school system where nobody may know you or your work. For this reason, ***yes*** you do want to investigate professional micro credentials and professional relationships with educational technology companies. These badges not only show that you are qualified to step in and support them, but it shows that you are a motivated self-learner.

Leveling Up Through Micro Credentials and Professional Learning Certifications

When looking at the landscape of professional learning networks that are available to educators there are, in my opinion, two tiers of programs. The first type are the ones that have been created by educational technology companies such as Google, Microsoft, Apple, ISTE, and ASCD. These are major programs that have dedicated staff and resources devoted to their maturity from the companies.

Tier 1 Professional Learning Communities

Google Education

Google Education has a tiered professional certification system. It starts with educators taking a series of online exams to earn their Level 1 and Level 2 badges. Once complete, the Google for Education program expands to include opportunities to become a Google Certified Coach, Google Certified Innovator, and Google Certified Trainer.

Apple Education

Apple Education has two tiers of professional certifications. The first is called Apple Teacher which educators can qualify for by completing a series of online tests about popular Apple apps. Once completed, educators can apply for the Apple Distinguished Educator Program which accepts candidates every other summer.

Microsoft Education

Microsoft Education has a robust professional learning network that begins with educators visiting the Microsoft Learning Center and completing a series of online courses. Once you have qualified as aMicrosoft Elevate for Educator, you can apply each summer to become a Microsoft Innovative Educators. Additional programs include the Microsoft Advanced Educator, Microsoft Educator Trainer, Microsoft Learn for Educator Program and Showcase Schools program.

ISTE

For many educators, ISTE is a conference that happens every summer, however, for a growing group of educators and educational leaders, the ISTE Community Leader program is a professional group that supports K20 learning year-round. Formerly called ISTE PLN's, the Community Leader group is an energetic network of educators that meet each month and showcase their passions and programs on the international stage through a variety of weekly programs and offerings.

ASCD

Are you an educational leader or aspiring to be one? The ASCD Emerging Leaders program which I joined in 2016, is a community of enthusiastic thinkers selected each year through a recommendation process that is designed to support everyone's career goals.

Tier 2 Professional Learning Communities

The second tier of Professional Learning Communities are made up of Educational Technology companies who have created ambassador programs to connect educators and support their products and applications. These are my favorite types of PLC's because they are usually more grass roots, and educators can form a tighter community due to their smaller sizes.

Often during educational conferences, these PLC's gather to share best practices and examples of work that is being created using their application. Over the years, I have been fortunate to be a part of ambassador programs for LEGO Education, PBS Learning Media, Canva, and PowerSchool. To become a part of these organizations' programs, usually there is a small form to fill out or often a requirement of proof that you have been using the product or application with your students.

What Should a District Look for in an Instructional Coaching Candidate?

Organized, Responsible, Multitasker, Well-Respected, Meticulous, Creative, Well Rounded, Growth-Mindset, Enthusiastic. These are all qualities of an Instructional Coach. Since becoming an Instructional Coach more than a decade ago, I have had the opportunity to collaborate with multiple school districts in search of Coaching candidates and have also been on several interview committees to select coaches for my own department. With each candidate search, there were questions that needed to be answered by the district before the job description was created and the position posted.

When searching for a coaching candidate, it is important that the district look for an Instructional Coach that fits the school's needs and culture and has a strong background in the district's digital philosophy. For example, if a school district was primarily running Microsoft technologies, it is helpful to ask that the Coaching candidate be a Microsoft Innovative Educator or Microsoft Trainer before applying.

Preparing for a Coaching Interview

If you are someone who has recently submitted a series of resumes for Instructional Coaching positions, there are several things that you can do to prepare for an upcoming interview. Having a strong resume on paper is one thing, but having your work stand out for you and being able to WOW a panel of administrators before you walk in the door is completely another. Let us look at some items you might need ready when applying for an Instructional Coaching position.

Resume

When it comes to resumes everyone has an opinion of what they should look like. For years, I went back and forth about what a resume should look like. My original resumes were simple one- or two-page documents, usually created in Microsoft Word or Google Docs. They looked plain and simple and just like everyone else's. I had some success with this format. It helped me land my first Coaching position and I was happy with the results.

When I created TeacherCast and had many accomplishments to add to my resume, I decided to jazz it up a bit by using a two-column approach, adding my photo up top, and adding color to it. I sent out this style of resume for many years. I had a version for Coaching and one for being an EdTech expert. Unfortunately, it didn't work, and I hardly received an invite for an interview.

More recently, I reverted to using a stylish two-page clean and well-organized resume. What I learned along the way, however, is that it is not the format of the resume that gets you in the door for an interview, it is the content that is on it.

For example, instead of saying "I created a PD for my teachers," instead, a coach should write "Create a PD on (insert subject) that created had a 75% increase in application adoption leading to a 40% increase in student achievement on their assessment.

It is always best to quantify with numbers rather than write a series of projects in bullet point form.

Cover Letter

Writing cover letters requires a delicate balance. They should be concise enough for quick reading, yet comprehensive enough to showcase why you're ideal for the role. A strong cover letter tells a compelling story about your interest in the position, explains how you'll fit into the organization, and demonstrates the value you'll bring. It's effective to reference key achievements from your resume to reinforce your qualifications.

Social Media

Social media, when it comes to Instructional Coaches, is often a tricky subject. I spoke with dozens of Instructional Coaches who said their social media status and relationship to edtech companies and conferences hurt their chances of being accepted for positions. When searching for a new position, social media is a great place to turn to because many of your online contacts may know of openings that you might not have seen in your search. However, always keep in mind that everything you say on social media can be used against you throughout the interview process.

Let's look at how best to use each of these platforms to search for your next Instructional Coaching position.

Facebook

Facebook is one of the most popular places to grow a professional learning community. It is easy to join one of the thousands of Facebook Groups or create one of your own on any topic and start sharing content with each other. However, just because it is plentiful, doesn't mean it's wise to build your professional brand on its walled gardens. If you decide to use Facebook as a professional tool, my advice is to keep it professional and not use it to share photos of your latest meal or silly vacation photos showing off something that might not be suitable for work. Always remember that the biggest platforms have all the eyeballs searching through them.

Twitter/X

Love it or hate it, Twitter/X has been and still is one of the biggest professional hangouts for educators. Everyone enjoys a good hashtag … right? When searching for your next coaching position, keep in mind that Twitter/X is an open platform where everything is not only search able but archivable. My advice for Twitter/X is to have both a personal and professional account. By doing this, you can keep one public for future employers to see and one private to keep in contact with friends and family.

Bluesky

Bluesky has emerged as a popular platform where educators gather online to form communities and connect—or reconnect—with colleagues. Through the hashtag #EduSky, teachers can access support, advice, and lesson resources from an expanding educational community.

LinkedIn

Are you looking for a PROFESSIONAL learning network? If so, LinkedIn is THE place to be. Everyone who is searching for a position, no matter what subject or location, should have a professional presence on LinkedIn.

With more than 85 million active users each day, LinkedIn is where I went to search for open positions and more school districts are posting their open positions on the platform due to this very fact.

My advice for LinkedIn is simple. Upload a professional photo and list your current and previous employers. Every now and again, update it with projects and artifacts that you are excited about. When the time does come to start searching, you will be glad to have a list of items that are all set and ready for you to show off and showcase. Who knows… perhaps your next employer has already checked them out before you even hit the apply button.

YouTube

If you are applying for an Instructional Coaching position, you MUST have a YouTube channel. One of the skills that school districts look for when vetting coaching candidates is the ability to tell a story, give a presentation, and hold a group's attention. This IS YouTube! Before you send out your first round of resumes to school districts, create a channel and upload some video tutorials. If you know you are applying to Microsoft focused schools, it is also best practice to have Microsoft tutorials on the top of your channel so that you can instantly be seen as an expert in the technologies the district has already invested in.

Portfolio

If you are active on Facebook, Twitter, LinkedIn, and YouTube then essentially, you have created a professional portfolio. Every interview that I have ever had has asked me to highlight something. Sometimes there is no warning for this request so I often, in the middle of the questions ask, "would you like me to share some examples?" A Portfolio could be a WordPress website, a Google Site or even a collection of links in the form of a Wakelet or Pinterest board. The best practice in creating a portfolio is to create it piece by piece as you go throughout the year rather than rush to get it done before a big interview. Most curation applications such as Wakelet have a Chrome Extension for quickly capturing links. In just a few clicks, you can have a nice-looking portfolio without taking a ton of time out of your day to organize a large-scale project.

Selecting the Best Interview Questions

The Instructional Coaches interview process should be well rounded and based on assorted topics rather than just technology skills. Often, a coaching candidate is asked to bring an artifact to the interview or engage in a performance task to highlight both digital learning and curricular skills. Above all, when interviewing a coaching candidate, it's important to look for people skills. Watching the candidate enter the room, greet the interview panel, and speak about their background are important things to look for as it is often first impressions that make-or-break Instructional Coaches when they are in the field providing professional development to both large and small groups of staff members.

Popular Interview Questions for Instructional Coaches

- Why do you want to leave the classroom to become a coach?
- Tell me about a situation where you were in a mentorship role with another teacher.
- Tell me about a relationship that you had with an administrator that you really enjoyed.
- Tell me about a relationship with an administrator that you did not enjoy.
- What was your biggest challenge as a classroom teacher?
- How have you used the SAMR model or 4C's to create a lesson or unit of lessons?
- Teacher "X" is working on "Y" project … how would you first approach that teacher and how could you help the teacher meet building and district goals through that project?
- Describe your most memorable professional development experience.

Popular Performance Tasks

- Create and give a demo lesson supporting your favorite curricular topic using "X" application that is popular in our school district.
- Create two PD sessions on a single topic. One for large group and one for a small group.
- Create a short video tutorial highlighting a popular application or skill.
- Bring a portfolio displaying previous work.

No matter the question, I always look for coaching candidates with a growth mindset. No candidate can know everything you want them to know, and it is often easy to find their strengths and weaknesses in each topic. There is a significant difference between hearing the words "no" and "not yet" when asking about certain skills that might not be strengths to a candidate.

Congratulations! The Search is Over ... What is the Next Step?

No matter if you are reading this chapter as an Instructional Coaching Candidate, a Coach searching for a new position, or an administrator getting ready to search for a new member of your team, the creation of an Instructional Coaching position is not one that should be taken lightly. Finding the right balance of people, pedagogy, and project management skills is difficult.

In this chapter we looked at the coaching candidacy process from both the school district and coaches' perspectives. We learned how to search for and prepare for a coaching position and what questions might be considered for a first or second interview.

Unfortunately, selecting the perfect candidate or getting selected for a coaching job is only the first step in helping a school district create a standards-based movement to bring a new and innovative culture of learning into your school district. In our next chapter, we are going to take a deep dive into the absolute most important piece about building a culture in your district ... relationships. To move a team forward and introduce a new culture, a school district must have a clear definition and delineation of roles for its Instructional Coaches and how position must be set up for success in the classroom as a mentor, with administration as a building leader, and in the community as an ambassador for innovation.

Chapter 10

The Importance of Building Relationships (Preparing for the Job)

"Nothing reinforces a professional relationship more than enjoying success with someone."
Harold Ramis

No matter if you are an Instructional Coach starting out in a new position, or a school district seeking to create and develop an Instructional Coaching Department, one of the first things that should be mapped out is the various relationships that each member of your school district will have with your coaches.

Relationship building is a key part of the ISTE Standards for Coaches (4.3 Collaborator) and ISTE Standards for Education Leaders (3.3 Empowering Leader).

Standards for Coaches

- 4.3a: Establish trusting and respectful coaching relationships that encourage educators to explore new instructional strategies.
- 4.3b: Partner with educators to identify digital learning content that is culturally relevant, developmentally appropriate and aligned to content standards.
- 4.3c: Partner with educators to evaluate the efficacy of digital learning content and tools to inform procurement decisions and adoption.
- 4.3d: Personalize support for educators by planning and modeling the effective use of technology to improve student learning.

Standards for Education Leaders

- 3.3a: Empower educators to exercise professional agency, build teacher leadership skills, and pursue personalized professional learning.
- 3.3b: Build the confidence and competency of educators to put the ISTE Standards for Students and Educators into practice.
- 3.3c: Inspire a culture of innovation and collaboration that allows the time and space to explore and experiment with digital tools.

These standards provide a blueprint for establishing a successful school district by defining the roles and responsibilities of the Instructional Coaching position. This framework enables coaches to excel both as mentors in the classroom and as leaders in the building, school district, and community.

In this chapter, we will explore these essential coaching relationships:

- Coach / Teacher Relationship
- Coach / Library Media Specialist Relationship
- Coach / Building Administrator Relationship
- Coach / Central Office Relationship
- Coach / IT Department Relationship
- Coach / Student Relationship

It Is All About Relationships

Why are relationships so crucial to the success of an Inst. Coaching program?

The Instructional Coach and the responsibilities required for the position are unlike the school district. For some school districts, the Coach is a core member of a school building serving by the side (and being evaluated by) the building principal. For other coaches, they serve at the side of Central Office and are assigned to one or more school buildings.

For each of these types of organization systems, the Coach will need to create key relationships with a variety of district employees as well as members of the student population.

Let's look at the relationships that an Instructional Coach will form with the following groups and describe how each of these relationships could or should be outlined or thought of from both the coach and the staff members' point of view.:

- Students
- Teachers
- Building Administrators
- Central Office Administrators
- IT Department
- Other Instructional Coaches

A key skill that Coaches must develop as they and their position evolve within the school district is the ability to work effectively across all levels of the organization. The capacity to communicate at various "altitudes" — from classroom-level details to district-wide strategies — is crucial. This versatility not only shapes the Coach's effectiveness but also determines how the school district can leverage the Instructional Coaching position both inside and outside the classroom.

The Teacher / Coach Relationship

Of all the relationships that an Instructional Coach has is the one between the Coach and the Teacher. The primary responsibility for Instructional Coaches is to work with and be a team member of the classroom teacher in and out of the classroom. The teacher needs to be able to trust their Instructional Coach and at times become vulnerable with them to allow the coaching process to naturally happen.

In return, the Coach needs to be able to collaborate with teachers of all ability levels, background specialties, and grade levels to make sure that each teacher has a plan to take their instructional abilities to the next level. The Coach needs to be not just a "guide on the side," but also a "sage on the stage."

In essence, a Coach and a Teacher share similar job descriptions, albeit from different perspectives. A Teacher's primary focus is to work with and enhance their students' abilities. A Coach, on the other hand, concentrates on working with and improving their adult learners —the teachers themselves.

How Can the Coach Support the Teachers?

Throughout the school year, a Coach can work with classroom teachers in a variety of ways. The Coach usually starts building their teacher relationships by having conversations, sometimes in the hallways, and sometimes in the classrooms. Often these conversations turn into classroom visits and eventually a series of co-teaching opportunities begin to happen.

The Coaches job in these situations is to support the curricular needs of the teacher. They are there to learn how the teacher teaches, how the classroom runs, and what their goals are in working with their students.

From this point, the Coach and Teacher can formulate a plan of action for the Teacher to learn how to create new and dynamic lessons for their students. This relationship is all about the many ways that a Coach can supply 1:1 professional development to the teacher in a safe and mutually respectable environment.

How Can the Teachers Support the Coach?

If the Coach's role in the Teacher/Coach relationship is to be supportive and provide guidance when needed, then the Teacher's role is to allow the process to unfold. When a teacher—whether new or experienced—first meets an Instructional Coach, it's natural for them to feel somewhat apprehensive about having someone else in their room "coaching" or assisting them. They might initially view this as an opportunity to let the coach take over instruction. Some teachers, particularly those with many years of experience, may resist the concept of having a coach.

In these situations, the best approach for teachers is to gradually open themselves to meeting and working with their coaches. This step-by-step process allows them to build the trust necessary to recognize that the coach is there to support them and help them grow as educators.

The Library Media Specialist / Coach Relationship

In the world of Instructional Coaching, the one relationship that is mostly the strongest in a school building is the one between the Instructional Coach and the Library Media Specialist (LMS). Often, it is found that the Coach and LMS are the two most "techy" people in the building, and they are also the ones that teachers will reach out to the most when something is broken or in need of fixing in their classrooms.

When working as a team, it is important that both the Coach and LMS understand and know their role in the building.

- The LMS's position is to support students by teaching them Digital Literacy skills.
- The Instructional Coach's position is to support the teachers by helping them learn how to bring digital literacy skills into their lessons.

I mention this because quite often both roles can easily become a two-headed "technology teacher" if the situation is left unchecked.

How Can the Coach Support The LMS?

In most school districts, the coach is the team member most closely in contact with Central Office and the IT department. For this reason, it is important for the Coach to keep the LMS up to date on district projects and initiatives.

The Coach can also support the LMS by keeping them up to date on what is happening in the classrooms. Quite often, a teacher might bring their students to the library and on short notice request that the LMS support a certain curricular topic (last minute). In working with teachers, the Coach can keep an eye out for any current or future classroom projects and help support student activities both in the classroom and in the library.

How Can the LMS Support the Coach?

The relationship between the LMS and the Coach can be thought of as both symbiotic and cooperative. If a Coach finds themselves in a school where there is a long-standing tradition of asking the LMS for digital learning support, the LMS can support the Coach by directing any of these types of questions over to the Coach. This will not only help the Coach become familiar with what is happening in the classrooms but also allow the coach to get into the classrooms and begin building relationships.

Additionally, the LMS is usually the best person for a Coach to practice their coaching skills. In many cases, the Coach/LMS relationship is extremely close and concepts such as "coaching" and "co-teaching" are out the window and in exchange, the two team members simply lock into one of total and complete support for each other's goals and objectives in the building.

The Building Administrator / Coach Relationship

The relationship between building administrators and Instructional Coaches is one of the most crucial discussed in this article. For some Coaches, the Building Administrator is their immediate supervisor, while for others, the Administrator serves as the building leader who influences the coaching program's success rather than as an evaluator.

As Joellen Killion, Chris Bryan, and Heather Clifton note in their book "Coaching Matters," the Building Administrator must first be a "Coach's Champion." This means they should actively support having a Coach in their building and have a clear vision for how the Coach will be utilized in classrooms.

Whether or not the Building Administrator directly evaluates the Coach, the success of the coaching program ultimately rests on their shoulders.

How Can the Coach Support the Building Administrator?

When defining the various relationships a Coach should have with their building administrator, one of the most important is that of a resource provider. A building principal typically has a clear vision for how learning should occur in classrooms. The coach serves as the vehicle through which this plan is implemented.

As a resource provider, the coach plays a crucial role in helping teachers understand their classroom objectives. They work alongside educators, demonstrating key concepts and aspects of digital learning skills to both students and teachers. This hands-on approach ensures that the principal's vision is effectively translated into classroom practice.

How Can the Building Administrator Support the Coach?

When a coach first arrives in a building, they are often looked at as an outsider. They are members of the school building community, but they do not follow the same schedule or have the same rules as teachers. This often puts the responsibility of creating meaningful relationships to start "the job" on the shoulders of the coach.

The process of building relationships and starting a coaching program is less on the coach and more on the way the position (and person) is introduced by the building administrator. The coaching position needs to be set up on day one by the building administration.

Teachers need to understand what the expectations are of the coach just as much as they need to know the expectations they have in the relationship.

The building administrator can support the coaching process by working with a coach as both a leader and mentor to share building and district goals. They can also go on classroom walkthroughs with the coach to point out what they see as positive and what they would like to see addressed in the building so the coach can begin to formulate a plan for improvement when working with teachers.

Above all, the building administrator must be the foremost champion of the coach and the coaching program. While the coaching program is voluntary, when implemented effectively, it becomes an invaluable resource—offering teachers personalized, one-on-one professional development during instructional time.

The Central Office / Coach Relationship

If the building administrator is responsible for setting the direction of an individual building, central office administrators are responsible for setting the direction for groups of buildings, entire grade levels, or individual curricular departments.

For this reason, to create a unified and supportive coaching program, central office administration should have a strong relationship with their coaching staff to alert them (first) of new district initiates, critical changes to technology applications, and adjustments to the curriculum so that they can be ready to train staff and field first-level questions when they come up in conversation.

How Can Central Office Support the Coach?

Often, during coaching sessions, or professional development sessions a question such as "why are we doing this" comes up from the teaching staff. When central office takes the time not just to share updates but also explains the theory and philosophy behind changes in policy it gives the coaching staff to stand up on the front line and provide important context for the decisions, they often become the face of in the classroom.

Central office administration should also allow coaches to have behind-the-scenes access to key technologies that they will be teaching. As an example, coaches should be given higher level access to applications that have district resource libraries so they can help manage classroom technologies. This not only takes the burden of doing this off the plate of central office staff, but also trains coaches to think at a higher altitude than they previously needed to when they were in the classrooms.

The IT Department / Coach Relationship

If you look at a school district the way you look at a football team, the Coaching and IT departments can be thought of as both your offense and your defense. The Instructional Coaching Department represents your offense. Coaches are responsible for moving instruction forward. When set up for success, coaches have a game plan set up by Central Office and adopted by building administrators charged with supporting in classrooms.

The IT Department on the other side is your defense. They are responsible for making sure that bad things do not happen to the network and digital infrastructure. When devices break down, it is the IT Departments' responsibility to repair and put back into action.

How Can the Coach Support the IT Department?

When working as a unit, the Coach should be assisting teachers with the creation of support tickets so that damaged technology gets cataloged quickly and put back into the hands of students for future use. Coaches should have a strong working relationship with their building technicians and meet with them often to alert them of what is happening in individual classrooms so that they are able to come out to the buildings with any additional cables or equipment needed to keep classrooms up and running smoothly.

How Can the IT Department Support the Coach?

In a traditional school district, the Technician position is one that rotates between multiple school buildings. They need to be able to quickly enter a school building, identify what needs to be addressed and be able to take care of a building as efficiently as possible.

They usually are entering a building with previous knowledge of a certain number of issues in mind due to what support tickets have been submitted but are also aware that at any moment they might be faced with several secondary challenges or requests for added services.

Much like the relationship with building and central office personnel, the Technician should enter a building and before leaving, seek conversation with the building coach. Traditionally this is the best way for a technician to learn about both major and minor issues happening in classrooms.

The Technician, who is often in technical meetings that the coach is not invited to, knows, and understands not just about their buildings, but about any issues happening across the district such as application issues, or Wi-Fi outages.

The Student / Coach Relationship

So far, we have looked at several relationships that a coach must form during a school year. The one thing that all these relationships have in common is that they are between two adults. However, there is one more important relationship that a coach must form and that is with the student population.

Traditionally, a coach is focused on and dedicated to supporting teachers. They meet teachers outside of the traditional classroom and spend time planning and preparing lessons. The next phase of the coaching program is when students come into play.

There is a fine line between a coach being a co-teacher or a mentor in the classroom and being the building's technology teacher. This is where it is important for a coach to clearly define their relationships with students.

How Can the Coach Support the Students?

Understanding that their role in the school district is to teach teachers and not students, the coach has the responsibility of supporting the students both during the times they are in the classrooms and the times they are in non-instructional meetings.

The coach is a believer in both Future Ready and ISTE (International Society for Technology in Education) standards and keeping them in mind strives to support the needs of the students when planning lessons and discussing instructional strategy with building and district administrators.

In many ways, the coach is the ultimate advocate for what the student needs to learn both on the micro and macro level, and thus why the coaching position exists in the first place.

How Can the Students Support the Coach?

Simply put, the students play a significant role in the success of any coaching program. They are the ones that show (directly or indirectly) a teacher how important it is to include digital learning skills in traditional lessons.

When students are working on a video project and they say, "this is awesome, can we try this again?" The teacher is going to then be encouraged to turn to the coach and ask for them to come back for additional lesson planning.

Is the Instructional Coach a Leadership Position?

In this section, we discussed a variety of roles and relationships that must be set up by a school district for the Instructional Coaching position to be successful. The Instructional Coach, while often on a teacher's contract, is very much a building leader and when the position is successfully created, a district leader. If you think of an hourglass with sand running down it, the Instructional Coach sits right in the middle of the two halves. On one side they are a mentor of staff members. On the other side, they are members of the leadership team.

By setting the Instructional Coaching position up as a leader, educational leaders provide their coaches with the ability to walk into a classroom and meet teachers with the knowledge and confidence that they are more than just a voluntary task for teachers.

Conclusion

When building successful Instructional Coaching programs, several important decisions must be made. Decisions that allow coaches to be successful in the classroom, successful in setting up their schedule, and successful in being productive and equal members of the leadership team.

To do this, it is vital for proper relationships to form for the coach at all levels of the greater district organizational chart. Having strong relationships at both the central and district level administrative levels allows the coach to speak not only to, but for the district as they are usually the ones who are tasked with implementing new initiatives and programs. The ability to know not only what is happening in the curriculum world but also in the greater technology world is also important and thus, it is important for coaches to be in constant communication with their district and building IT staff.

When these relationships are set up and communication channels are put in place it is not the coach that is successful, but ultimately the students who are put in the best position to succeed.

Chapter 11

What does an Instructional Coach Do? (Defining the Job)

It's the beginning of a new day. An Instructional Coach enters the building, drops their coat and backpack at their desk, and it's time to start the day. *What happens next?*

Every Instructional Coach has an answer to this question. In fact, it is more than likely that one of the questions that Coaching candidates ask most often during the later rounds of the interview process.

What will a typical day look like?

There are usually two responses to this. The first response is that a coach will be managed fully and given a set daily schedule. The other response is that a coach has full control over their day and has sets their own schedule.

For some coaches who perhaps are full-time teachers with coaching duties built into the day, it's logical to be in a position where coaching opportunities are fully scheduled, because their coaching role revolves around their teaching schedule. However, when an Instructional Coach is set up without a fixed schedule, their worlds are wide open and they can build relationships, make connections, and effect change as often as possible.

But *should* Coaches have an open schedule? Or should coaches be set up with a ridged schedule that is controlled by administration?

In this chapter, we will look at the daily schedule for Instructional Coaches and each of the many ways that a Coach connects and communicates their role to the classroom. We will identify key items that each coach should create to be successful when collaborating with staff, as well as how they can mold their practice based on professional feedback from staff, administrators, and students.

First, we will look at how the staff will view the coaching position. Many teachers are used to working by themselves. They teach in a classroom by themselves, create their lesson plans, and administer assessments by themselves. For many teachers, the only time someone walks into the room to watch them is when they are being officially observed.

For this reason, it is not unusual for a teacher to feel skittish or threatened when first approached by an Instructional Coach. No matter what discipline the Coach supports, it can be scary for a teacher suddenly to have someone come in and sit down to watch them.

Several questions might go through the teacher's mind:

- Why is this person here?
- What are they thinking about me and the way I am teaching this lesson?
- Is there something I should be doing when they are in the room?
- Is this person going to go back to my administrator and discuss this?
- What happens if a student does something and I react poorly?
- Why does this person keep walking around to look at students' work?

As mentioned in an earlier chapter, the way that the coaching position is presented by the administration is key for helping teachers become comfortable having a coach in the room. The administrator should not just introduce the coach once, but several times throughout the year. This process of constantly reminding teachers why the coach is there and how their skills can be used will help build relationships between the coach and teacher and not allow the coach to become an outsider in their own building.

Fortunately for coaches, there are several things that are within their control. Let's look at the best ways for coaches to become members of the school community and assimilate themselves into the school culture.

Building Your Brand as an Instructional Coach

What comes to your mind when you think of the word "brand?" It could be a symbol, a color, a logo. Have you ever stopped to think what makes a memorable brand?

Whether or not a coach is actively trying to create a brand for themselves, every time they walk into a building, classroom, or office area, they are building their brand. For the sake of argument, think of a coaching brand as a reputation. Everyone in the school, including administrators, is looking to see what the coach will be doing and how the coach will be serving and supporting in the classroom.

Sometimes a brand is built for the coach. The principal stands up and introduces them as "the coach" and that might be all the introduction they get. At that point, their brand is one of mystery amongst the staff. In another case, the principal might give a longer description of the coach's background, the reason for having the position in the school, a brief list of expectations, and then might share thoughts on how the staff should be interacting with the coach. This is my preferred way of having a coach – or any new position – be introduced, so that roles are established and expectations set from the start of the school year.

Sadly, not every Instructional Coach has a glowing introduction from their administrator. Sometimes, coaching departments are not set up well. Unfortunately, too often, a coach is hired at the district level and is assigned to a building where the building administrator is not fully sure of what their role is or what value they could bring to the staff.

No matter what type of introduction an Instructional Coach receives, it is ultimately the responsibility of the coach to build their own coaching brand; in doing so, they will set the stage for what will ultimately be their successes or failures throughout the school year. For this to be successful, a coach needs to first build their brand identity.

What is a Coaching Brand Identity?

An Instructional Coach wears many hats throughout the day. Some of these are teacher, leader, mentor, and problem solver. Some coaches might be better at wearing certain hats than others. No matter what hat they are wearing, they are reflecting to their staff what their coaching brand is.

To first create a brand identity, a coach and their administrator must first agree on a certain set of coaching goals. These goals will differ depending on who the coach is working with at any time. For example, a coach might have certain goals with the full teaching staff to help move the school in a certain direction, but the coach might also have other specific goals for a particular grade level or set of teachers based on the needs of the principal. When working with a building's office staff, another set of goals might be provided to help administrative assistants become more fluent in certain applications. In these examples, the coaches' brand identity is based on who they are interacting with at any given time.

Many coaches already have a brand identity and have a set routine for working with office staff, certified staff, special area staff and/or students. They might not even realize it. My suggestion to any Instructional Coach and/or coaching department is to take time to organize these goals, write them down, and then track their progress over time. (We will address this topic in a later chapter.)

There are several steps that a coach can take when organizing their brand identity to staff members.

1. Clarify your audience.
2. Define target goals for each audience member.
3. Set boundaries for when a coach will be working with those members on those goals.
4. Decide which hat each audience member will associate a coach with.
5. Craft a narrative with those audience members.
6. Bring your brand to life when interacting with those members.
7. Launch your brand.
8. Monitor your brand.
9. Optimize your brand.

In the marketing world, this is often referred to as the "customer journey." For Instructional Coaches, this journey can be thought of as a standards-driven adventure that assists staff members in moving from one side of the adoption curve to another.

When looking at the ISTE Coaching Standards, there are several that demonstrate the importance for a coach to create a customer journey for their staff.

- 4.1a: Create a shared vision and culture for using technology to learn and accelerate transformation through the coaching process.
- 4.1c: Cultivate a supportive coaching culture that encourages educators and leaders to achieve a shared vision and individual goals.
- 4.1d: Recognize educators across the organization who use technology effectively to enable high-impact teaching and learning.
- 4.2c: Establish shared goals with educators, reflect on successes and continually improve coaching and teaching practice.
- 4.3a: Establish trusting and respectful coaching relationships that encourage educators to explore new instructional strategies.
- 4.3b: Partner with educators to identify digital learning content that is culturally relevant, developmentally appropriate and aligned to content standards.
- 4.3c: Partner with educators to evaluate the efficacy of digital learning content and tools to inform procurement decisions and adoption.
- 4.3d: Personalize support for educators by planning and modeling the effective use of technology to improve student learning.

When we are building our coaching brand through the lens of the ISTE Coaching Standards, we can see how easy it is to bring each of your coaching goals into a well-organized and easily accessible rubric that will ultimately determine the success of the coaching program.

Clarify Your Audience

As an Instructional Coach, I generally break down my building staff members into one of three categories.

- Staff who work directly with students.
- Staff who work primarily at a desk.
- Staff who are in a leadership capacity.

This simple grouping can also be thought of as Teachers, Office Staff, and Administrators. Each of them has their own personal goals for being in the building and they also have goals put upon them by administrators above them.

Define Target Goals for each Audience Member

Now that we have our audience clearly defined, it is time to ask the question "What goals do these staff groups have and how can the coach help them successfully meet those goals?"

Ultimately, this is where the coach needs to think about how they can become valuable to those staff groups to build relationships and trust for future conversations.

Set Boundaries for when a Coach will be Working with those Members on coaching Goals.

This is a key factor in building a brand identity. There are times when a coach should be having a discussion with a particular staff group to satisfy the staff members' needs and times when they need to be having a conversation with that staff member to satisfy a coaching need. Most important, a coach needs to know when to have a conversation with that staff member or group simply to have a conversation and build a report with them.

Determine what Hat each Audience Member Thinks of when Associating the Coach with a Topic

Making sure that each group of staff members sees the coach the correct way is vital for building relationships. The teacher should look at the coach as a guide on the side who is a friendly mentor and supportive co-teacher that has the best interest of their students in mind. The office worker should think of the coach as a warm and fuzzy staff member who is always bringing them tips and tricks for how to help them be more efficient in their daily tasks. Finally, the administrator should always think of the coach as both a leader in the building and as a staff member who always gets the job done and is well trusted by the teaching staff.

Craft a Narrative with those Audience Members

When entering each staff member's daily circles, what is the running topic of conversation throughout the year? This could be something personal, or it could center around a topic such as music, movies, or sports. What “non-school” topic is available for a coach to use as small talk to build a personal relationship with another staff member.

Bring Your Brand to Life when Interacting with Those Members

For coaches, it is always important to remember that behind every interaction is another conversation. This conversation is the one where one staff member (sometimes an administrator) asks about or hears information about a coach. I often remind coaches that they are never “off” when they are in their buildings and that their coaching brand should always be always “on”.

Launch Your Brand - Monitor Your Brand - Optimize Your Brand

When creating a coaching brand and building relationships with your teachers, office staff members, and administrators, it is important to remember that once launched, your brand becomes a living thing.

The coaching brand is more than just the interactions that a coach has with staff members, it is everything that helps a coach make an impact in the classroom and ultimately be the one responsible for shifting the culture of a school building or district and it starts on your first day of school.

Introducing Yourself as an Instructional Coach

Congratulations! It is the beginning of the school year. Perhaps you are entering your third or fourth year as a Tech Coach, or perhaps you are getting ready to walk into a brand-new school for the first time. No matter what the scenario, it is always an exciting time of year and an incredibly stressful one.

When entering the first week, or even the first day, it is important to have a few things in mind. Your job as an Instructional Coach is always a bit shaky when it comes to relationships with your teachers and administrators and it's important that you start the year off on the best foot.

When thinking about my own first day of school I started thinking about the advice I had been given. In years past, I tried to meet each department on the first day. I thought it was my duty to stand up and give a killer presentation that would WOW them and make them love me. I wanted to prove to them that I was worthy of being their Coach. None of this worked. This year, instead of starting off with a fancy tech demo, my plan is to go in and say hello and ask them about their hopes for this year. My plan is to let them lead the conversation. Here is the reason.

When you are in a Coaching role, it's never about you. It is always about them and their goals. If you walk in and force a presentation on your teachers, you are simply doing it to show off.

Listen, Listen, Listen

At the start of the year, it's easy to want to jump into staff and faculty meetings and impress your staff with tech-heavy presentations. After all, you spent the summer trying to come up with the best way for teachers to learn about you and all that you can bring to their classroom. However, this might not be the best thing to start the year off with.

When thinking about the first ten minutes of the school year, teachers are extremely busy and burdened with all that goes into opening a fully functioning learning environment with very little time that another tech demo is simply another tech demo.

Instead of dazzling them with gizmos and gadgets, try another direction with your opening speech.

The most important thing you can do as a tech coach in any situation is to sit back, ask questions, and listen. I often start with two questions:

1. What was exciting about last year that you would like to emulate?
2. What frustrations did you have that you are looking to avoid this year?

In these two questions, you have the basis for a very good first 1:1 conversation with teachers, or the meat of a first email that you can then personalize for that teacher. If you can get in front of teachers in a group and ask those two questions, you have a strong possibility that a good percentage of them will respond to your emails because they know you are listening to them and that you are interested in learning about their needs.

Communicate Your Intentions for Supporting Their Goals

Once you have a conversation going that revolves around their needs, or the needs of their departments, it's important for you to continuously express your goals and how they are aligned to the goals of the district, building, and department.

Your goals are not to bring amazing tech into their classrooms and rock their world. Your goals should be to support the needs of the teachers that "just happens to be" through the lens of technology integration. If this philosophy is switched around, it might be difficult to get teachers excited. In general, teachers are not looking for that "one more thing" that they must learn at the beginning of the year. Instead, they are often excited by the ability to take one or more things off their plate so that they can have a great start to the school year with their students.

Showcase Your Resources Not Your Tech Skills

Right before leaving those early conversations, I always have something up my sleeve that can solve a particular problem for them. In many cases, this MUST be content specific. It doesn't make any sense to highlight something general that is abstract. I often start with some type of spreadsheet, video, or presentation slide deck trick that makes them say "how do you do that? I've been looking for something like that!"

This is generally when you take out your calendar and ask "When are you available? ... Let's work together!"

Building your coaching brand on those first few days of school is critical for setting the tone of a successful school year. Remember that these conversations have their own way of spreading throughout the school. If you have a great first interaction, that experience will make its way into conversations between other staff members and soon you will soon find yourself stopped in the hallway from a staff member you might not have met who referenced that conversation asking for your help with the same or similar topic.

The Instructional Coaches Dress Code

Before we dive into the various items that an Instructional often creates to support their position, I thought it was wise to take a moment and address the dress code of coaches. The topic of dress code is one that varies from position to position, and it will certainly depend on what the dress code philosophy is in any district.

For many coaches, the day is filled with interactions and activities. It is not uncommon for a coach to be sitting on the floor playing with kindergarten students one minute, and then be in an administrator's office soon after having a strategic planning meeting. For this reason, a dress code is critical for a coach's success.

When I first began my career as a coach, I wanted to dress casually so I would fit in with my teachers, but I also wanted to develop my own brand to support my role in the district as their Instructional Technology Coach. I wore Khaki's and jeans often paired with a polo from an edtech company such as Google or Microsoft that I received for being a member of their ambassador groups.

This choice of outfit unfortunately did not work. Teachers were taken back by the fact that I was inadvertently "bragging" about my tech knowledge, and many didn't understand that I was a member of the district staff. Many of them thought I was an employee of Google or Microsoft and were working in their schools, like a vendor from a different company, working in a Best Buy selling their brands. Because of this, I was not let into the teacher circles and had an extremely challenging time making connections and building relationships.

I then changed my daily attire to wearing button down shirts with a sports coat and dress pants. This also didn't work. Teachers looked at me as an administrator, and I spent more time convincing teachers that I was a member of their teacher union than having meaningful conversations about curricular or student topics.

In my previous role as an Instructional Coach, I choose to wear jeans and a button-down shirt when entering classrooms but always had with me a jacket that I could put on when entering the main office and/or working with principals and district level staff members.

I bring up these stories here to remind anyone in this position that your success often is built around your appearance. Success with students, especially young ones, requires you to look the part and provide you the ability to get down to their eye level, even if that means sitting on the floor to co-teach a lesson. When supporting upper-level decision makers, it is often proper to dress a bit more professionally so that you are not the odd person in the room without a tie on.

To summarize this section … always be prepared to play to your audience.

The Instructional Coaches Website

Take a moment and think of one of your favorite brands. It could be a food company, a technology company, or even a movie franchise. What do all these famous brands have in common?

They all have a website. A single place for their audience to visit to learn more information about their product that is dynamic. On this website, perhaps you find videos, blog posts, a newsletter and more to help connect you with their brand so you can become more familiar with them and become brand loyal.

For Instructional Coaches, a website should be thought of very much like a part of your marketing plan. It should be a place for staff members to visit to learn how to best infuse new and innovative strategies and technologies into their classroom. The Coaches website should also be a place where staff members can locate a coach's newsletter and find newly published blog posts and videos on any number of topics to help them best prepare lessons for their students.

That said, there is one significant difference between an Instructional Coaches website and those created by large marketing companies supporting restaurants, technology companies, and movie franchises. That difference is the fact restaurants, technology companies, and movie franchises have large fan bases who seek out information on those brands several times a week, if not daily, and so their websites need to be constantly updated and able to push out a large amount of dynamic content as quickly as possible.

The Instructional Coaches website, in contrast to these examples, needs to be both a destination website but also should be considered one of the most valuable tools in an Instructional Coaches backpack that they can use at a moment's notice to support any number of coaching situations.

Why Should You Create a Website?

For many Instructional Coaches, the purpose of the website is to create an online place to share tips and tricks with their staff members. In doing so, they create a robust website using a platform such as a Google Site, Weebly, or WordPress and spend hours filling it with every video, tutorial, link, and instructional strategy they can find.

But …

- Is this an effective strategy for Coaching Websites?
- Is the work being put into the creation of these websites paying off with users?

- Do staff members really take the time to benefit from the time spent building such a platform?

Where I would never discourage any Instructional Coach from creating the website of their dreams, I would like to offer a few points of advice on the creation of a coaching website to help them both maximize their time both during and after the website creation process.

Choosing Your Website Avatar

When we put together any marketing plan, we must first determine who our avatar, or audience is. Think about the members of your staff. Think about who your website is being created for. Is it teachers, administrators, or perhaps for other coaches?

Now ask yourself what types of information those staff members need and most importantly, how they need it. Do they need videos? Do they need blog posts? Do they need templates and tutorials?

Now ask yourself one of the most puzzling questions any web developer asks themselves … will your avatar care about what you are about to create?

This is often a challenging question. Over the last decade, I have worked with dozens of Instructional Coaches on their websites. The first thing I ask them to do is to add some type of analytics on their website to track usage. Many tools have analytics on them and it's easy to track how many people click on that first link and arrive on page, but to get a true picture of how effective a product, such as a website, is, it's important to see how many secondary clicks a website brings to truly find its value.

Unfortunately, most coaches find that the hours of work creating the perfect website never get seen. The coach then finds that they have created a website that, where it might look amazing, has no value in the eyes of their avatar and so it never sees its full potential.

Let's shift this concept a bit from one of giving, to one of supporting.

What if an Instructional Coaches website was designed not for the staff member the coach is working with, but as a true tool that was to be used to support the coach each day as they work their way throughout the school building.

Creating a site that can be shared AND used daily by the Instructional Coach

Picture this situation, a coach walks into a classroom to meet with a teacher. They sit down to discuss an upcoming lesson. The coach suddenly has an idea and starts searching through their online drive for the perfect document or presentation. Several minutes goes by as the teacher watches the coach search for this document. Finally, the file is opened, and they discuss the example in question. The coach then has another document they would like the teacher to see. The search starts over. Rinse and Repeat.

What if this situation played out a bit differently?

A coach walks into a classroom to meet with a teacher. They sit down to discuss an upcoming lesson. The coach quickly clicks on a bookmark in their browser to pull up their coaching website and clicks on a page called Artifacts. On this page are neatly curated links to files in the coach's online hard drive, embedded examples of templates available on many subjects, and a variety of student examples from previously created lessons with other teachers. Suddenly instead of the teacher watching the coach search through their drives, they have an entire buffet of possibilities to choose from. The coach can then pull up any number of project solutions from any number of subject areas and inspire the teacher to work together to create something magical for their class.

After the meeting is over, the coach sends the Artifacts page to the teacher with a message inviting the teacher to choose any one of the projects and make a second appointment to get started.

In which example would you like to be the Instructional Coach?

Creating a Hybrid Marketing Plan for your Instructional Coaching Website

When planning your Instructional Coaches website, I highly suggest that it be created both as a learning center for staff members AND a place where meaningful coaching & professional development can happen. You want to create a place where your teachers can learn but more important you want to create a vehicle from which your teachers will be inspired to not only try new things but invite you back into the classroom for additional meetings, planning sessions, and coteaching opportunities.

Once you have created your website both for your staff members and your coaching/ professional development practice it is also time to think about your administrative avatars who will be using this website as a potential evaluative tool and for this reason, it is important to make sure that your website can also be used as a data collection tool. This is a topic that we will cover later in this section in greater detail.

Final Thoughts on Instructional Coaching Websites

Often when coaches get together at conferences, they begin discussing their websites. They wear them as a status symbol. They create them to help them define their brand. I have had the opportunity to create several of my own coaching websites. Some of them were successful and others failed immensely. There was one year that I created an extremely detailed WordPress website. I was trying to take everything that I learned from building TeacherCast and tried to apply it to my coaching website. I thought it looked amazing.

Unfortunately, I realized that I was building a website for myself and not one for my staff to use. Ultimately after a few months I decided to scrap the entire thing and I started from scratch with a much simpler website created from Google Sites.

My best advice to Instructional Coaches is to create something that serves multiple purposes and multiple avatars. It is a far more arduous task to create an Instructional Coaches website than one for a restaurant, tech company or movie franchise.

Now that you have your website planned out and built, it's time to create the vehicle that will be sent out to your staff each week to draw people to it. It's time to build your brand through your Instructional Coaches Newsletter.

The Instructional Coaches Newsletter

As an Instructional Coach, we all know the value of communication with our teachers. No matter if you are supporting one or two buildings with a great deal of time to walk hallways, pop into classrooms, and get to know the staff members or if you happen to support more than a dozen buildings with very little free time on your hands, the struggle to make meaningful relationships is real and constantly on your mind.

One of the most important things that we can do as Instructional Coaches is to our teacher in a way that invites and encourages others to relax from their comfort zone and give new tech tools a try. (Coaching Standard 4.4: Learning Designer)

But …

- How do you do it?
- Where do you start?

Why Should You Create Weekly Email Newsletters?

For many coaches, the point of their newsletter is to share with their teachers the latest edtech news and highlights from applications they know and love. They might fill their newsletters with videos, blog post links, and other digital learning goodies. Coaches spend a good amount of time each week making sure that they maximize their designs and layouts to provide the best possible product to their teachers each Tuesday. They might even have a catchy name for the newsletters.

All of this is certainly well and good and I highly encourage coaches create something special for their staff members on a regular basis, but one question always comes out of the reading of a traditional newsletter …

After speaking with Instructional Coaches over the last decade, there seems to be an agreement that some type of newsletter is necessary. How long it should be and how often it should be sent will be discussed later in this section. Here are some reasons why an Instructional Coach should create some type of printed or digital communication system to keep their teachers updated each month.

To Attract More Teachers to Your Brand

If you are an Instructional Coaches tasked with supporting multiple buildings, you know that your brand is everything. You need to be thought of as someone to turn to for professional support both when you are in and out of the classroom. Try as you might to be everyone all the time and to be everything to everyone, it is just nearly impossible. This is where your email newsletter comes in.

By creating a weekly newsletter, you keep yourself and your brand in the inboxes of all your staff. You are the Jiminy Cricket of your subject each week. When you walk into a school for the first time after being away for a few days, your staff members might have questions for you based on things they read in your newsletter. This is something that you can always use to your advantage in both helping teachers you have a good rapport with and teachers you might not have the opportunity to get to know personally.

To Showcase New Additions to Your Favorite Apps

One of the easiest things you can do each week is to use a popular application used in your district to curate district news and updates each week. This could act as easy filler content for your newsletters. Do you have teachers in your school who are all using a fantastic app such as Wakelet? If so, you should make sure you are following the Wakelet blog so you can share news and updates and be able to walk into their classrooms ready to dazzle them with what the new hot features are.

To Promote Teacher & Student Success in The Classroom

Lastly, your newsletter could be, and more importantly, should be a place to highlight what is happening in the classrooms. A good Instructional Coaches weekly email newsletter has some type of section dedicated to what is happening in the classroom. If you want to take this a step further, ask the teachers permission to post an abbreviated version of their lesson or tech template in the newsletter for others to download.

The “teacher feature” section is something that is not only good for Newsletter sidebars but also a fantastic way to promote content by grade level or subject area. If you take something that a science teacher has done … see what you can do to manipulate that lesson in a way for other subjects and grade levels to take advantage of and then use that updated content to push into additional classrooms during the week.

Are All Weekly Email Newsletter's Created Equally?

There are several types of Email Newsletter applications available to Instructional Coaches:

- Some describe themselves as "apps that create newsletters."
- Some curate content for easy sharing and posting.
- Some provide the option of acting both as a newsletter and presentation tool.

No matter what option you select, it's not about the app, nor the content that you should be thinking about when creating your weekly newsletter. What is most important is how easy it is for your teachers to click on something … quickly glance over it and perhaps find one or two golden tickets that they can take with them or reach out to you about over the next few days that will make it an ultimate winning choice for you and your tech program.

How Can You Know If Your Newsletters Working?

Often when I work with a coach or read a thread of comments online about coaching newsletters, I ask the question "Is your newsletter working?" In other words, "is anyone reading your newsletter?"

For many coaches, the answer is "I don't know" or … "I doubt it" which is, to be honest, heartbreaking knowing how long a coach might spend each week putting together something wonderful for their staff.

If coaches are going to be working hard each week to create a weekly communication platform one question is left to be asked …

How Can Coaches Create a Better Newsletter?

In this section we are going to walk you through a brand-new philosophy for Coaching Newsletters. A philosophy based on marketing and entrepreneurship rather than on impulse emailing. This philosophy is designed on first remembering what the purpose of the Instructional Coach is (and is not) and defining the function of the newsletter in relationship to a coach's overall job description.

If this is confusing … it is ok … keep reading and we will work through your questions below.

What Are Coaches Currently Doing to Support Their Newsletters?

If you are like many coaches creating weekly or monthly newsletters, you might spend a few moments each day, or an hour on a Friday putting together your newsletter. You might do this in two steps.

- Curating & Creating Resources
- Designing and Publishing

I am always curious to learn how much time it takes for a coach to design the perfect newsletter (each week) using applications such as Canva, Google Slides, Bitmoji, or even Wakelet. I am sure that the process is fun and exciting but … I will ask again … *Is your newsletter working?*

What Can a Weekly Email Newsletter Do for A Coach?

When looking at the topic of Instructional Newsletters, there are several advantages to building a coaching brand through weekly digital communications.

Improve Teacher Interactions and Comfortability

When an email newsletter is created with not just the content in mind, but also the implementation of the provided activities, they can be especially useful for classroom teachers. For many teachers, newsletters are read and either saved or tossed so you have a 50/50 chance of user retention. However, after working as an Instructional Coach, I have noticed a trend of teachers reading Coaching newsletters and saving them for later use.

One of the things that should be kept in mind when creating your newsletter is your email subject and what text is used in the newsletter. Often these keywords are what your teachers search for weeks if not months after you send them the newsletter. If you "think in search" when creating your correspondences, it might be helpful to someone down the road.

How many times has a teacher come to you and said that they were looking through some old newsletters and thought to reach out with a question???

Develop Your Instructional Technology Curriculum

One of the things that your newsletter should be used for is to develop a drip campaign for your professional development content. If you just completed a big PD Day in your school then you now have a few weeks' worth of opportunities to follow up with your teachers on that content to distribute additional resources, templates, or examples of student work.

What Should You Include in Your Weekly Newsletter?

In order to create a unified newsletter that is created by all and is meant to be read by all, several factors must go into the creation of it.

Message From Administration

Traditionally the Instructional Coaches weekly email newsletter is just that. It's a weekly email that is created by the Coach and sent to the teachers. However, what if ….

What if each week, or even perhaps each month there was a short paragraph from your building/district administrator that features something positive about the district. How would it look if each week your principal did a short 30-second video praising a teacher or grade level inviting other teachers to join in and take part in the digital revolution?

In writing this, I can already hear you saying NOOOOO but … all I am asking here is… "*What if …?*"

Video Tutorials

One of the staples of every Instructional Coaches newsletter should be some type of video tutorial. While there is always a debate on if these videos should be created by the Coach or if they should be grabbed from YouTube, what is important is the understanding that videos help to add value to the newsletter.

My goal when creating newsletters is to put as much personal content as possible. This way the teachers see that YOU are the one putting in the time in their learning and YOU are the voice that is helping them out. While there are several great YouTube channels to get your videos from such as Teachers.Tech, Flipped Classroom Tutorials, and of course TeacherCast, no video tutorial will ever come close to something that you put together based on your own teachers' classrooms.

New App of The Week

This is a tricky one to include in your newsletter. Generally, you have two distinct types of teachers … the ones that will read your email newsletters and learn something from them, or the ones that don't read due to lack of time, interest, or frustration with technology in general.

As Instructional Coaches, we are generally on the cutting edge of what is new and amazing but one wrong move with this excitement and you might end up in hot water. Just remember many school districts can't move at the speed of Twitter Chats. If a new application opens today and you wish to use it in your class tomorrow, you might have to first ask for permission from your district administration. You should always be proactive about new technologies but at the same time, you shouldn't ever be promoting something that isn't district approved.

How Is a Coaching Newsletter Created?

Let us look at both a traditional coach's newsletter and compare it to a slightly unique way of looking at your digital communications platform.

The Traditional Coaches Newsletter:

The traditional Instructional Coaches newsletter might be outlined like this.

- Audience
    - Teacher
- Content
    - Cool Tools
    - New Updates
- Platform
    - Popular Applications
- Release Schedule
    - Weekly / Monthly
- Purpose
    - To Help Teachers Learn about "something."

In a traditional newsletter, the teacher is the primary audience member. It is only natural to think so given the way that a coach might define their roles in the school. In addition, the newsletter is traditionally made up of the latest and greatest in educational technology, supporting videos, and maybe a few templates created by the tech coach to show off what they can do in the classroom with teachers. The newsletter is released on a" Tech Tuesday." (Why?? Who Knows) When asked, the coach might say that the reason for the newsletter is to share something with their teachers, drop some value bombs and hope and pray that a teacher fills out a sign-up form.

But … again … does the traditional method work?

Your New Instructional Coaches Newsletter

When looking at your newsletter philosophy with a bit of a marketing eye, you might outline your product like this.

- Audience
  - District Leadership
- Content
  - District – Strategic Goals
- Building – Principal Directives
- Platform
  - District Initiative
- Release Schedule
  - Based on PD (Professional Development) Schedule
- Purpose
  - To Get Coaches into the Classroom to Support District and Building Goals and Initiatives

When looking at your newsletter from a slightly different lens, you might see your newsletter as a way for your administrator to support their building and district-mandated goals. The newsletter is not yours (exactly) but their way of getting teachers on board with new directives that they wish to show up inside of the classroom.

The audience for your newsletter, rather than being the passive teacher is the active administrator who is on a mission to bring forth change in their staff. The content of your newsletter is designed to support their primary goals and directions. In other words, whatever they are asking of the teachers … should be what is inside of the newsletter so you (the coach) can be seen as supportive of their wishes and demands of classroom instruction.

When choosing a platform, it is best to select something that your district is trying to get behind. If your district for example is pushing the use of Google Applications, it does not make any sense to use Canva or SMORE to create your newsletter. That will not give the teachers the ability to see the district-mandated application in action or to see what the possibilities of that application are.

Lastly, when looking at your newsletter with a marketing eye, it is important to make sure that you are doing it to meet the needs of your professional development schedule and are doing everything in your power to create a newsletter to service one goal … to get you in the classroom, so you can help teachers meet the needs of the principal and district goals for (digital) learning.

Do you see a slight difference between these two approaches?

Understanding The Role of The Instructional Coach in Relation to The District?

Before we break down the components of your new Instructional Coaches Newsletter, we must first take a step back and ask the question, "What is the role of the Instructional Coach?"

For many coaches, they say something like "I'm here to help teachers learn how to use technology in their classrooms." However, this is not the correct answer. Helping teachers learn about technology and digital learning skills is what a coach "does" not what the coach's role is in the district.

Long and short, a coach's role is to help the district to achieve the goals and initiatives set forth and agreed upon in the Strategic Plan. Nothing more ... nothing less.

The district might have a goal to improve their science scores. The function then of the Science Coach is to support this goal by working with teachers in the classroom to improve science scores.

In another example, the district might have Future Ready or Digital Learning goals. The district then might bring on Digital Learning, or Tech Coaches to support those goals. Those coaches will then collaborate with teachers in the classroom to help the district meet their needs.

See the difference?

If the function of a coach is to help support the district and to help the district leadership team meat their directives ... we must think of the Coaches Newsletter, simply as a tool to make those goals become achievable.

Does this make sense?

The Three-Part Coaching Newsletter

To create a newsletter to fit the needs of the strategic goals, curricular goals, and teacher it is only rational that we create our coaching newsletters in three parts.

Part 1: District Goals

The first part of our newsletter strategy is to help our teachers understand and promote various school districts and building level goals and objectives and how they might be included in classroom activities. This might be curricular in nature or might be wrapped around a specific suite of. Applications (Microsoft & Google) or a Learning Management System that needs to be installed and trained on.

Part 2: Curricular & Digital Learning Goals

The second part of the newsletter might focus on helping teachers meet the standards of either their curriculum or the ISTE (International Society for Technology in Education) Standards for Digital Learning.

Part 3: Teacher & Student Goals

The third part of the newsletter revolves around providing something to the teachers that they or their students are interested in. This not only is designed to keep their attention, but also gives them something to look forward to each time your newsletter comes out.

What Should Be Included in The Coaches Newsletter?

When looking at your Instructional Coaching Newsletter as a resource and tool to support your administration's goals and directives, the next step is to decide what should be placed inside the newsletter.

Initiative Quick Tips (Ways to help teachers meet the needs of administration)

- Calendar of Events (To keep them updated on district events)
- Instructional Videos
- Templates for Curricular Activities
- Advice For Coaches Creating Newsletters This Year

For many coaches, the newsletter is something that they enjoy doing. My recommendation, if I can suggest anything with this blog post, is to make your newsletter a supportive vehicle for your administrators rather than a weekly email that your teacher must quickly look at and decide if it is of interest to them. When you create it as “the answer” for how to successfully have a great school year rather than a colorful document with links, they will be more adventurous in the contents that are in the newsletter.

What Apps Are Perfect for Tech Coach Newsletters?

SMORE

One of my favorite platforms for creating and sharing lesson plans is SMORE. SMORE offers a freemium pricing model and allows teachers to create amazing looking infographics, online posters, and newsletters. The designs are easy on the eye and each SMORE is completely responsive which means that it looks great on a desktop or mobile device. If you want to share your SMORE with your school, it's easy to import a CSV file to ensure all contacts are notified.

Google Sites

Have you ever thought about creating a website and using THAT simply as your newsletter? If the answer to this is YES, then you're not alone. Many Tech Coaches are turning to Google Sites as their newsletter choice. Through Google Sites, you can create a beautiful newsletter that can serve as either a landing page for additional content or a series of informational blocks from which you are sharing your content with your teachers.

By using Google Sites as both the home for your content and your newsletter landing page you save yourself the added step of creating content AND formatting an additional email program. All you need to do is copy your published link and send it off in a Gmail message and BAM you are done!

Canva

Canva is one of those apps that I am proud to say that I am a long-time paid subscriber. It's my app of choice for just about all the images and graphics on TeacherCast. It has made this website look much better than I could ever make it look on my own. Like other applications on this list, Canva offers a Freemium pricing model. Trust me… its paid features by far outweigh its free features which is why I decided to become a subscriber. However, you can certainly do a ton with it on the free version.

Creating a newsletter in Canva is super easy and barely an inconvenience. Simply select a template, add your information, and click the publish button. Canva offers the opportunity to either download your project as a PDF or image file but the true power of Canva is the ability for you to embed graphics into your website directly OR create full websites from your projects.

Google Slides

Are you looking to double up all the time you spend creating weekly PR Presentations? IMO, Google Slides is one of the most underrated apps on the G-Suite roster. Many people, even to this day think of Google Slides as "The PowerPoint of Google Apps" which is just silly these days. With thousands of teachers and Tech Coaches sharing their Google Slides Hacks, all you have to do is click on the File button and select Page Setup to turn your 4:3 or 16:9 into a beautiful 8.5/11 design that you can not only share with your teachers or send to Google Classroom, but also present from at your next department meeting.

SWAY

If you take a SMORE and add some additional design features to it, you might only start to understand the beautiful newsletter application that is Microsoft SWAY. Much like Google Slides, SWAY (in my opinion) doesn't nearly get the love that it deserves.

Using Microsoft SWAY, you can easily turn your digital documents into dynamic websites for sharing and emailing to your teachers. It also makes a great presentation tool that you can stand in front of and share information with your teachers.

Email

Last is a simple email. Yes, it is true that for many Coaches, hours each week are spent creating beautiful-looking newsletters that simply aren't read or given any thought by our teachers. Where all the apps above are great in their own rights, nothing beats the time saved by sitting down to write a 3 (short) paragraph email to your teachers with a few links to websites that you didn't even write yourself to show off what is new and exciting. The chances are … you will have the same percentage of interaction while saving a ton of time each week.

Email Newsletter Bonus Tips: Create A Weekly Call to Action

Tip #1: Encourage Social Sharing of Projects

One of the things that you should consider adding to your weekly email newsletters is a Call to Action. This could come in the form of "please share" or "send me copies of what you are doing so I can share" and go a long way in creating not just a weekly email chain but a culture of staff supporting staff.

Tip #2: Establish Your Hashtag

Does your school have a Social Media presence? What if you created a special hashtag that focused on student achievement and activities during the school day? This could then be something that teachers are encouraged to post to each week with various photos, projects, and other digital encouragement.

Final Thoughts on Instructional Coaching Newsletters

One of the things that I have been thinking about over the last few years of being an Instructional Coach is … "Why shouldn't Tech Coaches use the power of email marketing to their advantage?" We are all out there every day selling ourselves and creating a branded product that we are hoping our teachers decide to invest in. It takes a ton of time each week to research, curate, and distribute a quality newsletter. Why not figure out a way to do things even more efficiently?

As you can see, the Instructional Coaching Newsletter is one of the most powerful tools in that a coach should have available to support teachers. The Newsletter, along with a well-thought-out website, cannot help a coach create a strong brand identity but saves them hours of time over a long school year and supports their professional development goals.

The Art of Professional Development

When it comes to professional development there can be a million ways to do it correctly and a million ways to turn your staff members off so that they never accept voluntary assistance from a coach during their prep times. It is often not an easy task to engage with staff members who may be on their only 30-minute break each day. I have had the opportunity to collaborate with several coaches who have been extremely successful in their buildings. They created amazing relationships with their staff members who were willing to give up their planning time to sit and discuss pedagogy over morning coffee or inside the hallowed walls of the teachers' break room. On the flipside, I have also witnessed firsthand instructional coaches go out of their way and spend their time, energy, and money out of their own pocket to supply snacks, gift cards, and more only to find that teachers were unwilling to join a study session.

Let's look at several ways that you can create a successful day time professional development program in your school that supports not only a coaches need to build positive relationships with staff members but also the creation of a culture for collaborative professional learning amongst peers.

The Lunch and Learn

Often when a coach enters a building for the first time, they seek ways to gather teachers together for quick and exciting professional development. Knowing that half day or full day professional learning days are very rare, it is natural for a coach to attempt to create a lunch and learn style event either during the day or before/after school to build their brand. This is an extremely exciting opportunity to get staff members together to build experiences that could then lead into meaningful classroom interactions.

For many coaches, the Lunch and Learn is an extremely easy program to put together. It is created as a voluntary event that often attracts a few staff members at first and then grows into a weekly event where teachers gather with assorted snacks to learn something new while interacting in a dynamic social situation.

Are Lunch and Learns Effective?

The effectiveness of the lunch-and-learn session is often determined by three factors.

- The motivation of the Instructional Coach
- The support of the administrator
- The culture of the building staff

Over the years, I have had the opportunity to collaborate with coaches who had a ton of motivation to get their lunch and learn programs up and running. They would stop by the local bagel shop each morning to gather breakfast and have some tasty goodies set up in a community room before the day starts. Teachers would be invited to show up and learn something new formally or to simply meet with the coach. All participants enjoyed the experience immensely.

Successful Lunch-and-Learn programs are often promoted by building administration. Not necessarily in writing or verbally at a staff meeting (more on this below) but supported simply by being present during the lunch-and-Learn session. This is a fantastic opportunity for the administrator to participate as an equal to the teacher and set the tone for everyone being a lifelong learner. This is the chance for the administrator to let the coach function as a building leader and influence how staff members see the coach.

I mentioned building culture above for an extremely specific reason. For many coaches, the Lunch and Learn is an organic professional learning experience that starts small and has the potential to grow as big as the building allows. In other situations, unfortunately, the building's culture may not allow it to get off the ground. This could be due to any number of factors such as contract status, the relationship between staff and administration, or the idea that attending an extracurricular professional development session would be considered working outside of contract hours. It's unfortunate when these things happen, but the fact is that they do happen, and a coach should always have the blessing and advice from an administrator before taking the first step into this arena.

Tips For Lunch and Learns

All these pros and cons being on the table, let's look at several ways that you can be successful with your lunch-and-learn Program.

Location, Location, Location

One of the first things that a coach thinks of when planning a Lunch and Learn is where they should be holding it. It is natural to want to hold a Lunch and Learn in the lunchroom or staff break room, but I would caution against this as it's often the one room where teachers go to unwind and get away from the world for a few minutes. They might not want to walk into the break room to see that the coach has turned it into a social classroom.

Instead, it might be best to hold the Lunch and Learn session in an empty classroom. This would give you an opportunity to have desks and chairs and if needed a board to project to. You can keep the sessions in the same room each week or rotate classrooms so teachers can see other classrooms they might not experience throughout the week.

Topics, Topics, Topics

Lunch and Learn topics depend greatly on the audience and the culture of the staff you are working with. When planning my own Lunch and Learn sessions, I tend to plan a mixture of topics that vary between ones that the staff is interested in, topics that may come up during coaching conversations, and topics that are "suggestions" from the administration team.

If you find that several teachers are asking you about creating video lessons, that would be a great topic for a session. You could do one week on how to use video in the classroom and another week on a specific video application used in your district. Finally, you could do a lesson where everyone comes and together you create something fun with video. These are all great ways to satisfy the curiosity of your staff and meet the needs of both curricular and digital learning standards.

Format, Format, Format

For some coaches, Lunch and Learns are a way to provide extra professional development for their staff disguised as social situations. I would encourage any coach thinking about putting together a Lunch and Learn to think of them more as a social situation first with a bit of professional development sprinkled in.

In my first year as an Instructional Coach, I created a series of Lunch and Learn opportunities. I came into school with a very well-prepared slide deck and had several examples. I was able to get a few teachers to join but only for a few minutes and when they were in the room, we found ourselves having meaningful conversations. It was effective, but thinking about it now, there was no need to have a highly detailed slide deck. I wasn't impressing anyone and never found myself using the slides.

What attracted staff members to the sessions was the community building experience and the conversations that happened in the room. The learning was simply a byproduct of the environment that I created for them.

Presentations, Presentations, Presentations

Building on the previous topic, it's important that a coach creates a positive communal environment during their lunch-and-learn sessions. I once asked a teacher to get up in front of the group and show everyone a project that we had been working on. It didn't go well at all. Putting the teacher on the spot was certainly not a selling point and the teacher unfortunately didn't come back the following week. I then switched my presentations to being hyper social and I always followed them up with a visit to the classroom thanking each teacher for attending the session followed by an offer to meet with them later to answer any questions they might have had on the topic.

Feedback, Feedback, Feedback

The true secret to creating any robust and sustainable professional learning community is feedback. For this reason, I always recommend asking a ton of questions to all staff members about their interests and their pain points. Once you start finding trends in certain topics or once you identify a hot topic that is exciting everyone … plan your Lunch and Learn and have fun!

Final Thoughts on Lunch and Learns

Daytime professional development, or lunch-and-learns can be an extremely exciting weekly event for staff members. It can be a terrific way to help a coach build their brand in the school community by bringing staff members together for a social hour that just happens to have a learning component.

Lunch-and-Learns are not easy. It takes the right balance of administrative support and staff acceptance to make it happen. Not every building is ready for additional professional development, especially if they feel that they should be paid extra for coming into school early for a learning session. Always look to your building leaders for advice before proceeding.

All things being equal, the lunch-and-learn, when combined with the marketing plan you create through your Instructional Coaching newsletter and website can be a terrific way to help get a coach into the classroom and set them up for a successful coaching career.

Using Data to Support Your Coaches, Professional Learning Practices, and Raise Student Achievement

Every day, Instructional Coaches enter their schools bright-eyed and ready to go. They spend the early part of their day interacting with teachers in their buildings to make sure they are caught up on what is happening in classrooms while at the same time trying to schedule visits and coaching conversations to support the curricular needs of both teachers and students. They may also spend time in the main office mingling with the office staff hoping to get a green light to visit their principals to discuss the latest building initiatives.

At some point in the school year, the coach might sit down with their administrator or supervisor to discuss the progress they have been making in the classrooms.

What happens next is usually one of two things:

1. The coach says "let me show you my calendar ... it's full of events, meetings, and other interesting things ... and look ... It is colorful!

2. The coach opens their coaching data dashboard and presents a series of charts, graphs, and meaningful information about what they have done during the school year complete with links to artifacts to projects they have worked on with both teachers and students.

The question today is ... "Are you currently Coach #1, or Coach #2?"

To be honest, in my first year of coaching, I wasn't either of those coaches. I spent my first full year as an Instructional Coach busy beyond belief. I was constantly moving from classroom to classroom and building to building not thinking anything about the future and only experiencing each moment as it was happening.

At the end of the year, my Superintendent sat me down and I learned an extremely valuable lesson about the importance of collecting data and being able to present to an audience exactly how valuable you have been to the organization.

ISTE Standard 4.6 reminds us that Coaches should be data-driven decision makers. It describes Instructional Coaches as needing to use data to inform their own instructional and professional learning practices. It was during that meeting with my Superintendent that I decided that to become a valuable staff member to central office, I would need to incorporate some type of data collection process in my daily habits so that I could support the district in making both financial, curricular, and instructional decisions.

Why Is Data Collection Important?

To answer the question about the importance of having a solid data collection system, it is important to ask two particularly important questions.

What is the role of the Instructional Coach in your district and/or school building?

As we learned in our Instructional Coaching Newsletter section above, the Instructional Coaching position is an extension of the school district's Strategic Plan.

Nothing more ... Nothing Less

At some point, the district leadership team and the Board of Education came together and approved a series of Strategic Goals that would set the stage for all activities that will be happening in the school district for one, two, or even up to five years. The members of the district's senior leadership team are then tasked with meeting those goals and improving the school district.

Let's say that one of your district's goals is to improve scores in both Mathematics and English, it might be logical that the district then provides support for teachers so that they have the ability to raise those test scores. One of the support systems put in place might be the Math or ELA Instructional Coach.

Additionally, many school districts have digital learning goals to improve the Future Readiness of their students. To support both teachers in learning how to implement these skills and technology-based goals, the district might create a Digital Learning department and support teachers through "Instructional Coaches."

In this example, the "role of the Instructional Coach" is to serve the district's strategic goals. You as a coach, are "the answer" to the question "how do we raise test scores and support our teachers in the classroom."

How does an Instructional Coach support their role in the district?

If the role of the Instructional Coach and its main function in the district is to be the vehicle from which the strategic plan is carried out and its goals achieved, then the coach must find a way to do this. In meeting this role's requirements, the coach then goes into classrooms, meets with teachers, sets up coaching cycles, and provides professional development sessions to support their goals of (for example) raising test scores.

How Can Data Be Collected by Instructional Coaches?

Over the last few years, I have seen a variety of methods for keeping track of teacher and staff interactions, and where they are all good, each of them seems to have its good and bad points.

So, what do you do?

A few years ago, I created a simple Daily Teacher Interaction Tracker using Google Forms and *believe me* ... it saved me a ton of time each day AND it provided me, my digital learning team, and my principal with the data that we needed to support our teachers and students. I have since created this system using Microsoft Forms and both are available as downloads on the TeacherCast website.

What Is a Daily Teacher Interaction Tracking System?

A Daily Teacher Interaction Tracking System is a data curation tool that coaches use every day ... in fact, several times a day to account, not just for the work that they do with teachers, but what type of work they do as an Instructional Coach.

Sample Questions Include:

- Type of Coaching
  - 1:1 Coaching
  - Co-Teaching
  - Supporting Students
  - Building Lessons & Resources with Teacher
- Time Spent with Teacher
  - 5 Min
  - 15 Min
  - 30 Min
- Topics Covered
  - Curricular Topics
  - Digital Learning Topics
- Follow Up Topics
  - Action Items for Future Conversations

By having and using a tool such as a Daily Teacher Interaction Tracking System, you can quickly analyze the data and know which staff members need additional information, or what topics you might want to build Professional Development around.

What Happens to The Data Collected?

Once your data is collected, it is time to make some sense of it so you can present it to your building and district leaders. This is where your Instructional Coaches Data Dashboard comes in handy. A Data Dashboard could be as simple as a Google Sheet with a few graphs on it or it could be a detailed Google Site with those charts and graphs embedded and surrounded by additional materials and resources to support the data.

Why Are Instructional Coaching Data Tracking Systems Important?

It can be argued that the primary function of an Instructional Coach is to help our administration meet their district and building goals. Coaches do this by interacting with teachers and supporting them in the classroom. If Coaches are not doing everything, they can support their administrators, they might wake up one day without their administrators supporting them or worse yet, without administrators to support at all.

By creating a data dashboard, coaches can not only have data-based conversations with our district administrators, but we can also give THEM data to then show to their supervisors to justify the need for an Instructional Coaching position in the district.

Coaching Cycles: The Standard Definition

Another strategic way for Coaches to build their brand is through Coaching Cycles. A Coaching Cycle is a series of staff member interactions that build upon one another that ultimately lead to a change in instructional strategies for the teacher. Another way of defining a Coaching Cycle is a process where a teacher and a coach work collaboratively on agreed upon learning goals together over the course of several interactions. Coaching cycles can happen after a coach and teacher build a strategic relationship or through the actions and support of a building administrator.

Traditionally, a Coaching Cycle has four phases:

1. A Pre-Conference or Goal Setting conversation.
2. A Support Phase where the coach visits the classroom to learn more about what type of support the teacher may need.
3. An Action Phase where the coach is collaborating with the classroom teacher as a model instructor or a co-teacher.
4. A Reflection Phase where the teacher and coach discuss the learning experience during a post-conference conversation.

As mentioned in the subtitle above, this is the standard and traditional definition of the term Coaching Cycle. It is a process that traditionally includes one teacher and one coach in a very personal collaborative setting to support the teacher in implementing a new skill or strategy they may be asked to use in their classroom. However, in thinking about the term Coaching Cycle, I often like to use it to describe an entirely different type of coaching model. One that supports many staff members and is much more collaborative due to its size and function.

Coaching Cycles: The Unheard-of Definition

In Chapter 4 of this book, we learned that there are several types of professional learning experiences. Some experiences are small and intimate sessions between a coach and one or a few staff members. They allow coaches to enter a classroom and create meaningful conversations that directly impact student learning and teacher confidence with new technologies and curricular tools.

In contrast, some professional learning experiences are supported in a large room with dozens if not hundreds of staff members. These require a different approach to preparing and presenting the learning materials and require the coach to be much more dynamic and charismatic due to the sheer size of the group.

No matter what type of learning experience the coach is preparing for, they all must have the same goal ... to get the coach into the classroom to collaborate directly with the teacher in front of students.

For this reason, I'd like to offer a different version of the term "coaching cycle." In this version, the coach works in partnership with building administrators to create a series of interactions. While these might appear to be simply ongoing professional development sessions, they are actually a carefully orchestrated set of coaching opportunities designed to support dynamic classroom interactions—all backed by data and verified through classroom observations by the administrator.

Additionally, by setting up these series of professional learning and individualized coaching events, the coach has an extremely strong opportunity to create a brand and positive reputation in the district because they are seen both as a leader in the building and as a member of the teaching staff simply by the way that the process is designed.

How to Create a Standards-Based Coaching Cycle with Support of Administration

ISTE Coaching Standard 4.4 Learning Designer, and 4.5 Professional Learning Facilitator share with coaches the importance of being expert at creating learning opportunities for both large and small groups. When Coaches and Administrators collaborate on a series of staff learning opportunities, a coach can create a coaching cycle that includes an entire building and by doing so helps the building administrator flatten their innovation curve quite a bit faster than if a coach had to do individual meetings using grass roots techniques every day.

Thinking of a Coaching Cycle like a Funnel

As mentioned, several times in this book. The Instructional Coaching position and the success of the Instructional Coach is completely based on one premise. Can the Coach successfully market themselves to staff members so that they find enough value in the coach to invite them into their classrooms for a discussion. This is often not something that a coach can do all by themselves. Where there are some situations where a coach and a building are all moving in the same direction, there are times where the building has a slight resistance to the coaching position. No matter how the building and the coach relate to each other, one way that a coach can successfully support an entire building is through the creation of a funnel system.

Much like in marketing, the term funnel is used to describe a system where information flows through a series of steps, usually general to specific, to capture the attention of someone with the intent to get them to eventually purchase a product or service. Usually, the funnel starts when a user goes to a website and is enticed to sign up for a mailing list. To get someone to sign up for the list, a free giveaway is usually offered as an incentive. This is called a lead-magnet. Once in the funnel, a series of emails gets automatically generated in hopes that a user clicks on them and travels back to the website. As time goes on, more emails are automatically generated that are more specific to the users' interests based on the specific clicks that the user has made throughout the funnel series.

The point of this funnel is that each new email that gets sent to the user is created and ready to be sent before the user even arrives at the website and signs up for the newsletter. It is an automatic process that saves time and allows the website owner to market their product while they are away from their desk.

Can this same system be used in education to support Instructional Coaches?

YES!

Let's look at what a Coaching Funnel might look like. Traditionally, a coach can meet with their staff as a large group presentation during a weekly faculty meeting. Sometimes the topic is given to them by an administrator and other times the coach is asked to come up with a topic for presentation. The coach gets up in front of teachers who may or may not be familiar with the topic and provides an exciting lesson. When the coach ends the presentation, they invite the staff to contact them with any questions. They sit back down, the session is over, and the staff gets up to go back to their day. It could be argued that while this may be a traditional coaching story, it may not be the best way to help an instructional coach get meaningful time with their teachers in a classroom situation.

On the other hand, ...

Let's look at this same situation from a slightly different approach. One that is predefined and predetermined and allows the coach to create personalized professional learning opportunities that target certain groups of staff members based on data that will ultimately have an impact on students in the classroom.

In this situation, the coach and the administrator meet and discuss topics that are pressing on the school district or building for the next few weeks. After looking through test scores and other data points, it is determined that there is a need for additional support in ELA in the 2nd and 4th grades. The coach and administrator determine that the best way to support this is by creating a series of learning opportunities together. Leading up to the next staff meeting, the coach prepares a newsletter with hints on how to support students through an upcoming math unit and shares examples of how all grade levels can raise student scores in that lesson.

During the staff meeting, the coach provides a demonstration lesson to the entire faculty that covers several ways to teach this skill. After the coach is finished, they end by announcing that grades 1, 2, 3, and 4 will be meeting as an entire grade level with the instructional coach to go over lesson plans and set a schedule for when the coach will be observing those lessons in the classrooms of grades 2 and 4.

During each of those grade level meetings, the coach sets up a time to meet individually with a few teachers that were previously identified during the coach/principal meeting as having low test scores in math. Throughout this process, the coach prepares and sends the entire faculty a series of newsletters to support this math topic.

Which of these two methods do you feel will be more successful in raising student achievement in math class?

When looking at professional development the same way that you might create a funnel, you can see how one action automatically leads to another action. Before the group session ever started, there was a plan in place to get the coach from the large group (staff meeting) into the medium group (grade level meetings) directly into the classroom through a series of preplanned collaborations between the coach and administration.

By creating a funnel system, or a vertical coaching cycle, the teacher will be better prepared to support students in the classroom and the instructional coach will not be left begging teachers to sign up for them after a staff development session. All building, grade level, and 1:1 staff interaction is preplanned, and the system ultimately sets the student up for success based on analytical data. (Coaching Standard 4.6, Data-Driven Decision Maker & Instructional Leader Standard 3.2, Visionary Planner)

How do you Create a Successful Coaching Cycle?

Building your coaching brand through the creation of a successful coaching cycle is not a difficult task, it simply takes time, planning, and a professional working relationship with your building administration. The key to success is knowing where your building administrator wants to go and what they would like to see improved in the classroom. This system works even better when the principal alerts the teaching staff that they will be looking for certain skills, or teaching methods during evaluative walkthroughs. By doing this, the coach automatically shifts from being another person entering the classroom and disrupting the flow of instruction to becoming the best safety and security blanket in the school because they will be able to help the teacher "pass the admin test" during evaluation season.

Long Form and Multi-Hour Professional Development Workshops

In the previous section, we learned how to build a coaching brand by first starting at the large group level and creating a funnel that assists an Instructional Coach in getting into the classroom while being able to support as many teachers as possible. In this section, we will look in the opposite direction and investigate how long form professional development sessions can be used for a coach to grow their brand not just in a school building but throughout an entire school district.

A few years ago, my Instructional Coaching department was tasks with creating a district wide training system to introduce Microsoft Teams and demonstrate how it can effectively be used at the district, building, and classroom levels for staff communication, file sharing, and instruction. My coaches and I created a platform that could run both synchronous and asynchronous and covered 6 major features of the platform.

To accomplish this, we created a SharePoint website from which our staff members could sign up for our live training sessions. Each of our coaches was tasked with creating a slide deck and an after-session quiz to go along with their topic. At the end of each of the training sessions, those who attended filled out a form and were sent a custom designed badge to say THANK YOU for attending the session.

At the end of the day, everyone walked away learning something and had a wonderful time doing so. Our coaches looked like rock stars and staff members not only had a chance to learn a new tool for their building but had the opportunity to see our coaches working together as a team to support a common goal. This was building at its best!

How to Develop a Successful Long Form Professional Development Project

In order to successfully develop a session that met the needs both of the district and of each staff member attending, we asked our coaches to go through a six-step process. By doing so, we were then able to come together as a group and map out an experience that directly spoke to the goals of each party included.

- **Step 1:** Identify learning objects that directly or indirectly correlate to district & building goals and initiatives.
- **Step 2:** Develop a Curriculum that matches the strengths of the presenters.
- **Step 3:** Integrate staff member needs and wants into the creation of learning modules.
- **Step 4:** Decide on a proper framework and workflow for the staff member to complete the training.
- **Step 5:** Provide both users and presenters with time to self-reflect and share new experiences.
- **Step 6:** Highlight staff member and presenter accomplishments at the conclusion of the session.

The Key to Developing High Quality and Successful Large Scale Professional Development

What made this training project successful wasn't the fact that our staff members attended 6 different training sessions over three months to complete the training. The thing that made this successful was that much like we described in the previous section, our coaches had their calendars already book with building level, department level, and classroom training sessions before we even opened our doors for registration. By creating a funnel out of district wide asynchronous training sessions, everyone at the session knew from the start that the material being covered is something that the district is serious in having them learn and that it would be discussed later in meetings and by both the coach.

Building Coaching Momentum through Staff Feedback

Being an Instructional Coach is difficult. On the surface, a coach has no schedule, they have little daily responsibility, they are often driving across the district each day trying to support multiple buildings and multiple administrators and rarely do they leave their schools at the end of the day with stacks of papers to grade or lesson plans to create.

For this reason, the Instructional Coaching position often comes across as being easy and because of that the easiness creates a brand that the coach might never be where the teacher needs them to be because teacher isn't aware of all that a coach actually is charged with doing in a day.

Because of this, a coach must build their brand based on feedback they receive throughout the week and during the course of a year. They must always be asking qualifying questions to both certified staff office staff, and their administrators to make sure that the needs of everyone is being met and that there are supportive of new curricular demands and new technologies that might enter the classroom.

Asking for feedback could mean asking a staff member a simple question about what they find difficult in their classroom, or it could also be a more formal feedback process where a staff member is given an online survey after a PD session. No matter what type of medium is used to gather feedback, it is crucial that an instructional coach be making decisions about coaching topics based on any type of feedback available.

What should a Coach do with Feedback?

Once a coach has gathered feedback from a professional development session, or through conversation, it is important to organize the feedback to create a data trail and formulate a roadmap that addresses both large group, small group, and individual staff member needs. Once the staff sees that you are helping them meet their needs and become successful in their classrooms, the Instructional Coaches brand will grow for them due to positive teacher-to-teacher interactions about your work.

Final Thoughts on Instructional Coaching Brands

In this chapter, we learned several ways that an Instructional Coach can grow and maintain their Coaching Brand. A brand is not simply something that a coach can wear on their clothing. A brand or reputation could start with a simple conversation, the sending of a newsletter, an email with a link back to a support page on a coach's website or even the knowledge and assurance to staff that there is a process happening and a method to professional development.

For many coaches, they see professional development sessions, the website, and the newsletter as a way to show off how much they know about being a great coach. The reality is that this couldn't be farther from the way to be successful in the classroom. To successfully build a coaching brand, the coach must first begin with a listening tour to learn what is on the mind of both administrators and staff members and then, in collaboration with administration, create a professional learning system that meets, hits, and exceeds the expectations of staff members on both sides of the innovation curve. By doing so, an Instructional Coach will create long lasting professional relationships, earn the trust of teachers, and ultimately, create experiences that lead to a rise in student achievement.

Chapter 12

Coaching the People ... Not the Technology

(Doing the Job)

"Don't let the world define you. In the world of acting, and I think in any profession, really, people are really eager to put you in a box and categorize you as one particular thing."
Jonathan Groff

When I first took on the role of a Coach in a 5-building, K12 Regional School District, to be fair, I really didn't know what I was doing … at first. I was given the titles of Tech Coach and Coordinator of Instructional Technology. I spent my first year on the job meeting teachers and administrators. I did the traditional listening tour to ask questions about the school building and district to get an idea of what type of role I should be playing. Even looking back more than a decade later, I think I had a fairly good first year.

However, there was one thing that kept coming up in conversations both with teachers and administrators that I was never able to shake. One topic that no matter how I tried to approach it with staff members, always seemed to get in my way.

It wasn't my actions. It wasn't the work that I was doing. And even though I stumbled at times in my first year, it wasn't even me. The one thing that stood in my way of being successful was the title. It was the way the position was defined both on paper and in front of others. The title of "tech coach" implied that I was literally coaching technology. On the other hand, when I started using Coordinator of Instructional Technology, that again brought out the wrong concept in teacher and administrator minds. How can someone be coordinating technology?

In order to create a successful coaching program that both has teeth in the classroom and in the conference room, roles have to be clearly defined, developed, and distributed. Too many times during those first few years, I entered a classroom to support teachers only for teachers to think that I was there (no matter how many conversations I had about this subject) to help fix the technology. There was no one pushing me with the staff as a leader in instruction and pedagogy. It was truly an uphill battle.

Has this situation ever happened to you or one of your coaches?

To prevent these situations from happening, I decided in my second year and beyond that I needed to rebrand. I stopped referring to myself as a Tech Coach at the time and started using a newer term, Instructional Coach. Just this subtle name change gave others the opportunity to see me as someone who was here to support instruction rather than technology and it had a major impact in the work that I was originally struggling to accomplish with teachers and administrators.

Coaching is a People Business ... NOT a Technology Business

No matter what title you put on your email signature, whether it is the one given to you by your job description, or something that you make up yourself to look good in front of others, the fact remains that the world of Instructional Coaching is, in reality, a people position. The job starts by building relationships, and it ends with building relationships. It's just that simple.

I say it is simple because if you walk into a classroom and start a conversation with a human being about themselves, their families, and what they did over the weekend you will have a far greater chance of supporting them than if you walk into a classroom and ask them if they need any help building their next set of lesson plans. Coaching is a people business. Successful coaches are the ones who can interact for hours with their colleagues without ever having to ask a question about pedagogy.

Supporting Your People When Your People Cannot Support Themselves

In my first year as an Instructional Coach, in my very first month, I was asked by an elementary building principal to join them for a staff meeting in September and do a small demo so that I could introduce myself to the staff. This was my first time working with a full building staff, and I was extremely excited about it. I planned a 30-minute session where I would have the teachers sit in grade level groups and interact with each other. I placed a few tubs of modeling clay on their tables before they walked in and as an ice breaker, I invited them to work together to build something fun while we waited to get started.

I started the session by introducing myself and sharing some personal things about the triplets so I could get them a bit more comfortable with me. I then shared that they would be working as a group to create a stop motion animation project using Google Slides. For the next ten minutes they worked collaboratively with each other to create a series of slides that showed how the modeling clay could be manipulated.

One component of this was a request for them to use the Google Slides app on their phones so that they could take photos directly into Google Slides. I made this request because I knew the building would soon be getting iPads and I was trying to prepare them for how they could use the devices with their students.

The session went well, and it seemed everyone was having an enjoyable time. When the session was over, we did a small show-and-tell session where I displayed their slide decks on the projector screen, and we ended the session on a high note.

A few days later, I walked into a teacher's room and tried to make friends by asking random questions. The teacher gave me the professional cold shoulder and I said my goodbyes and walked away after a few minutes.

A few days after that encounter, I went back to visit the teacher to try to make friends a second time. I was able to get a few more feet into the teacher's classroom and that is when the conversation happened. I had a feeling that something was wrong while we were talking so turned the subject from being personal to a bit more professional. I asked the teacher what she thought about the staff session. It was then when the teacher unloaded on me about her feelings for me and my session.

"How dare you." she said. "How dare you ask me to take out my phone and use it in front of everyone." It turned out that the teacher took quite an offense to me asking her to use her personal device during the session. I apologized and did my best to turn her frown upside down and after a few minutes we parted ways.

This did not stop me, however, from coming back and giving the coach/teacher relationship another try. Over many weeks, we started having a few nice conversations. I learned about her family and eventually was invited into the back of her classroom to support her with a science lesson. After weeks of stopping into her classroom to talk about anything ... *anything* other than technology and pedagogy, I finally decided to ask one question that had to do with something computer related. I asked her if she had any questions about an upcoming lesson and that's when she finally allowed me to enter her circle of trust.

Somewhere in the middle of that wonderful conversation, she sat down and told me that she was embarrassed. She said that she comes to school every day nervous that her students would eventually figure out that she didn't know anything about Google or how to use educational technology in her lessons. Then she paused and said to me that she felt helpless because she didn't know how to create a doc and share it with her students.

Rewind several months to our first staff meeting and it turns out that she wasn't mad at me, she was feeling embarrassed because she didn't want her peers to know that she couldn't do the technology driven lessons that she was being asked by her principal to do. She was embarrassed because my role as a technology coach was being promoted as an authority figure in the building (behind my back) and she thought of me as a threat to her teaching career which was soon ending.

It took me several months and dozens of conversations to get her to open up and become vulnerable with me. Once she did this, we were able to find a starting point together. I spent the next three years working with this teacher weekly both in the classroom and in 1:1 meetings to help her and her students. It was an amazing journey. It took a ton of courage for her to admit to me that she wasn't able to do what she was being asked to do. But, once we started building a professional relationship, everything moved in a wonderful direction and her students benefited greatly from it.

It's all about the people. It is never about the technology.

Coaching is a Vision Process ... *Their* Vision, Not Yours

A coach walks into a classroom and says, "Here is how I would like to see you teach your students."

A coach walks into a classroom and asks, "What are you struggling with each day, how can I help?"

When collaborating with adult learners, coaching has to be about *their* vision and *their* need to find support for their daily pain points. It's true that a coach always needs to be supporting the districts overall vision for what classroom instruction should look like, but on the day-to-day levels, it has to be completely about the teacher and how you can support their needs. Coaching is a process that starts first with examining whatever environment that a teacher is in and learning how you can support them in their visions and goals for their classrooms. Only then can you begin to make suggestions based on preplanned programs and suggested outcomes that will help the teacher and ultimately their students.

Supporting Your Teachers Vision even when they can't See their Vision for Themselves

I remember an encounter with a teacher a few years ago. I approached the teacher by setting up a meeting to discuss an idea that I thought they would be excited to participate in. I started the idea by pitching the concept and laying out the entire plan. With each new concept and idea that was introduced, I noticed that the teacher recoiling about adding anything new into their worlds and they had serious concerns about the amount of time it would take to collaborate on this project.

Sensing that this would be a short conversation, I paused and took a step back. I asked the teacher what their biggest pain points were for the program and what the group's goals were. I learned that the teacher had a goal to increase membership in her writing program by 10% the following year. It was then that I decided to pivot from sharing what my goals were for her group to sharing how this new concept would help her grow her program because it would allow students to become more interested in her club. Once I shifted the conversation from my vision to the teachers' vision, I was able to move the conversation forward and ultimately the next year, her club grew by 15% due to increased promotion for the groups work in the community.

Coaching is a Game of Time Management ... So, Manage it Well

For years I was a K12 teacher. Every day my life revolved around getting to school at a certain time and waiting for the homeroom bell to go off so I could stand in the hallway to greet my students. After a set number of minutes, the bell would ring, and the next teaching period would start.

Rinse and Repeat

Day after Day … after Day

Then suddenly, all of this went away. I was an Instructional Coach, and I oversaw my own schedule. Some days would require me to be sitting in my office and other days would require me to drive to multiple schools. Every day was an adventure but at the same time, every day was an exercise in time management.

Supporting Your Teachers by Supporting Your Calendars

Time management is a skill that needs to be learned and mastered by every Instructional Coach. Because the position is susceptible for others to ask, "what is it that you actually do?" A Coach needs to make sure they are finding the proper balance of office work and classroom activities built into their day. For many coaches this isn't a problem. They naturally gravitate to the classroom, make themselves at home and interact seamlessly with both teachers and students. For other coaches, (me for example) the thought of entering a classroom unannounced and interacting with a teacher is somewhat terrifying.

I have found that the best way to become experts in time management is to become experts in your calendar. When you are a teacher, your schedule is managed for you. When you are in an open calendar position such as an Instructional Coach often is, you need to produce a way for others to fill up your calendar. For this reason, many coaches set up booking calendars.

Coaching is about Transforming Teachers "Why Is" into "Why Not"

I once heard an instructional leader during a conference presentation say the phrase "attitude is contagious." This took me by surprise. What does this mean? How can this be applied?

- Supporting the Culture Shift of Digital Learning
- Helping students create Authentic Learning Experiences

When we consider the phrase "attitude is contagious," it becomes clear that a coach's positive mindset can significantly influence teachers' perspectives on educational technology and innovation.

Creating a Culture of "Why Not?"

One of the most powerful transformations in educational technology coaching occurs when teachers undergo a fundamental shift in their approach to innovation. Initially, many educators approach new technologies and methodologies with skepticism, often asking "Why is this necessary?" This defensive stance can create barriers to growth and learning.

However, through careful coaching and relationship building, teachers can develop a more open mindset. When they begin asking "Why not try something new?" instead, it signals a crucial turning point in their professional development. This shift indicates they've moved from a place of resistance to one of curiosity and possibility.

This transformation doesn't happen overnight - it's the result of building trust, demonstrating value, and creating safe spaces for experimentation. When teachers feel supported and empowered, they're more likely to embrace new possibilities and take calculated risks in their teaching practice. This mindset shift opens doors to innovation, creative problem-solving, and growth opportunities that benefit both educators and their students.

Building Confidence Through Small Wins

The journey from resistance to enthusiasm in educational technology begins with carefully planned, manageable successes. When teachers first encounter new tools or methods, the key is to start with simple, low-stakes activities that align with their existing teaching style. These initial experiences create a foundation of confidence upon which more complex innovations can be built.

Think of it like learning to ride a bicycle - you start with training wheels before attempting more challenging maneuvers. In the same way, teachers who successfully implement basic technology tools in their classroom are more likely to explore advanced applications on their own initiative. Each positive experience reinforces their belief in their ability to adapt and grow.

The confidence gained through these early victories often leads to a snowball effect. Teachers who master one new tool or technique naturally become curious about other possibilities. They begin to see technology not as an obstacle to overcome, but as a valuable resource that can enhance their teaching practice.

Strategies for Transforming Mindsets

The transformation from tech-hesitant to tech-enthusiast requires a thoughtful, systematic approach. Here are several key strategies that have proven effective:

- Start with teachers' comfort zones and gradually expand
    - Begin with familiar tools or methods they already use

    - Introduce new elements that naturally extend their current practice
- Celebrate small victories and progress
    - Acknowledge even minor technological achievements
    - Document growth through portfolios or reflection journals
- Share success stories from peer educators
    - Create opportunities for teacher-to-teacher mentoring
    - Facilitate professional learning communities focused on tech integration
- Provide ongoing support and encouragement
    - Offer just-in-time assistance when needed
    - Maintain regular check-ins to address concerns and celebrate progress

The Ripple Effect of Coaching Success

When one teacher undergoes a transformative shift in their mindset and begins to enthusiastically embrace new possibilities in their classroom, it creates a powerful ripple effect that reverberates throughout the entire school community, touching every aspect of the educational environment. As this educator implements innovative approaches and experiences success in their teaching practice, their enthusiasm becomes remarkably contagious, spreading from classroom to classroom like a positive wave of change. Other educators, witnessing these positive changes in their colleague's classroom environment, teaching methods, and most importantly, student engagement levels, naturally become more curious and receptive to exploring innovative approaches themselves. They begin to see firsthand how embracing new teaching methodologies can revolutionize their own practice. This organic spread of openness to new ideas often leads to spontaneous collaborations and peer-to-peer learning opportunities, with teachers actively seeking out chances to observe and learn from one another. These interactions create a self-sustaining cycle of growth and innovation within the school, where each successful implementation builds upon previous achievements and inspires further experimentation and development. The resulting collaborative atmosphere transforms the school into a vibrant learning community where both teachers and students thrive on the energy of continuous improvement and shared discovery.

Measuring Transformation Success

Success in coaching isn't just about implementing new technologies - it's about creating sustainable change in teaching practices and mindsets. This can be observed through:

- Increased teacher-initiated requests for support
- More collaborative projects between teachers
- Greater willingness to experiment with new teaching methods
- Improved student engagement and outcomes

Conclusion: The Heart of Coaching

At its core, instructional coaching is about empowering teachers to discover and unlock their full potential, helping them see beyond perceived limitations and embrace the endless possibilities that lie ahead in their educational journey. Through a carefully crafted approach that puts people at the center of every interaction, actively supports their unique vision for their classroom, implements effective time management strategies, and deliberately cultivates positive mindsets, coaches can create meaningful and lasting transformations within their educational communities. This human-centered approach ensures that technological integration becomes a natural extension of teaching rather than an imposed requirement.

The pivotal transformation from asking "Why is this necessary?" to wondering "Why not try something new?" represents far more than a simple shift in terminology or attitude - it embodies a fundamental evolution in how educators perceive their role, approach their practice, and envision their potential for professional growth and development. When this profound transformation takes root in a school community, it catalyzes a chain reaction of positive changes that ripple through every aspect of the educational environment. The resulting impact on student engagement, learning outcomes, and overall school culture proves not only profound and far-reaching but also creates a sustainable foundation for continued growth and innovation that can benefit generations of students and educators to come.

As we conclude our exploration of coaching people rather than technology, it's important to recognize that the impact of effective coaching often grows beyond what one person can handle. When coaching programs demonstrate success, districts often look to scale up their initiatives to reach more teachers and students effectively. This natural progression leads us to consider how to build and manage larger coaching teams while maintaining the human-centered approach we've discussed.

The challenges of coaching at scale are unique and require careful consideration of team dynamics, organizational structure, and leadership roles. As we move into the next chapter, we'll explore how to transition from individual coaching to building and managing an effective Digital Learning team that can support an entire district while maintaining the personal touch that makes coaching truly transformative.

The principles we've covered - focusing on people, managing time effectively, and transforming mindsets - become even more critical when working with a team of coaches. These fundamentals serve as the foundation for creating a cohesive coaching department that can effect change across multiple buildings and thousands of students.

Chapter 13

Building a Digital Learning Team (Scaling up the Job)

It was the summer of 2020. The pandemic had just started, and I was asked to leave the confines of my classroom and become the first (and only) Instructional Coach for Digital Learning in a school district that supported 20+ buildings, 11,000+ students and almost 2,000 employees. This was an amazing opportunity and one that I spent the summer preparing for. I had only been in the district for a year prior, but because it was the year when the world shut down, I hadn't met anyone outside of my immediate teaching hallway, let alone made meaningful contacts with others across the district. Nevertheless, I started to create a plan that could allow me to be in multiple places at the same time and could allow the district quick and easy access to the resources I was creating at any point in the day.

Then the phone call came in. It was the call from my supervisor in central office that shared the big news that we were going to be able to expand the Digital Learning coaching program into a full department. I remember this conversation happened in the middle of October after I had already begun working my way across the district and had made great connections with both building and district leadership to essentially build a brand for myself in the eyes of the school district and community. The time had come to now think beyond one person and build a team that would be able to cover all buildings, all the time, and support all students, teachers, building leaders and the community.

The only question that remained was … where do you start?

It turns out, you start by creating a mission and vision statement.

What is an Instructional Coaching Department Mission and Vision Statement?

A Mission Statement is not simply something that gets drafted and approved, they are vital documents that should be created with the help and (more importantly) the involvement of all stakeholders in the district so that, when sent into the school building and classroom, there is no doubt what the role, purpose, and function of the Instructional Coach is and what they should be doing. To do this, we must first ask the question … "What is a Mission Statement?"

What is a Mission Statement?

According to the Dictionary, a Mission Statement is:

- An official document that sets out the goals, purpose, and work of an organization.
- A written statement that sets out personal goals for the future.

Your Instructional Coaching Department Mission Statement, reflecting this definition, must be crafted as an official document and widely recognized in the school district by all members.

Do you find that your administrator treats you differently than how another administrator treats their coaches? This is the consequence of not having an agreed upon mission statement.

One defining feature of a Mission Statement is that it is a declaration of both the "what," "how," and "why" of a department. The Mission Statement should not be confused with a Vision Statement.

What is a Vision Statement?

If a Mission Statement sets the role and responsibility for the department, what does a Vision Statement Do?

A Vision Statement is a separate document that describes the long-term goals for a company. Vision Statements are usually created after the Mission Statement has been completed and agreed upon so that the group has benchmarks and a very loose roadmap to follow.

Note that a Vision Statement is to be created using broad terms.

Example Short Term Goals

- To establish an understanding of educational technology standards and ISTE standards to set benchmarks and personal goals for buildings, staff, and students.
- To establish Microsoft Teams as a Digital and Professional Learning platform
- Establish school and district Professional Learning Communities focused on measuring and improving instructional practice using digital resources.
- To create a pathway of learning for staff members to become members of globally recognized professional learning communities.
- To curate and deploy digital learning resources and instructional tools to meet the needs of PreK12 staff members and curricular standards.
- To create and deploy a model for professional coaching and collaboration.

Example Long Term Goals

- To create an Instructional Technology Integration Plan based on District Strategic Plan to serve as a Professional Development roadmap and guide for digital learning in our school district.
- To develop and deploy a K-8 Digital Citizenship curriculum that is based on Common Sense Education guidelines and ISTE Standards for Students and Teachers
- Develop a pathway for being recognized as a:
- Common Sense Media School District
- Microsoft Showcase School District
- Future Ready School District

What is the difference between a Mission Statement and a Vision Statement?

One of biggest differences between a Mission and a Vision statement is that one could be thought of as a public declaration, while the other one can be left private between the members of the group or organization. For example:

Mission Statement

- A public document agreed upon by the district.
- Shared with the School District (website).
- States the purpose of the department.

Vision Statement

- A series of benchmarks agreed upon by the department.
- Shared with only the department for internal motivations.
- States where the department wishes to be in the future.
- Includes long-term and short-term goals.

How To Create a Mission Statement?

When composing your Instructional Coaching Department's Mission Statement, the goal should not only be to plant your flag in your digital soil but also incorporate your overall goals and with the inclusion of a concise description of what an Instructional Coach looks like.

Where there traditionally is no true definable template for what a Mission Statement looks like, below is an example of what a Mission Statement should look like.

The mission statement is composed of the following segments:

- A clearly definable snapshot of your school district.
- A statement of what your role is in the structure of the district.
- A brief description of the qualifications of an Instructional Coach.
- A statement of what the role of the Instructional Coach will be in the classroom environment.

When planning your mission statement, it is important to have clear discussions with your stake holders, but also with your greater administration team to determine what the function of the Instructional Coaching department be both in the eyes of teachers, building administrators, and central office.

Example Mission Statement

"My School District" is comprised of "X" students and "X" staff members serving more than "X" families across "X" educational campuses. The mission of the Digital Learning department is to serve as an equitable conduit for both Curricular and Educational Technology standards to provide a comprehensive professional learning program for teachers to succeed in the classroom and for students to become college and career ready.

Digital Learning Coaches are first exemplary educators who, in addition to being experts in their subject areas and fields of study, are recognized for their achievement in the educational technology community. The role of the Digital Learning Coach in Norwalk Public Schools is to work in collaboration with peers and building administrators to inspire excellence in the classroom by providing staff members with opportunities for collaboration, reflection, and growth.

Why This Mission Statement?

When creating your Instructional Coaching Mission Statement, it is important to be both concise and direct. Here is a breakdown of why and how the above Mission Statement was created:

A clearly definable snapshot of your school district.

"My School District" is comprised of "X" students and "X" staff members serving more than "X" families across "X" educational campuses.

When crafting a Mission Statement, it's important to first build the box from which your world will live in. With this sentence, your mission is defined by the scope of the project. Your department, your mission, and your ultimate vision for success is going to support a school district of "X" size and "X" shape across "X" number of buildings.

A statement of what your role is in the structure of the district.

The mission of the Digital Learning department is to serve as an equitable conduit for both Curricular and Educational Technology standards to provide a comprehensive professional learning program for teachers to succeed in the classroom and for students to become college and career ready.

For many Instructional Coaches, their day is spent defending and defining their role in their school districts. By using words such as "equitable conduit" you are declaring that you are going to be looked at, thought of, and directed equally by both what happens in the technology and curricular departments. In essence, your focus in the classroom will be both on "what is" being taught in the classroom and "how" it is being taught.

The term "comprehensive professional learning program" is being used to demonstrate that the role of the coach is not to simply be around for "tech needs" and is in fact to be thought of as a 1:1 and individualized professional development partner in the classroom. This type of partnership should be happening in a variety of places and times throughout the school day and school year.

By adding "teachers to succeed in the classroom" allows the department to highlight where their strength is when supporting this partnership. Coaches are primary to be thought of as "educators that …" rather than "tech people who …" which is often another point of frustration for coaching programs.

Ultimately, this sentence leaves users with the true mission of an Instructional Coaching program which is to help students become successful both in and out of the classroom and well beyond the boundaries of their time in the school district.

A brief description of the qualifications of an Instructional Coach.

Digital Learning Coaches are first exemplary educators who, in addition to being experts in their subject areas and fields of study, are recognized for their achievement in the educational technology community.

This part of the mission statement is designed to support current coaches in the program and define what the job description is of coaches. The term "exemplary educator" is used to support the idea of teachers being seen as mentors to other teachers beyond the traditional duties of the coaching model. By using "experts in their subject areas and fields of study" it is another declaration that, although the greater knowledge of educational technology is important, teachers will not be interested in working with anyone who doesn't have at least a loose grasp of the subjects they are teaching. Coaches should be first seen as curricular partners before they are seen as "edtechnicians."

The theme of this section is not only how teachers will like, know, and trust their coaches, but also how administrators will like, know, and trust their coaches. For this reason, we add the phrase “achievement in the educational technology community.” This is designed to support those teachers in the school district who are always doing great things and whose natural next progression of their careers would be to transition from being a classroom teacher to being a building level coach.

A statement of what the role of the Instructional Coach will be in the classroom environment.

The role of the Digital Learning Coach in “X District” is to work in collaboration with peers and building administrators to inspire excellence in the classroom by providing staff members with opportunities for collaboration, reflection, and growth.

This phrase, in the middle of the mission statement, is designed to set up what the coach should be responsible for and expected to be doing every day. “Working in collaboration with peers and building administrators” is a declaration that the coach should be not seen as an equal to the teacher but as a supporting professional who has the full support of the administrator whom they are in constant contact with. By ending this statement with “opportunities for collaboration, reflection, and growth,” again reminds us that the mission is to be a constant partnership between two professionals rather than a “occasionally when a teacher needs something” type of relationship.

How to leverage your Essential Question and District Snapshot?

If we step back and look at a school district as a triangle, you end up having three key directives.

- What
- How
- Through

In creating an EdTech Integration Plan a district first creates the “what” when it approves its strategic plan. The “how” is the roadmap that will be answered at the end of the EdTech Integration Plan process. It is only after those two things are set that the “through” can be created in the mission of the Instructional Coaching program. It is the coaches that provide the “through” because they are the ones directly working in the classroom with both the teachers and the students.

When creating an Instructional Coaching program and making an investment in both personal and programs, it is important to have a clear definition of who you are, what your role is in the district, and how teachers will be supported. Is the above Instructional Coaching Mission Statement perfect? Of course not, but my hope is to provide a structure and framework for you to build and create your own instructional coaching mission statements.

Defining Your Digital Learning Brand to Your School District

- Does Your Instructional Coaching Program Have a Logo?
- If Your Instructional Coaching Program had a Logo ... *What would it look like?*

Take a moment and think of your favorite sports team. How about your favorite sports drink? Think about the last time you drove down the road. Did anything catch your eye from your favorite fast-food restaurant?

What does your favorite sports team, sports drink, and restaurant all have in common? They all have eye catching and clearly definable logos that quickly identify who they are, capture your attention, and spark your enthusiasm for their brand.

Think for a second about your own community of Instructional Coaches. Does your Instructional Coaching Department have its very own logo?

What is a Logo? What does it Represent?

A logo, to put it succinctly, is a symbol that represents an idea or a group of people. Logos can be colorful or monochromatic. What all logos have in common is that they represent something. They represent an idea that a group or entity stands for.

Think of one of the most iconic logos on the planet, the NIKE Swoosh. Anytime you see that you probably say to yourself "Just Do It."

But ...

If Logos are designed to be simple, does this mean that their meanings must also be simple?

Below, we have an image of several popular logos, many of which you are familiar with.

Each of these has a hidden meaning behind them.

On the surface these images might look simple, but when you take a second look you might just find something hidden.

- Do you see a hidden arrow inside of the FEDEX logo?
- Do you see a bicycle rider in the Tour de France logo?
- Did you notice that the number 31 is hidden inside the Baskin-Robbins logo?

So, what does this have to do with your Instructional Coaching Department?

How to Create a Logo for Instructional Coaching

When discussing the creation of your Instructional Coaching Department Mission Statement, we learned that the position of the Instructional Coach should be a hybrid of what is happening both the Technology AND Curriculum departments. We also learned that professional learning when it is supported by curricular activities (rather than applications) can be the catalyst for raising student achievement. Because of this, it is important to create a logo that represents all these components of your school district plan.

For these reasons, when the planning and creation of your Instructional Coaching Department logo should include all these concepts when creating your department image.

Let's look at one example.

What Does an Instructional Coaching Department Logo Look Like?

Here is an example of an example logo designed to not only support but provide meaning to their Instructional Coaching Department.

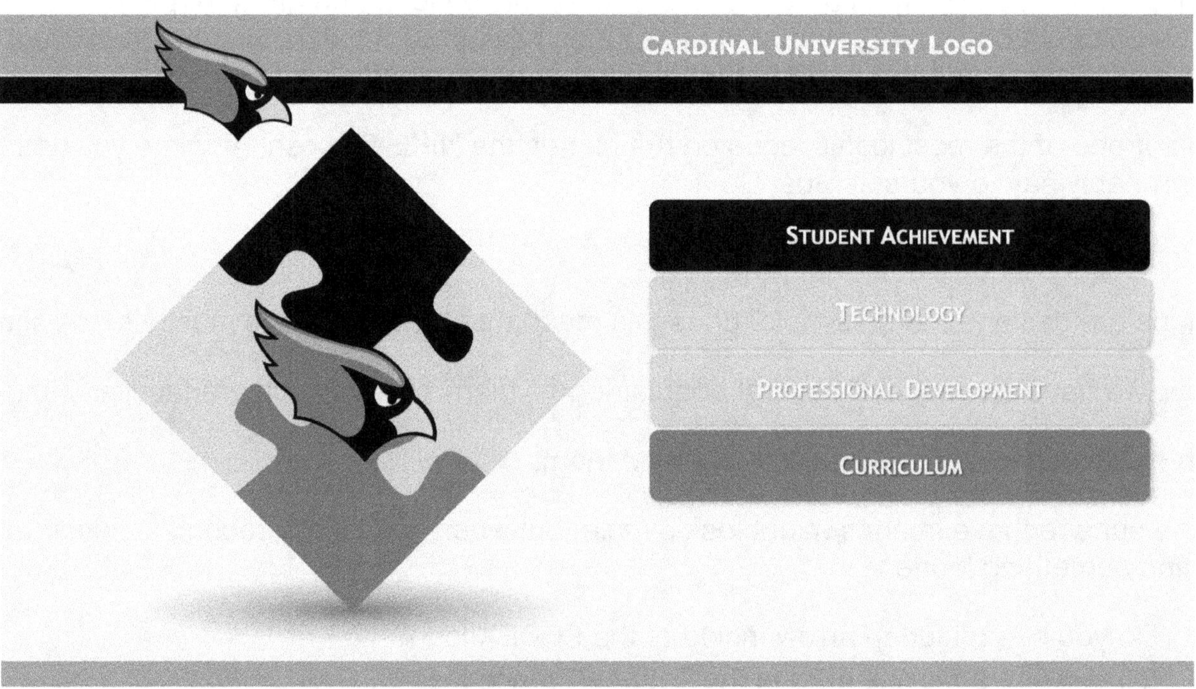

Let's break down the example above. Here we see a simple logo of a Cardinal logo overlapping a puzzle composed of four pieces. Each piece of the puzzle is a different color. This might seem simple, but there was a great deal of work that went into creating it and crafting the meaning behind each of these unique sections.

The Cardinal

At the center of this logo is the school's mascot, the Cardinal. In this school district, every school has the same Cardinal mascot as its building emblem and because of this the Instructional Coaching logo was designed to represent the entire school district both in graphic representation and in its color scheme.

The Four Puzzle Pieces

Each of the four pieces of this puzzle are designed to represent different aspects of the school district's instructional plan and are placed strategically on the logo to represent what their function is in the school district.

The Curriculum

The Curriculum Department is located on the bottom of the logo to represent strength and to signify that it is the Curriculum that grounds the entire school district. Everything that a student learns and that a teacher instructs is designed by an agreed upon curriculum. It is the Curriculum which both holds up a school district and supports the most fragile component of this logo.

Student Achievement

At the very top of the logo is Student Achievement. The goal for everyone and every program in the school should be to raise student achievement. For this reason, the logo has been designed to show that the Curriculum is the main aspect of the school district that supports Students and Student Achievement.

Technology

Placed on the left side of the logo is Technology. It is the Technology Department and the devices in the hands of both teachers and students that connect the students to the Curriculum. This part of the logo is also designed to show that it is the Technology Department that propels both the Curriculum and Student Achievement forward throughout the year.

Professional Learning / Instructional Coaching

Placed on the right side of the logo and serving as the glue between Curriculum and Student Achievement is the Professional Learning Department, otherwise known as your Instructional Coaches. If the Technology Department is what is propelling the district forward, it is the Instructional Coaches that are providing guidance and direction in a process that is grounded by Curriculum.

The Importance of District Buy-in on Instructional Coaching Logos

The creation of an Instructional Coaching Logo is something that should be on the list of every department, but as we can see in the example above, should not be created in a silo. Just as we discussed in our post about an Instructional Coaching Mission & Vision Statement, the Instructional Coaching Department is the glue that propels a district forward by supporting the goals of all educational departments.

On the surface, an Instructional Coaching Department mission, vision, and logo are great however if a team is ever going to form an identify in the eyes of building, district, and community leaders, there needs to be a central point person to not only represent the department in administrative level meetings, but also become the departments biggest advocate.

The Coach Champion

I first came across the term "Coach Champion" while reading the book "Coaching Matters" written by Joellen Killion, Chris Bryan, and Heather Clifton and available from Learning Forward. Essentially, the Coach Champion is someone inside the district who is the primary advocate for Instructional Coaches. They ensure that the coaching program is successfully implemented and that there are building, or district wide conditions put in place to make sure that Instructional Coaches have the best opportunity to be successful in the classroom while working with teachers and students. They serve the coaching department both as mentors, supervisors (often), and points of contact between central office and the department.

What are the Responsibilities of a Coach Champion?

Depending on how a school district sets up an Instructional Coaching department the Coach Champion can take on several roles and responsibilities including but not limited to:

- Making sure that the department is designed and set up for success.
    - Creating department Goals
    - Developing an infrastructure of roles and responsibilities within the coaching department
    - Setting expectations both long term and short term
- Establishing Relationships both within the department and with other school groups.
    - Setting up short- and long-term schedules for individual coaches.
    - Providing support with coaches need assistance in the school building.
    - Sharing coaching celebrations and positive experiences with both building and district leadership.
- Creating and Setting up Department Meetings

- Creating action steps that focus on how coaches can meet building and district level goals.
    - Organizing department media and digital assets for cross referencing and future planning.
    - Allowing the department the opportunity to work as a team rather than a group of individuals.
- Serves as a mentor to Instructional Coaches
    - Takes on the responsibility of being a second set of eyes when coaches need support.
    - Helping coaches set up programs in their own buildings.
    - Being an objective voice during difficult conversations across a variety of district levels.

The Importance of having a Coach Champion

As mentioned in the book Coaching Matters, the main reason for someone in the Coach Champion role is to ensure that at least one person in the district is ultimately responsible for the program's success. The Coach Champion does not need to be a coach's direct supervisor; however, it is often most useful if this is the case. When setting up your primary Coach Champion as a district level employee with supervisor ability, a coaching department has the opportunity to not only feel like they are part of the conversation, but that there is someone at the central office level that has their back and is fighting for and supporting them at the big table.

Building the Right Team for Your District

Choosing the right candidates to interview and develop an Instructional Coaching Department around is an amazing experience. There are several things that need to be taken into consideration when doing so ranging from coaching experience, teaching experience, leadership experience, and from what subjects the coaches background comes from. Where you may be focused on building a team of Instructional Coaches, you are, in reality, doing so much more.

If you ever have the chance to design and develop your own Instructional Coaching Department, you can shape not just a team of digital learning leaders but the way every classroom in your school district operates. Because these are the people that will ultimately enter each classroom in each building and sit in leadership meetings as an advocate for your Educational Technology Strategic Plan and Digital Learning Curriculum, it is imperative that the right group of individuals be selected to not only compliment the system you have chosen to put together but ultimately complement each other.

When searching for instructional coaching candidates, I liken the experience to building a sports team. You need both a strong pitcher and catcher to control the game, but you also need solid position players that can communicate with each other and support each other even when the ball isn't being hit in their direction. You also need to think about who will play the team captain's role and how that member will interact with the team as a group leader and with administration as a team representative. If team building were a sport, I would liken it to baseball much more than any other sport. The team that has the ball is on defense. It is the only sport where the defensive team controls the ball and the game's flow. When playing defense, they must work together and complement each other. However, on offense (or, when they are working with teachers in the classroom) they are often alone with the single goal of moving into the position to eventually score a run.

Making Personality Recommendations

There are a few ways to think about building an effective instructional coaching team. The first way is based on individual personality and character traits of the individual. When doing so, you might build a team with these types of traits.

- **The Lieutenant** – The Lieutenant is someone whom the Coach Champion can always count on. They possess years of experience doing the job and are now ready to step up into a leadership position. They can serve as team captains when the Coach Champion is away but also as a mentor to other coaches when opportunities call for team meetings.

- **The Chameleon** – A Chameleon is a team member who isn't afraid to think about the big picture and be willing to adjust their plans at a moment's notice. When other coaches are focused on one single task, the Chameleon is constantly thinking about Plan B, C, and D just in case it is ever needed.

- **The Charmer** – The Charmer is the one person on the team who excels at moving the communications needle to be pointed in and focused on a new direction. They are listeners first and supporters second. They understand the vision of the department and have a good grasp of what other plans the Chameleon might be planning as they enter strategic meetings. Because they can quickly build a rapport with others, they are often listened to and often followed.

- **The Go-Getter** – The Go-Getter is an individual that is always seeking new challenges and adventures both for themselves and the group. They will enter classrooms trying to strategize not only how they can help the teacher, but how they can help the group formulate a plan to support other teachers across the district, like this one. They have both the micro and macro in mind at all times.

Making Skill Based Recommendations

In looking over and analyzing this list above, it is easy to dream up your ideal team and create a series of interview questions to help you create a successful and complete department. But what happens if you don't have the opportunity to build a team based on individual personality traits?

There is another way to build your Instructional Coaches team based on their individual skillset. Using this guide, you can also create a well-rounded team but base your hiring decisions around the focus of your Digital Learning Plan and Strategic Plan's goals so ensure that you are bringing on the right members to support your ideal classroom learning environment.

- **The Creator** – Someone who excels at Audio and Video and can be the point person for teaching media skills to both coaches and teachers.
- **The Designer** – Someone who can look at a project and quickly break it down into its various components to build a professional development and coaching game plan.
- **The Technician** – Someone who has a knowledge of hardware and can be the one to speak directly to the IT staff and support the training of the coaches on quick and easy device issues.
- The Jack of all Trades – Someone who knows a lot about many things.

Now that you have your team in place it is time to align both your Digital Learning Departments and your Informational Technology Departments so that each of them has their own function, purpose, and role within the school district.

Supporting Your Defense with a Great Offense

Let's take a moment and switch sports from Baseball to Football. Football is a sport that is played on a "gridiron" and is designed in a way where the offense has a finite series of downs to move the ball forward, hopefully into scoring position before the opposing defense either forces the offensive team to punt or in a worse case takes the ball out of the offenses position to begin moving the ball in the opposite direction.

If this is confusing, let me pose a question to you and every other Instructional Coach that has ever entered a school building.

Have you ever been introduced as "the tech guy" or "the IT guy?" Let's be honest, we all have. One of the hardest things that an Instructional Coach must face is the perception that someone has of you when they don't truly understand what your position, title, or role is in the district and why you are standing in front of them having that very conversation.

In order to support this mindset transformation in my teaching staff, I started explaining what I do in terms of Offense and Defense.

Helping Staff Members Understand Which Side of the Ball You Play On

Every time I get referred to as "The IT Guy" I simply say "no, I'm offense… I am here to help you. The other guy is defense. His job is to stop terrible things from happening. There are of course other ways to describe the difference between the two departments, but this often does the trick and allows me to move forward.

It is from this philosophy where I first started introducing myself in a lead coaching position as the district Offensive Coordinator. It was my job to support the forward movement of our Digital Learning Curriculum to help teachers meet the needs of their students by supporting standards-based instructional strategies. (It's a long way of saying "I'm here to help you get better at what you do.")

Using this as an example, the Defensive Coordinator role goes to whoever is the IT Director of Director of Technology. Their job is to make sure that the district has all of the filters, SPAM blockers, and virus catchers in place to not allow anyone wishing to cause harm to the district to score on the offense.

Creating a Unified Game Plan ... Together

Bottom line … in order to be successful, both the Offense and the Defense need to be on the same page working together so that they can support each other both in the classrooms and in the application dashboards. If a coach knows and understands why the IT department has made certain decisions about blocking websites, or allowing certain features to be used, they can then formulate how they can ultimately coach their teachers.

Have you as a coach ever suggested an application and had a teacher get excited about it only to then be told by IT that it wasn't available to use? When your Coaching Department and your IT department are kicking on all cylinders, this never happens.

The Art of Defining Your Team to Your School District

Just as it is difficult to define your role as an Instructional Coach to your building as we discussed in a previous chapter, it is also difficult to define your role as an Instructional Coaching Department to your entire school district. There needs to come a time at the beginning of each school year, usually in the summer, where your Coach Champion should clearly outline the department to the entire administration team and together create a list of annual goals for the department. These goals should revolve not just around ways to support teachers in the classroom, but also include ways for the department to be a part of building level School Improvement Plans (SIP's) and the District Improvement Plan (DIP). It is through these meetings where your Coach Champion can truly shine as the department advocate.

If this is done correctly, by the time that the coach returns from summer break, their building administrators are all set with a clear idea of how to use them and they are ready to sit down as discussed in our previous chapters to plan out a successful year with their Instructional Coaching team.

Having explored how to build an effective coaching team that positively impacts schools and shapes district culture, let's examine how the Coaching Department can serve as community members and district ambassadors beyond school walls.

As we transition into the next chapter, we'll explore how your coaching team can extend their impact beyond the classroom walls and into the broader community. Building on the foundation of a well-structured coaching department, we'll examine specific strategies and programs that allow coaches to serve as ambassadors for digital learning while promoting the vital role they play in educational transformation.

The following chapter will demonstrate how coaching teams can create lasting connections with parents, community members, and stakeholders through innovative programs like Parent University, professional development initiatives, and student leadership opportunities. These outreach efforts not only enhance the visibility of your coaching program but also create a robust support network that strengthens the entire educational ecosystem.

Chapter 14

Using Your Coaching Team to Support Your Community (Promoting the Job)

It was the summer of 2020, and I was in the planning stages of becoming my district's first (and only) Instructional Coach for Digital Learning. The Pandemic had just hit and was only a few months old when I received a call from one of our district administrators asking me to meet about a new project that was starting to be formulated in one of the elementary buildings.

The concept that we discussed with the creation of a series of after school online community sessions to help parents learn how hybrid instruction would be happening in the district. I thought this was a great idea and immediately started to work on a plan to make this program come to life. A few days later, that same administrator called me back and told me that they liked my proposal, but the scope of the project had changed a bit. Instead of designing this program for only one school, it was now going to be a district wide event. This was the start of our Parent University Program.

Over the next 10 months of the school year, our district created a program that taught parents not only how to support their hybrid learning student, but also helped them learn many other topics ranging from "how-to Google" topics to "how to support young readers at home." This program was supported in the district by administrators, core-curricular Instructional Coaches, Library Media Specialists, and general subject teachers. It was a fantastic way for our school district to connect with the community and a wonderful way for me as a new district level coach to grow roots in the school district, which would only prove to be useful in the years that followed.

In this chapter, we will explore how to leverage your Instructional Coaching Department to support your community, as well as examine various ways your coaches can contribute to the broader district-wide educational program.

Parent University

A Parent University is an opportunity for a community to come together and provide a service to itself. Parent Universities come in a variety of shapes and sizes depending on the needs of the community, but the basic idea is for the school district to be a conduit for community learning. When it comes to adult learning, and creating programs to support adult learners, it is a logical choice to turn to your Instructional Coaching Department. Not only can your Instructional Coaches design and develop a multitude of online courses for community members but they also have the flexibility in their schedules to meet with others in the district who might also be able to support the program and become either instructors or promoters in the community.

The mission of the Parent University that we built was to provide caregivers with experiences to create a lasting learning partnership with our district that will transfer to positive outcomes for our students.

Parent University Goals

Traditionally, the goal of a Parent University is to create a community driven, interactive learning experience for caregivers. Here are the three goals that we decided would guide our program.

- Goal One: Provide opportunities for parents and the community to engage in the learning process and be active participants in the education of our students.
- Goal Two: Create an environment for parents and community that provides access to needed services and resources.
- Goal Three: To provide the community with an opportunity to support each other through interactive workshops.

Types of Instruction

In order to facilitate a program that met the needs of all parents we developed a structure to support both synchronous and asynchronous learning opportunities.

Our Parent University included:

- Live Instructional sessions
- Online courses that were scheduled live and streamed on district YouTube channel.
- Live chats that supported community involvement and engagement.
- Pre-Recorded Instructional videos that were translated into multiple languages.
- Presentation slide decks and infographics that were designed to drip to the community each week as and supported by district newsletter and the district YouTube channel.

How To Choose Your Parent University Session Topics

Many school districts set up a Parent University to teach Tech Topics. For us, it started out that way too. We ran classes on how to support students using Google Classroom, Microsoft Teams, Google Meet, and other popular classroom applications. Sessions were broken down so that one topic would have two sessions each supporting older and younger student populations.

But this is not the only value that a Parent University has. When created properly, a Parent University can be set up to include sessions where community members teach other community members.

Let's say that you have an active parent who is very knowledgeable about taxes or legal matters. A great idea would be to invite that parent to give a session on tax prep or college financing options.

Parent University does not just have to be about parents teaching parents. It is also a fantastic way for parents to tutor students as well. For example, if you have someone in the community who is great with audio and video, perhaps they can run a "how to make a podcast" session for students.

How can Instructional Coaches Support Parent University?

When we first created our Parent University our instructors were our Instructional Coaches and our Library Media Specialists. This was a wonderful way to get the program started and gave our team an opportunity to work together outside of their normal teaching positions.

One advantage of inviting your coaches and LMS's to participate in this is that it gives them "face time" with the community. Having your Coaches and LMS's staff be the visual face of the program provides a terrific way for them to act as digital ambassadors and conduits between what is happening in the classroom and what might be possible at home. It also provides parents with a friendly face to seek help from in case something needs to be addressed with digital technologies at home while on distance learning.

Organizing and Promoting your Parent University

Website

To create something that was able to grow at scale, we created a website for our Parent University. To make things simple for us, we used Google Sites so that we could create a product that was easy for parents to navigate through and would be scalable over time. Each session had a page dedicated to it that held information about the topic, the registration link, and our session recordings for viewing in case parents were not able to watch something live.

Zoom Webinars

We also used Zoom Webinar's to host and manage our sessions. By using Zoom as our video delivery platform, we were able to have access to a scheduling system, attendance tracker, and easy to download recordings of each event. Additionally, when called for, we were also able to use Zoom's translation feature to bring in additional languages into our presentations to reach a wider audience and support our MLL community.

Promoting through CoachMoji's

To help make things fun and exciting, we used Bitmoji (or what we called CoachMoji) to provide a family friendly environment to the project and to share a bit about who our presenters are in the program.

Promoting Through Social Media

Each week, Parent University ran between 2-5 sessions in the evening. We found that the best time would be to run two sessions to support families with different schedules so that we could support our entire community. Each week, families received a calendar of upcoming Parent University sessions in the weekly district newsletter.

Should You Create a Parent University?

If you are looking to support your community, I would highly consider starting a Parent University. Much like Student Tech Teams are used to support what happens inside of the school district, a Parent University is designed to support learning outside of the school district.

By using your Instructional Coaches and Library Media Specialists, you have an amazing opportunity to create and deliver high quality sessions that are going to be used by both district families and community members that support both instructional and global topics.

If you or anyone in your district would be interested in discussing this topic further, please do not hesitate to reach out and make an appointment with me to discuss the topic. I am extremely proud of the program that was created, and I would love to help you and your district create one of your own.

New Employee Orientation

Imagine yourself as a new teacher. You go through the process of being interviewed, you receive an offer of employment and are now accepted into a new position in a brand-new school district.

It is usually at that point when a million questions start to flood your mind. Questions about your classroom, your students, and your new schedule are usually on the front of your minds, but somewhere in the back, you are also thinking about items like salary, benefits, and how to make the most out of the new relationships you will soon be forming.

This is where New Employee Orientation (NEO) comes into play.

Traditionally, NEO is a wonderful, and well-planned event that happens each summer as the new school approaches. At that time, new hires to the district gather to learn about the new district and are generally greeted with speech after speech from all the key people in the district.

Recently however, there has been a growing trend in education to support staff members entering the district throughout the course of the school year by holding NEO sessions sometimes once a month and more so once a week as turnover in school district is often on the high side.

- What should NEO look like to a staff member?
- Why is it important?
- What is the purpose of putting on a show each week to support new staff members?
- What is the role of the Instructional Coach and how can coaches be leveraged to support not only the orientation event but use it to springboard important relationships that have a lasting effect on students in the classroom?

In this section, we are going to look at how your school district can build and support a dynamic New Employee Orientation program that provides new hires with exactly what they need, how they need it, and when they need it.

In the Beginning …

In the winter of 2020, I was asked by my school district to help develop a brand-new way of welcoming staff members into the district. The previous way of doing this was to bring new hires into a central office conference room and provide them with a half day of informational sessions provided by members of our leadership team.

The NEO session as a whole was very effective. The day started off with our IT team sharing a bit about the technologies that we use and helping new hires log into their new accounts. Throughout the morning, members from our Human Resources, Finance, Safety and Security, and Communications team gave presentations about how the district works, how to access important tax and financial information, and after a few hours, the staff members were released at lunch time and officially welcomed into the district.

It was from this blueprint where we started crafting a more efficient and effective model for NEO. We knew that we had all the key ingredients, but some things were missing in order to give our new employees their best advantage for that first day when they entered their new careers.

Creating a Vision for New Employee Orientation

To begin the transformation of our New Employee Orientation program, we first asked the question "What does a new hire need to know on their first day of employment?" We knew that it was important for everyone to have the basic knowledge of their financial plan and some basic rules of engagement with our district policies, but we realized that the topics that were being discussed in NEO were not meeting the needs of someone entering the classroom the next day.

Keeping in mind that the rethinking and recreation of our NEO program was happening at a time where teachers were being asked to teach in a new hybrid learning environment where students were both physically in front of teachers as well as distance learning at home, we knew that teachers would be walking into the classroom the next day needing to be prepared for every possible situation so that students and families would have the best opportunity to learn together.

In order to do this, we needed more time.

Expanding the Schedule to Support all Learning Styles.

The first thing that was agreed upon was that NEO needed to shift from being a weekly half day event to a full day PD (Professional Development) session. In order to properly prepare our staff members for both their internal and professional responsibilities a second half of the day was created specifically for certified staff members, (teachers and support staff working with students in the classroom) to help them learn about how to use our digital learning tools such as our EdTech applications, interactive boards, and document cameras.

By adding this second half, we were able to focus our training on supporting teachers directly to provide them with the answers and resources to get them up and running so they would have the best chance of succeeding in the classroom.

Enter .... The Instructional Coaching Department

The addition of this teacher-focused PD portion of the day not only supported classroom-based employees directly, but also made it possible to include our Instructional Coaches in the NEO day.

Because this second half of the day was led by our Instructional Coaches, it gave the Digital Learning department two key advantages that were not there before.

1. Coaches are able to introduce themselves to new hires and begin the mentor relationship with new staff members that will continue into the classroom and throughout the year.

2. New staff members now have a name and a face to be able to ask questions both during the day and during the school year.

Breaking down NEO into Teacher Focused Sessions

The second half of the day now consisted of 3 unique sessions:

- Microsoft/Google 101 (Classroom, Teams, Email, etc.)
- Hardware (Interactive Boards, Laptops, Document Cameras etc.)
- Practical Applications for use in classroom activities (Nearpod, WeVideo, etc.)

By breaking down the second half of NEO this way, Coaches are able to learn more about their new teaching staff and promote the use of partnering with new teachers across the district even if they aren't physically working (during NEO) with new staff members that will be stationed in their traditional buildings.

How Can New Employee Orientation Support Your Students?

As the school begins to turn the corner and we all look ahead to a summer of regrowth and rebirth, I would encourage every school district to look at the way they are bringing in new hires. New Employee Orientation isn't simply a day to provide presentation after presentation to new hires to make their heads spin uncontrollably, it's an opportunity to help everyone learn how to be successful at the very first moment they step foot into their classroom or sit down at their desk.

At the heart of this training is your Instructional Coaching Department. The Instructional Coach is your key figure in supporting staff members both in and out of the classroom. By creating opportunities for long lasting relationships early, new staff members not only walk away from NEO knowing that they have someone on their side but have a face and a name to call upon in their first few days to help them get settled into the building and become successful with their students.

Daytime PD Programs

For many school districts, the ability to create a dynamic and effective Instructional Coaching program is a challenge. You have a few hundred teachers scattered across several school buildings, each with their own comfort level digital learning, and only one or a few coaches to support everyone.

When creating your EdTech Integration Plan one of the options that should be discussed and considered is a Day Time Professional Development Program. However, to conceive of a program requires a little bit of planning and buy-in from every level of administration.

Creating a daytime professional development program where teachers leave their schools to spend time in classes and workshops takes not only staff coordination but also a financial commitment from the district because of the number of substitutes that would have to be involved.

While in my first coaching position, I attended a series of PD sessions at a local high school. I thought it was very well organized and extremely well thought out. Each week, the coaches in that school district prepared a series of in-person classes and the sessions were made available to both teachers in that district and, for a small fee, teachers in other districts could attend as well.

After attending a class and speaking with the coach instructors I decided to create my own daytime professional system in my district. We called the system "Cardinal University" and developed a series of face-to-face daytime sessions called "Cardinal Classes" which turned out to be an extremely successful adventure both for myself, my program, and the entire school district.

Planning from the Top Down

When planning any type of professional development, a strong consideration of important topics should first come the district Strategic Plan. As we learned about when planning the EdTech Integration Plan, the Strategic Plan is the district blueprint that not only gives the district a vision for what should be happening in classrooms, but why it is important for students to be taught a certain way.

The next series of topics that should be considered for group professional development sessions are the goals and vision that each building administrator and curriculum office leader has for their staff members. One of the best ways to build daytime workshop sessions is with the understanding that the sessions will help administrators meet their yearly goals.

Surveying Your Staff

Once you have discussed PD topics with both central office and building level administrators, it is also important that staff members have a choice of sessions that serve their interests and needs. Creating sessions based on a single application or project is critical in getting teacher buy-in. Keeping in mind that attending these sessions means that a teacher must provide extra work for a substitute, your session should always be designed to help both teachers and administrators meet their goals in addition to being positive learning experiences.

The question often is, "How do you know what types of sessions and topics are of interest to staff members?" Some of the best ways of knowing what sessions to offer are by creating self-assessments and by simply sending staff members short-form interest surveys.

Pre-Workshop Documents and Surveys

Short-Form Staff Self-Assessment

What is a Short-Form Staff Self-Assessment?

One of the best ways to take a quick temperature check of your district's comfort level or use in digital learning applications is through a simple "what do you know and what do you want to know" assessment activity. For many staff members, this is a non-stressful way of sharing what applications are meaningful to them. This also is a terrific way to show off a new way of using an application that you are looking to focus on throughout the school year.

How does the Short-Form Staff Self-Assessment Work?

In this example, a Google Apps assessment has been created using Google Drawings. The user is asked to then place the icon of each application in one of four boxes to demonstrate their comfort level of that application.

One of the best ways to distribute an assessment such as this is by first creating a template (using Google Drawings in this case) and then distributing it through Google Classroom. This will give staff members the opportunity to quickly take the assignment and submit it. Additionally, using Google Classroom's thumbnail view of assignments you can see all the assessments in one scrolling window without the need of opening each individual Google Drawing file.

The PD Topic Interest Survey

What is a PD Topic Interest Survey?

The Professional Development Topic Survey is one of the first tools that a coach can use when deciding what PD sessions to offer. This is an invaluable tool to not only take a quick temperature check of a building or school district, but also for the coach to get an idea of what topics and applications are on the minds of their teachers.

One thing to keep in mind when looking at the example provided is that the survey asks two simple questions. One question focuses on specific applications. The other focuses on more curriculum and project-oriented goals.

How does the PD Topic Survey Work?

The focus of this survey is to do a quick check of what your teachers are thinking about doing in their classrooms. This form can be shared with staff members by email, but often it is best done in a staff meeting situation so that you can very quickly get your entire group to answer it all at the same time.

One thing to notice about this survey is that it asks for the teacher's name and email. Not all surveys in this process will be staff member specific. The reason this survey asks for the name of the staff member is that, even if the staff member does not sign up for a PD class with the coach, they will still be contacted for potential coaching meetings. Additionally, a coach can relate the data provided by the staff by building or department so that additional group PD can be discussed and planned between the coach and administration.

Choosing Your PD Sessions

The PD Course Catalog

What is a Professional Development Course Catalog?

The PD Course Catalogue is a key component in the planning and development of the Day Time Professional Development Program. The catalog can be as simple as a Google Doc with session titles, a Google Form with checkboxes, or in the case of the example provided, a Google Slide that provides a visual "e-book like" viewing experience.

No matter how the course catalog is created, it is important to remember that every staff member learns and searches differently. In the case of the example provided, courses are listed throughout the catalog in at least two ways.

How is the Catalog Organized?

The first way that courses are listed is by application. Teachers can search for an application they may be working on or would like to learn about and can search through courses that will address a particular application.

Additionally, each course is organized by a category based on (in this case) the 4 C's which will help teachers choose classes based on curricular and digital learning goals.

Advice on Topics and Descriptions

One piece of advice when creating a catalog for your school district is to keep things simple. We all have been to regional and national conferences where we see session titles and descriptions such as "Iron Chef Google Apps" and have been impressed with the way things are worded enough to stop by the session.

Where those fancy and flashy titles might be good for conferences, they do not always work when working in a K12 district. Many teachers will not know what it means and even though you are creating a good session focused on staff needs … if they do not feel comfortable signing up for a course and leaving their teaching day to attend … the course will not be successful. (See tree falling in the woods)

PD Course Registration Form

No matter if daytime workshops are mandatory or volunteer, the PD Course Registration Form is a coach's last offensive opportunity to entice staff members to sign up for daytime professional development workshops.

If the form is too long, nobody will fill it out. If the form is too short, you might not have enough courses to spark enough interest from teachers to sign up.

In creating the PD Course Registration Form, there are always two thoughts:

- Create a form for each month.
- Create a form for the entire semester and adjust it as time passes.

No matter what option you choose, the form should provide your coaching staff and administrators with exactly what is interesting to your teachers. It should have sessions available that meet the needs and goals of building administration as well as having fun and engaging sessions that spark interest in collaborating with you as a coach.

In designing this form, it is best to have as many multiple-choice questions as possible so that you can graph out the responses. Additionally, this is one of the best places to add the "what do you want to learn" question before hitting submit. This will not only get staff members thinking about why they want to attend but is also valuable feedback when asking administrators for the opportunity to run additional classes on certain topics.

Running Your Workshops

Workshop Pre-Test

The PD Course Pre-Test is a useful quick assessment tool that is given just before the workshop begins. You might think of the Pre-Test as an Entry Ticket given at the beginning of a class period.

Why Start with a Pre-Test?

The purpose of the Pre-Test is to get the attendees to think about the topics that will be covered during the workshop session. I generally use grid-type questions. The reason for this is that the information is outlined clearly on the form, and it also looks great when a teacher takes the form on their mobile device.

The second part of the Pre-Test is to ask one final "what do you want to learn" or "what questions do you have about today's topic" type of question so that you can make sure that you address everyone's questions and concerns during the presentation.

Why Use a Rating System?

In creating the Pre-Test, it is important to create your main questions with a rating scale. This allows you to later give the Post-Test which will be the same exact assessment as the pre-test. This will help you show the growth of your attendees over the course of the session. This is immensely helpful for any coach who wishes to use their PD as part of their Student Learning Objectives (SLO) during evaluation season.

Workshop Post-Test

The PD Course Post-Test is remarkably like the Pre-Test except that it is given directly after the workshop has finalized. The Post-Test should be created using the same exact question format as the Pre-Test so that you can easily show the growth of the participant.

How does the Post-Test differ from the Pre-Test?

One additional feature of the Post-Test is the ability to collect examples of any work that was created during the workshop. This is a fantastic way of archiving what happened during the session.

Additionally, the Post-Test is a wonderful place to ask your workshop attendees if they would like to book the coach for a classroom visit.

Collecting Data and Feedback after the Workshop

The Post-PD Workshop Feedback Form

What is a Post Workshop Feedback Form?

An important part of any professional development session for both presenter and participants is the ability to provide (and accept) open and honest feedback about how the experience went.

Traditionally, the Post Workshop Feedback Form is one that is anonymous so that the participant can share openly about their experiences. It is also designed to have a surprise ending. (More on this below.)

How does the Post Workshop Feedback Form Work?

The focus of the Post Workshop Feedback Form is to gather quick and effective reactions on how the session went and what needs to be improved on. A feedback survey could be given out directly after the workshop, but it is often best to email this survey to participants an hour or more after the workshop, so they have time to think about and process their experiences.

One thing to notice about this survey is that it comes in two parts. The first part of the survey is the actual feedback survey that asks participants to share their thoughts about the event. Once the participant clicks the submit button the form, they are then provided with a link to an additional form where they can sign up for times to meet with the coach.

Conclusion

When done correctly, ongoing day time professional development is a tremendous plus for any coaching program. Not only do your coaches can work with both large and small groups of staff members, but workshop interactions also can springboard into meaningful 1:1 coaching relationships.

Student Tech Teams

Growing up, I loved to tinker. I was always that kid with my head in the tech books at school and every night when I was home, I was pulling apart some type of technology to fiddle with.

When I was 14, my father gave me his old computer. A very tall Gateway machine and it was my job to "fix it." It was through that machine that I learned to take apart a machine piece by piece. I swapped out hard drives, upgraded CR-ROM's and put more video cards in it than I should have. That computer was my little

piece of heaven. Ironically, looking back, that computer was the start of a career that would not happen for a few decades.

My story is not one that could have happened alone. It took someone giving me an opportunity to learn more about something that I was interested in and providing a hands-on "can't break this if you tried" approach which gave me the opportunity to test drive everything to as many lengths as possible so I could build the Frankenstein computer of my dreams.

In this section, we are going to help you and your school district provide students with the same opportunities and responsibilities that I had growing up. One of the best ways to do this is through the creation of a Student Tech Team, a group of students who, when guided by a mentor, have the potential to support both their fellow students AND teachers in making sure that digital technology in the classroom is up and running as it needs to be and most importantly, where it should be.

What are Student Tech Teams?

In today's world of ever-changing technology and revolving door of cables and computer parts, it is increasingly difficult for an IT staff to be everywhere or for an Instructional Coach to be on call 24/7 for minor inventory issues. For this reason, it is a great idea to install a Student Tech Team in your building.

Student Tech Teams not only can be designed to help relieve the stress and duties of both the Coaching and IT staff, but also help students learn about responsibility, budgeting, entrepreneurship, and marketing. Verizon Innovative Learning Student Tech Team Overview

How to Get Started Creating a Student Tech Team?

The process of creating your own Student Tech Team is not difficult at all. If your district has a vision for what you are seeking additional support for, you can create a program that fits the needs of both students, teachers, and the community.

Step 1: Select a Student Tech Team Mentor

When it comes to creating a student tech team, your advisor needs to be not only excited to work on technology but is also able to serve as a mentor to young minds. Often, the Student Tech Team Mentor (STTM) is a teacher who also has a desire to learn themselves and has no problem going the extra mile to set up learning opportunities for students with district IT staff and community members so that students have an opportunity to learn from all areas of technology subjects.

It is also important that the STTM be able to set up learning situations and stand back as students both succeed and fail in the process. Therefore, it is important to think of your STTM as a mentor and not an advisor.

Step 2: Secure Administrative Support

The creation of a Student Tech Team, on the surface, does not need to be a heavily budgeted program. Teaching students how to fix iPad screens, onboard new students, and providing some simple digital learning supports are some examples of how a STT can be deployed at the beginning of the program.

Once your STT, however, gets more experience and comfortable being in a support role, there are a few items that might be needed to make the program useful to the school building and exciting for the students. This is where administrative support comes into play.

The goal of any STT is to provide students with the opportunity to gain leadership experience. By working with administration, STT's can be deployed in a variety of ways throughout the school day and school year to help them learn how to come together as a unit, form a team, and lead the digital learning experiences happening in the classroom.

A second and equally important goal for any STT is to learn about the technologies that are being used in and around the classrooms. This requires a time commitment to the program that only a building administrator can grant. Ultimately, your student tech team might be able to serve the school community during lunch periods, recess, after school, and if the situation presents itself, after school hours at community functions.

Step 3: Recruit Outstanding and Creative Students

Are you interested in creating a Student Tech Team? Why not make it a big deal? When recruiting, create posters that fill the hallway, video commercials for the school social media channel, and put announcements in every teacher's mailbox.

The beauty of a STT is that there is no single type of student that stands out and all students have an equal opportunity to join, participate, and become a school leader.

Let the application also be a fun way for students to highlight their creativity and passions about educational technology and digital learning. You might find students who love to code, love building in Minecraft, or even enjoy fixing hardware.

Providing Experiences and Opportunities for Student Tech Teams

One of the first things that you want to do once you have your initial group of students is to start brainstorming how they might be helpful and useful within the school community. This conversation should be completely open-ended and led by the students. Students should all take turns speaking, listening, and writing down what was said in the meeting. This will help the group begin to form a team.

Once several short-term and long-term projects are identified, the STTM should plan to create learning opportunities for students to learn more about popular applications that are being used in the classroom and how to do simple IT requests that do not require too much background knowledge. This is a terrific opportunity for students to start working with your IT department on supporting common Tech Tickets.

Students Teaching Students

One of my favorite ways to support students and build a community is by inviting students to share about what they love the most about technology. Perhaps one of your students is interested in Minecraft. This is a fantastic opportunity for them to take 10 minutes and highlight something they built for the group. By having students highlight their passions to each other it helps them become comfortable standing in front of others and begins their leadership journey within the STT and the school community.

Teachers Teaching Students

Another way for STT's to learn how to work together is by role playing. One wonderful way to do this is by asking a fellow teacher to come in and provide a situation from which the STT needs to decide how to trouble shoot.

Administrator Teaching Students

Are you looking to kick your student's motivation up a notch? Invite your principal or Tech Director into a meeting where they would give the students a "mission" to complete and help them through the process of creating a project or program to meet the needs of their building or department.

Community Teaching Students

One of the best ways for students to begin learning about how technology is used is by providing real world situations that require both long-term and short-term planning.

Suggestions for supporting STT development:

- Allow students to participate in "app approval" meetings.
- Create a situation for students to instruct other students about their favorite applications.
- Provide student to teacher training and interactions during lunch time.

What are the Benefits of Student Tech Teams

The creation of a Student Tech Team supports not just the students but the entire community and quite possibly could have long-lasting effects on all that are involved.

Benefit #1: Maturity and Leadership

As mentioned above, the biggest benefit for creating STT's is the ability to have students work with and learn from each other. It is quite possible that the students who join the STT are the ones who are not often found in group activities such as Band/Orchestra and Athletics (although, this is completely generalizing)

Benefit #2: Digital Learning / Digital Citizenship / Digital Responsibility

The ability for students to learn and grow as individuals and a team is the one thing that every STT strives for, but it is not the reason students join in the first place. Students join the STT program looking to learn more about technology and how to build something awesome. There is no greater opportunity to teach digital learning and digital citizenship skills than through the teamwork provided by the STT and the STTM.

Benefit #3: A Decreased dependency on Coaches and IT staff for certain items and activities.

By bringing in a STT to support new technologies, especially at scale, it frees up the need to expend a large number of Techs to a situation. One Tech can simply train the STT to support a task such as Chromebook setup or password resets and a job can get completed much more efficiently.

Should Your District Create Student Tech Teams?

Many (many) years ago when I was given my first computer, I didn't know what to do with it. It was cold, clunky, and outdated. Over the course of a few years, I had so much fun learning about it and tinkering my way through all the upgrades.

Looking back, I wish that I had a Student Tech Team to work with on projects like this and a mentor to help point me in the right direction. By creating a Student Tech Team in your school, it provides an opportunity to engage students in a variety of ways that other programs are not able to. Leadership skills, presentation skills, and teamwork building skills are all essential parts of growing up and growing into what we now call "College and Career Ready."

Conclusion

Throughout this chapter, you have learned about several ways that your Instructional Coaching Department can show its value in the school district and community. One of the most difficult parts about having an Instructional Coaching Department is keeping your Instructional Coaching Department. Because Instructional Coaches are not directly tied to students or student achievement, it is always one of the first things that gets discussed during budget season. It's often too easy to create budget cuts by reducing the number of Instructional Coaches a district has.

For this reason, it is imperative that your Coaches be seen as members of the teaching staff that are supportive at ALL levels. From 1:1 mentors to teachers in the classroom to being the first person that a new employee meets when entering the district, to creating a community wide instructional program, the Coach should always be seen as a jack of all trades and the first department called on when a new initiative is discussed and created.

Over the last few years since the end of the Pandemic and the reduction of federal funds in education, I have had the opportunity to unfortunately see too many coaching programs go away or be reduced in force. When a school district sets up their instructional coaching program with the right personnel, a supportive coach champion, and provides them every opportunity to become leaders in the classroom, building, district, and community, the results will be phenomenal.

But how do you do this? How do you create all of this coaching success and build a program that will allow students, teachers, administrators, and community members to see the value that an Instructional Coaching department can have on student impact?

In our next chapter, we will wrap up this section by showing several ways to build your standards-based Instructional Coaching program by first doing the one thing that many school districts fail to do.

Chapter 15

Defining the Instructional Coaching Position (Reflecting on the Job)

"Map out your future, but do it in pencil."
Jon Bon Jovi

Growing up I always wanted to be in a position where I woke up every morning with the opportunity to help others. Watching someone on the receiving end of an action or gesture smile is one of the greatest joys in the world. Perhaps this was the reason I love playing music and get excited every time someone comes to one of my performances just to get away from their world for a few minutes.

From 2001 when I earned my undergraduate degree to 2010 when I completed my graduate program, the only thing I wanted to was to play music and work with students who wanted to do the same.

However, not everything goes as planned. Things change. Situations change. The world changes.

In 2015, I left the world of Music Education and embarked on a 12-year career as an Instructional Coach, working for two amazing school districts. In my first district, I built a program completely from scratch. I entered with fresh eyes and no external expectations—only those I set for myself. From the ground up, I created a support group, developed a professional development system, and established a program robust enough to weather the pandemic, even after my departure.

In my second district, I had the incredible opportunity to not just build another program, but to build a team. Together, we developed an instructional coaching department that didn't merely survive the pandemic—it thrived. We created both in-person and virtual training sessions that supported students and teachers while providing leadership and direction to Connecticut's second-largest city.

I later transitioned briefly to a district-level administrator role, a position I embraced wholeheartedly. Looking back on my career as an Instructional Coach, I've had time to contemplate my journey—its experiences, challenges, and victories. None of this success would have been possible alone. The supportive community I built around me was instrumental in both my personal success and the enduring impact of the programs we created together.

I was recently asked the popular question "If you could speak to your 2015 self about what you know now, what would you share?" That advice brings me to this chapter. A chapter of thoughts, fears, successes, and stories to hopefully help you build the coaching program of your dreams.

The 10 Most Important Rules for Instructional Coaches to Follow

Rule #1: It's always best to begin in the beginning.

Always start with a plan. It's too easy for coaches to be hired and fail in the first year. Traditionally administrators come in two varieties. You either have administrators who don't know what to do with you or you have administrators who don't put you in the proper position for success in the classroom. For this reason, it's always important to get everyone on the same page and have those important, yet often awkward conversations about how the year will be run and what your role is.

Rule #2: You are only defined by how you are defined.

When having those first few meetings with your building leaders, it is critical to agree on how your role will be defined in the building and in the district. More important, it is hyper critical to agree on how your position will be introduced to the staff. More often than not, the administrator will try to brush this one off as "no big deal" but that only (and often) leads to confusion of staff members as to what you are supposed to be doing and doing with them. Coaches need to be confident in their roles in the building and in the district. Everyone needs to be on the same page in order for a coaching program to be successful BEFORE the start of the school year.

Rule #3: Instructional Coaching is all about Building Relationships.

No matter what your official title is in the district or how many buildings you support, the most important thing to remember is that the job is all about building relationships. Having strong relationships with teachers and students will lead to meaningful and positive interactions with your administrators. The better your relationship is with your administrators, the more opportunities they will support you taking on at the district level and in the community.

Rule #4: Instructional Coaching is a Seesaw!

One of the things that I loved about being an Instructional Coach was that I never knew what the day was going to be like. I could have a completely empty calendar while driving into school but could also walk out of school with wall-to-wall staff interactions. Each day was a challenge filled with ups and downs. What works between you and one staff member might not work between you and another. The expectations that one principal has for you don't have to match up with the expectations that another administrator might have. This is both the beauty and the struggle of the job.

One of the things that I started doing each day to help me gauge my experiences was bullet journaling. Having a simple planner or online form where I could write down some basic SEL (Social Emotional Learning) information and private notes from the day was an extremely helpful daily exercise that got me through a TON of stressful days.

Rule #5: Meet Your Teachers Where They Are

One of the most complex parts of the Instructional Coaching position is the moment when a coach sits down with a teacher to plan out a lesson. At that moment, the coach needs to carefully navigate a number of things including the ability of the students, the comfort level of the teacher, the current schedule and climate of the school, the support a teacher has from their peers, and above all, the expectations that an administrator has on the teaching staff to work with the coach. A Coach never knows what type of learning environment they are going to be walking into until they sit down.

Because of this, it is important for coaches to always begin teacher meetings by having a short conversation to learn where they are and what their goals are for the upcoming collaboration. After you know where the teacher and the students are, you can then formulate a plan to support and move forward with the lesson or project.

Rule #6: The Key to a Successful Coaching Program is in the Data

Creating a positive and supportive coaching program that provides teachers with the resources they need, when they need it is important, but if you want to build your program, you need to build it in the administrative offices and conference rooms. The best way to do that is through using standards-based data models to not only tell the story about your program but provide a persuasive argument for how you can grow your program. Keeping track of teacher interactions, workshop attendance, and how it affects student performance is key to speaking the language of central office.

Rule #7: You are not alone ... ever!

When I first started as a coach, I had to learn, (quickly), how to stand on my own two feet and become a leader. The only reason I started the "Ask the Tech Coach" podcast was so that I had someone to talk to. The reason for me having a steady cohost on the show was because I needed someone to bounce ideas off of. The fact that the show was recorded and distributed was simply a byproduct of the platform. The biggest thing that I learned from doing over 250 episodes of the podcast is that my situation is not unique and that there are plenty of other coaches who are also going through the same fears, frustrations, triumphs, and successes that I was going through.

No matter where you are in your coaching career, it's important to have a professional network to support you. Groups such as the ISTE Community Leaders, Microsoft Innovative Experts, Google Trainers and Coaches, and Apple Educators, are just a few of the many community-based organizations have been created to provide resources and support and face to face conversations on a wide range of topics. The best advice I can share with you is to take advantage of them… often!

Rule #8: Don't get Discouraged when your Teachers Don't "Get it"

Change is not easy. Culture change is difficult. The one piece of advice that I often find myself giving to new (and veteran) coaches is to not get discouraged. Not everyone picks up new skills at the same time. This is one of the reasons why, in this book, I have shared the reasons for creating a vertically aligned professional development system. By first showing new topics in a large group session, followed by grade level and finally 1:1 meetings, it allows staff members to see something new from a variety of lenses with the hope that they can grasp the concept by the time that a coach sits down to formulate a classroom lesson together.

In order to help coaches support all learning styles, it is important to be able to read the room when giving presentations. Before starting a presentation, ask the principal what the overall temperature of the staff is for the topic. Poll some members of the staff either through an electronic form or through casual conversation to get a feel for how excited they are to learn something new. By taking these steps, it might help you to have a successful learning session or 1:1 meeting with a teacher. If they don't "get it" the first time you explain it, never get discouraged. Stop, reflect, go back and always adjust as needed.

Rule #9: It's all about the Culture … not the Coach

One of the hardest lessons that I learned in my first few years of being a Coach was that the program wasn't about me. It wasn't about my accomplishments, my badges, my podcast, or my ISTE presentations. In order to shift a culture and build a program that elevates everyone in the organization, it must be about them. Coaching is a service-based position. You are a member of the district who comes to school every day with the single focus of helping students become high achievers. You do this by collaborating with all staff members to assist them in improving their skills. Culture shift isn't easy. It is difficult and it takes time. It is only after the school district, and its staff members, have a clear understanding that you are there to help *THEM* that the culture shift can happen.

Rule #10: It is Completely Ok to ask for Help and Support

There will be a time, perhaps even a few times a week, or at least once a day where someone comes to you as their coach and asks a question that you simply do not know the answer to. It's ok not to know the answer. There are plenty of ways to respond to this staff member. Inviting them to walk through the research process together is a fantastic way to build relationships while also teaching search skills. Another terrific way to respond is to simply state that you don't know the answer, but you would be happy to do the research and get back to them as quickly as possible. Just remember that if you do use this response, it is imperative to get back to that staff member sometime soon even if it's just to let them know that you are currently in the process of checking up on the request. This not only helps build your coaching brand with that teacher, but it will help others like, know, and trust you as their coach because they will know that you have their backs and are a great resource for them when they have questions.

Part 3 Summary

It's no secret that my background in instructional technology runs through my passion for being a music educator. I have countless memories of rehearsal sessions and amazing performances of the world's greatest pieces of music. About 10 years ago (or more) I decided that I wanted to get up and instead of sitting in the orchestra, I wanted to start down a path that allowed me to stand in front of the orchestra and work alongside them to perform sonata's, symphonies, and operas.

It was during that time that I started taking formal conducting lessons from several amazing teachers. From there, I learned how to physically stand and present myself to not only an orchestra, but a paying audience, and of course work alongside a board of directors to help promote my vision, the orchestras vision, and most importantly, the composers' visions.

Of All the Things That I Learned in The World of Conducting, These Lessons Stand Out:

- The conductor is the only one on stage that doesn't make noise, yet his actions are what tie the group together.
- The musicians do not need a conductor to know what to do. A conductor's job is simply to start everyone and guide them through transitions.
- Treat every musician with respect but understand that different instruments require different needs.

It has been through these lessons that I approach every day as a Tech Coach. It is through these lessons that I find myself more becoming a Tech Conductor. Let me try and explain how these lessons can be applied in a school system.

From Podium to Classroom … And Back Again

When you break down everything that happens on the podium, it starts and stops with the simple concept of Respect. I can honestly say that I have my good days, and I have had my bad days as I learn how to be a Tech Coach to over 400 staff members. As a conductor, you have your good days and bad days too. You have your rehearsals where everything goes well, and you have those times where someone puts you on the spot in a rehearsal and you simply don't know the answer. This happens in the classroom all the time.

What is important is that you come prepared to every rehearsal, meeting, classroom, as prepared as possible. If you don't know the answer to a question, you always make sure you have a resource (your PLN) that can help you find the answer quickly.

From early on in my conductor training, I learned that the word Maestro is one that gets placed upon you from day one, but the concept of Maestro, a word that literally translates into Teacher, (or coach) is one that is earned day after day, rehearsal after rehearsal and is earned only through respect. This is extremely true for Technology Coaches who not only work with everyone in a district at all levels but must also be walking talking resource centers of technology and pedagogy that are essentially on call 24/7.

You Are the Only One Who Doesn't Make Any Sound

In an orchestra setting, the violin players play the violin, the tuba players play the tuba, and the bass players play the bass. Each of these musicians or groups of musicians has an instrument that they can pick up anytime and practice. A Conductor, on the other hand, has the orchestra. There is no try way to practice late at night with an imaginary group of 50 people. The preparation for Conductors is mostly mental and requires you to study scores of music and practice "gestures" in the air, sometimes in front of mirrors to make sure that the one single time you are in front of a group you get it right.

As a Tech Coach, it is very much the same. Teachers have the opportunity to learn from their students every day. They learn how their classrooms work, act, and interact with each other. As a Tech Coach, you have just one moment to walk into a classroom and nail your lesson. When you are given an opportunity to present in front of a building, you are given an opportunity to showcase yourself in front of 150 (or more) strangers who are all there to learn from and support you. They know you are in front of them to help them become better educators, but there might not be the same friendly connection that a teacher and a group of students have, or a principal and a faculty have.

Walking into a building to give PD is very much like being asked to come into a new orchestra and guest conduct a rehearsal or performance without ever getting to meet the musicians.

Your Teachers … They Don't Need You

Let's face the fact that teachers have been teaching for hundreds of years without the need for a "Technology Integration Specialist." They don't need "Tech Coaching." But … do they?

One of the first rules of conducting is … Show Up When Needed, and Get Out of The Way …

There are times when you can simply tell a musician how to play something, times when you can describe a sound, and times where you have to grab an instrument from the violin section and demonstrate it for a group.

This couldn't be truer as a Tech Coach. There are times where I have worked with a teacher and my role was simply to answer a question or two and back away. Other situations lead me to help them create a co-teaching lesson where together, we worked with the students on an innovative lesson.

In the classroom, the role of a Tech Coach is to quickly enter and assess a situation and provide whatever the teacher needs when they need it. Perhaps it's by simply answering a question and other times it's by picking up the instrument to demonstrate how something should look or sound.

If you choose the right method of support, the group/teacher will appreciate your help and together the rehearsal/lesson will move forward. If you choose the wrong method at the wrong time, you are libel to insult someone and create a situation you never intended to have started. As a Conductor and as a Tech Coach, it's always important to know the personalities you are working with so you can quickly make the right decisions and choices.

Some Teachers Are Section Players … Some Are Soloists

If you really think about it, a school district is very much like an orchestra. To conceptualize this, let's break down the various parts of each.

The Orchestra

The Strings

In the front of a symphony orchestra lies a massive section known as the Strings. Altogether, their instruments are in the "violin family." Their instruments look similar, they play with a bow, and there could be as many as 24 of the same instruments in each of the 5 distinct sections. Together, they can be broken down into string quartets, trios, and often, composers write for them as either a full section or as soli sections. Each of the subsections (violins, viola, cello, bass) are seated by rank (ability level) and there is a section leader who is for conversation's sake, "the boss" of that section.

The Winds

The next group of musicians behind the strings is the Woodwinds. This section is composed of your Flutes, Oboes, Clarinets, and Bassoons. They are your mid-range, mid-level instruments who are put in the awkward position of sitting behind the massive string section, yet they sit in front of the mighty brass and percussion sections so it's often possible that while playing loud and proud they don't get heard when the entire group is playing together.

The Brass, Percussion, etc. …

Composed of the Trumpets, Trombones, and Tubas, Drums, Marimbas, Cymbals, and all other instruments these musicians are highly specialized and are only in your group because, like the winds, they passed an audition based on their ability to be leaders and soloists. When addressing these musicians, a conductor should simply be able to describe in as few words as possible the sound or quality they wish to hear, and it should happen with as little retakes as possible. These are HIGHLY skilled and trained musicians who spend hours in a practice room learning what is known as “excerpts” or very tiny solo passages just to have the opportunity to audition for the group.

A School District

Elementary Teachers

Elementary Teachers should be approached as a group. In any building, for example, you have several 4th-grade teachers all teaching their own class but teaching a common curriculum to the classroom next door. They meet in departments to plan common activities, but they often do their lesson plans on their own. When you work with one and not the others, it is often not looked on highly. Sometimes it’s best to talk about concepts such as blended learning, or SAMR models, but they are also the first to allow a Tech Coach to pick up their instrument (classroom) and come in to demonstrate something new and amazing in the world of Technology.

Elementary teachers often have degrees in general elementary education rather than a specialized degree in a subject area and for that reason, it’s often best to show a wide variety of examples and build lessons together. Elementary Teachers and Buildings should be approached the same way a string section is approached. It’s always best when you are able to demonstrate the concept as well as describe.

Middle School

Much like the proud woodwinds, Middle School teachers are caught between elementary and high school teachers. They have the hardest job because without them students don’t have a solid direction when they get into the older grades. Also much like the Woodwinds, Middle School teachers are soloists who often times are remembered the most when a student looks back at their favorite years in school Their hardest job is that they often have to work with a group of students who came from multiple elementary schools and haven’t yet jelled together as individuals yet … and oh, did we mention those wonderful puberty years.

High School

Much like a conductor should never (unless specialized themselves in the instrument) tell a brass player how to play the trumpet, a good Tech Coach should never (or hardly ever) approach a high school teacher and tell them how to teach their subject. . . Trust me ...

High School Teachers are HIGHLY talented, and HIGHLY Specialized educators who command the respect of teenagers every day and for those reasons I love popping my head into classrooms each day, asking if they need anything and moving on. Often, I find myself sitting down with high school teachers to plan out lessons the same way I would sit down with a soloist to plan out a solo passage in a symphony. If you show them respect, they will reciprocate and come back repeatedly because their only goal each year is to produce the best students and pass them on to college.

Tech Coaching or Conducting ... What Do You Think?

Why does the Instructional Coaching position exist in a school district? When we step back and really dive into this question, you will see that the coaching position is truly developed to help staff members working directly with students meet those impact standards. To do this, a coach needs to be passionate, dynamic, and organized. Every character trait you hope to see in a music director. They need to be stealthy and silent, but when given the opportunity, they need to be able to help a school district perform at the top of its ability.

In our next and closing section of this book, we are going to take what we have learned up to this point about building a standards-aligned and culture changing digital learning curriculum and share some thoughts and real-world stories to help you in creating positive change in your own school district.

Part 4

Making an Impact in the Classroom and Community

Chapter 16

Defining a Successful Digital Learning Culture

Culture … what is it? What defines it? How do you create one?

Up to this point, this book has broken down a data-driven systematic approach for creating a dramatic culture change in a school district that focuses on helping teachers and students meet and exceed both curricular and digital learning standards.

To accomplish this, we first needed to ask our district how it defines itself and through that definition, create strategic goals from which it will then go on a journey to meet those goals as a community. We then learned that the key to meeting those goals is by using both core-curricular and digital learning standards as a guide both in the classroom and in the community.

To help a district reach those goals, this book outlined how the creation of an Instructional Coaching Department could be built and deployed to support not only learning in the classrooms, but at the district level and in the community.

Let's assume that your school district was to follow every instruction in this book and take every piece of advice that this book offers. What happens next? Does that define success? Does that mean that culture has changed?

The hard truth about the contents of this book and the philosophy built into its teachings is that culture is not something you can simply create overnight. Culture is a living breathing thing that is fragile at its core but ridged when provoked.

For example, think about a school who has had the same leadership group for a number of years. The building knows what to expect at the beginning of the school year. Staff members are comfortable with the way that policy and procedures are set, and they do not have any worries about anything breaking their culture and spirit due to the fact that they look and act as a unit. One day the news breaks that a member of the leadership team is moving on to another position. All of a sudden, that one crack in the system leads to a number of questions from the staff. People feel that they might lose key positions in the building and social groups start to form when the new leadership team eventually gets formed.

- What happens next?
- How did this one minor change affect the culture of a building?
- How do you think this change could affect students?

As you can see from this example, culture change can be difficult. But it does not always have to be.

Success is Always how you Define Success

How do you define success? For many, success is often described as getting from Point A to Point B. It is starting the race and at the end of the year, getting past the finish line. It sounds so simple. For many leaders, success is often viewed at the macro level. Where this line of sight might work for some tasks and topics, it is not always the best advice for culture change.

I cannot tell you how many times I have been told by my leadership mentors to take things slow and to remember that change is difficult. You can't expect to move the herd all at once. But, by taking one task at a time and clearly defining its goals and meeting those goals one by one, you can then turn around to look at all that has been accomplished.

For this reason, culture shift will always start with the school district's Strategic Plan. The

Strategic Plan provides an overview of where a district wants to be in 4-5 years but is then broken down into year-by-year goals each with its own steps that will ultimately create a culture shift in the entire educational community.

The thing about Strategic Plans, Digital Learning Plans, and how a school district ultimately defines how successful they are is that it's all on a sliding scale. These mile markers are constantly in motion and are able to be adjusted at any point during the school year. For that reason, success and the success of your program is ultimately whatever and however you choose to define success. There is nothing wrong with that. Success is however it ends up being defined.

That being said, there are a few items that have been discussed in this book that should be brought up one last time.

Goals Should Be Measurable and Attainable

It is extremely possible that the first year after setting goals is going to involve creating systems and strategies for helping your district, building, and teachers meet those goals. This not only gives a school district the opportunity to discuss and promote these goals, but also provides staff members with a method for tracking and reporting on the status of these goals.

Goals should support standard-based instruction that highlights student achievement.

Whenever a district is in the middle of formulating its goals for the upcoming school year, they should always look at the standards to lead the process. The Core Curricular and Digital Learning standards provide not only a nationally recognized blueprint but a complete roadmap for how to set your goals and objectives for classroom instruction and teacher professional development.

Goals should be Presentable and Reflectable

At the end of the day, Goals are only as good as the way that the staff and community perceive them to be. Too often do you see school districts create a set of goals only to have community members and even the teaching staff ask the question "what does that mean?" In order to create a true culture shift, every goal and objective needs to be easily presentable. They need to be well thought out and easily understandable by everyone in the community.

In addition to being professionally written and easily understandable, Goals must be reflected on by both staff members and those in the community who support them. Goals that require long term planning with a number of resources attached to their success usually also come with a price tag and for this reason, it is important for the community to understand what they are ultimately voting on and paying for when it comes time to vote on the annual school budget.

Defining Success from Every Level of the Leadership Ladder

So, where do you start? How do you begin this process? If success is defined by those who have the power to define it what tools should we use to define success?

Let's take a quick look at the various levels of educational leadership that have already been discussed here and develop ways to define and determine if your program could be considered successful.

The Superintendent Level

How could a Superintendent and other C-Level Administrators define a successful culture shift? The easy answer is through Data. It would be too easy for me to write about how data is the ultimate definition of success when there are so many other factors that a Superintendent needs to have their eyes on.

Some of these factors are obvious and some of these are hidden in places you wouldn't expect. For example, if a school district is in the middle of a positive culture shift where every member of the staff is on the same page, and every administrator has their buildings falling in line with clearly outlined district policies, you might tend to have less staff turnover. Additionally, you might have fewer staff issues and concerns in Human Resources. If these numbers were seen to be on the decline, would that be a contender for defining a successful culture shift? Would that be something that a Superintendent might be able to share with others when touting the accomplishments of their strategic plan?

The Curricular Level

Are there ways that your Curricular leaders can take pride in the success of a strong digital learning culture shift? Certainly! A shift to successfully meeting digital learning standards is also a shift to how teachers and students are meeting core curricular content standards. When aligned to both core curricular and digital learning standards, a vertically aligned and standards-based curriculum can clearly help teachers, students, and parents understand where their place is in the greater educational picture at any point in the school year. They know what topics will come ahead and how those topics will interact with concepts being taught in other classes not just in the students' current grade but subjects the student will progress to in their academic futures. Success then can be defined clearly because everyone from teachers to students and community members can understand the path that each student is on and how it will help them prepare not just for the next grade level but into their college and career path upon graduation.

The Technology Level

Defining success at the Technology level is all about how often devices are used, applications are put into play during curricular lessons and having the ability to make offensive decisions about defensive issues that might come up throughout the year. Because a shift to becoming more technology dependent also comes with a greater need for devices, WIFI, security, and technical support, success is easily defined as "how busy is everyone?" The more a district relies on their devices the greater the need for additional technicians, security monitoring experts, data managers, and device management tools. Ultimately the technology department should hope to see a shift from being a keyboard fixer to being more of a support professional to the Instructional Coaching Department when they work with teachers and students in the classroom.

The Instructional Coaching Level

At its core, the Instructional Coaching Department's job is to make one simple transformation in the school district. They need to shift one question in order to be considered successful. The question that needs to be shifted is the question of "How do I…" and it needs to be shifted to "What is…" The "how do I" questions are very personalized questions usually constructed for a teacher to get a quick answer and move on with their day. "What is" questions on the other hand are often the start of long conversations that result in meaningful long-lasting coaching sessions.

- "What is one way that I can bring video into my classroom?"

- “What is an application that I can use with my students for this chapter?”
- “What is a better way to teach this lesson?”

Once a coach has teachers asking questions that invite long conversations, they know that they are being successful. This is not easy, and it does take time for a coach to actually coach their staff members into asking questions this way but, once the system is clicking the coach is unstoppable.

The Principal Level

I remember having a conversation with one of my principals a few years ago. I was in my third year as an Instructional Coach in the district and we were discussing the fact that the principal wasn’t sure if I was making an impact in their building. During that conversation, we happened to be walking down the hallway and came to a bulletin board where the principal commented to me that the work being displayed was at a higher level than had ever been in the past. I shared that I had been working with that particular teacher for the last few weeks. Wondering why the work then wasn’t presented in a digital format, I shared that in order for me to meet my goals as a coach, I first needed to get myself to their level and start from there. The fact that the teacher started to, in my third year, work with her in the classroom on any type of lesson was a huge improvement. This was a turning point in my relationship with that principal because they started at that moment to understand that the culture shift, I was attempting to make was going to be not measured in lessons, but in school years.

The Teacher Level

Defining success for a teacher is pretty easy. There is a simple formula that helps to define success. The formula is “distance over effort.” Meaning, how much can a teacher accomplish in the last amount of time? If a teacher can buy into a new system that allows them to get more done and bring less home at the end of the week, they will do it with a big smile on their face. Traditionally, culture shift is the most difficult for the teacher because so much of what is being shifted and moved around directly falls at the classroom level.

- Analog turns to digital.
- State Standards turn into National Standards.
- New procedures turn into policy

Everything that ultimately is affected by a culture change lands at the feet of the teacher. Their definition of success is often the hardest of all educational levels, and it should be. Too often change is created at the district level to support the district and not the teacher. This then leads to unrest in the staffing ranks which leads to turn over which … well … let’s jump up and reread the Superintendent section one more time.

The Student Level

The last, largest, and most important population in the school district are the students. They are the ones usually with the smallest voice but have the largest series of accomplishments to brag about when a district successfully goes through a dynamic and dramatic culture shift.

Students can define a successful culture shift by touting their graduation numbers, their increased SAT scores, and their high percent of college acceptance letters all they want, but that isn't the only way that a student body can share the fact that their school district has gone through a tremendous transformation at every level of the educational system.

So, how do students determine the success of a digital transformation?

They ultimately show the success of their district's transformation and the success of the Strategic Plan by being great kids. They show up for after school study sessions and they attend their school musicals. They stay at school late on a Friday to cheer their football team on in the blistering cold and they do so each and every week. They come to school wearing their school spirit and they paint their faces during homecoming. They do this not because it is a fun thing to do. They do this because the school has provided an environment where ultimately, the students ARE the culture of the school. They set the stage for what learning should be and how teachers should be teaching them. They bring their knowledge of how to be a digital native with them and invite teachers, coaches, and administrators to meet them where *they* are to help *them* prepare for *their* futures … together. They do this because they come to school every day to remind us that it's not about the data, it's not about the standards, it's not about the devices, and it's not about the bulletin boards. Successful transformation starts and ends with our students. Each and every day … and we can't skip one.

Chapter 17

Stories from Instructional Coaches and Digital Learning Leaders

In 2011 I had an idea to create a podcast where I would bring on educators from around the world to learn more about the world of educational technology and together, we would share the stories of classrooms, teachers, and students. Since then, I have had the privilege of interviewing thousands of amazing teachers, administrators, educational technology companies and students.

When the TeacherCast website was first launched and for every day of the next 12 years, it had one slogan on the top of every page. "A Place for Teachers to Help other Teachers." I did that by creating a network of educators who would contribute to the website through their writing, research, experiences, videos, and professional resources.

When I decided to write a book, I wanted to not just write a story about how Instructional Coaches and Digital Learning Leaders can successfully change the culture of their school districts, I wanted to do so with the help, voices, and stories of other teachers, coaches, and administrators to create "a book for teachers to help other teachers."

In order to make this possible, I reached out to several members of my professional and personal learning network and asked them a series of questions with the hopes that you may learn from them and their experiences, the same way that you might if you were listening to the podcast.

Impact Standards Instructional Coach and Digital Learning Leaders Q&A

Getting the Job

What prepared you to become an Instructional Coach or Digital Learning Leader?

- It was a combination of my own early experiences as a teacher. I needed help and couldn't find a support system- then I moved schools and was part of the first cadre of Critical Friends Groups and I really saw the power of collegial coaching. I wanted to do THAT, so I found a graduate program that helped me understand what that meant and how to do it well. - Laura Thomas

- Graduate school propelled me to start thinking differently about my classroom. This is especially true when integrating ISTE standards and the SAMR model into the Social Science courses I was teaching. My school site recognized me as the "tech guy", but this quickly moved me into being utilized at the school site leadership level and the district level of with various committees looking after technology, grading practices, and curriculum. These opportunities pushed me to be better and learn more about what was going on in education. I read. I read a lot from authors who knew more than I did about Edtech, but more importantly pedagogy. Stacey Roshan comes to mind, as her book was one of the first ones that I encountered that resonated with my flipped classroom and consider the problem/student before the tool. The relationship I had with Scott Nunes helped me consider being part of a larger community (PLN) than my own school and district. The world is big with phenomenal educators and leaders that are more than willing to support the work we are all doing. This led me to build relationships with Microsoft friends via the MIE Expert community, Edpuzzle coaches, and the Kami community on their Facebook group and ambassador program (Kami Heroes). All of this led me to find the confidence to speak more at conferences, which made me feel ready to lead more in the area of education. The more I speak (even now), the more I learn about what teachers need, what teachers say, and what teachers feel in the remarkable work that they do every single day beyond my memory of my classroom. While I never became an instructional coach in the traditional sense, I eventually found myself a Teacher Success Champion at Kami where I support teachers across the United States in Edtech. - Steve Martinez

- I shadowed my digital learning coach on my campus. I talked to her about scenarios and how the job worked. I read coaching books to prepare for this job. I asked my principal for support and leadership opportunities. She let me present at staff meetings for our book study. I worked on this for 2 years to be ready for my coaching position. - Lisa Hockenberry

- As a second-grade teacher, I was hungry to learn new technology tools and instructional strategies. Any time we received PD that included either of these things, I would race back to my classroom and plan a way to use something new that day. I knew if I didn't, I would quickly forget what I'd learned. Over time, I developed a reputation as a trailblazer. When a district-level technology coaching position was created, my administrator recommended me for the job. - McKenzie Fuller

- My years in the classroom were the best preparation for becoming a coach. No course or theory will prepare you better than the practical experience of having your own classroom - regardless of the content. The comment I heard most often at the beginning of my coaching career was, "You were in the classroom. You understand." I have kept that forefront in my mind with all I do. To have walked in their shoes - learning new faces, pivoting with change, the parents, the demands from admin, the planning and prep work, and so much more - allows me to empathize with them and see ways in which I can help them. - Sarah Kiefer

- I was the first Instructional Coach hired in our district. I was likely chosen because I had experience as a curriculum designer and had used this skill on numerous occasions within school projects and district-led projects - Cammie Kannekens

What advice would you have for educators going through the job interview process?

- Remember- you're interviewing them as much as they're interviewing you. - Laura Thomas

- Lead with learning, never with tech. Focus on student moves and student engagement - Adam Juarez

- The big skill set that I think has been most important in recent years is classroom management. For me, and perhaps relevant here, is HOW do you as a teacher connect with students in a meaningful way & WHY do you have the desire to make that connection in the first place. I have seen educators enter the classroom because they love their content. I have seen educators enter the classroom because they love helping students. Ideally, and hopefully, you want both. If this is you, make that known in an interview. – Steve Martinez

- I would say to truly listen and observe for opportunities in your building. There is always a coaching opportunity in your building. Listen to the coaches in your building and strive to understand the nuances of this role. – Lisa Hockenberry

- Do your research - know the district's priorities and be prepared to share strategies you might use to support those in your role. It's also helpful to know what other successful districts are doing, and how their practices might be implemented locally.

Ask a lot of questions and be prepared to wear a lot of hats. Your job won't be exactly the same as anyone else's, and that's okay! – McKenzie Fuller

- Be honest. Being a coach is HARD. You can be a great classroom instructor, but that doesn't always mean coaching is a good fit. Display and share your accomplishments, but also be willing to learn. Relationships are the key to being a successful coach. - Sarah Kiefer

- While it is important to show that you are competent with technology, it is important to also make an even bigger effort to show your competencies in instructional and strategic design. Show that you can work with relatively little supervision and that you are a problem solver -there will always be lots of problems to address in a role like this! And more than anything else, be prepared to have examples of how you can build and maintain relationships. - Cammie Kannekens

Things To Do Once You Get the Job

What was one of the first things you did once you accepted the position to get ready for the upcoming school year?

- Listen and learn- figure out what the "preserve and protects" are for the community, what the cornerstones of the foundation are, and what the growing edges may be. Start with the assets and the strengths of the community and if you can't find any? Keep learning. - Laura Thomas

- I signed up for a 3-day Google Workspace boot camp. I wanted to learn how to use the tools better, but I also wanted to watch an expert teach technology over a sustained period of time. The content and skills were great, but more importantly, I learned instructional strategies that worked well in a PD setting, and ones to avoid. – McKenzie Fuller

- I was visible. There wasn't any space for an office, so I didn't really have a choice ... BUT I am glad I didn't have one. I was in the elementary buildings, so I "camped" in the media centers, so I was highly visible to the teachers as they cycled through classrooms on their media times. Just BEING there allowed me to start building relationships and getting to know the teachers. It was also an exciting time for them to ask quick questions. Building relationships is KEY to a coaching position. - Sarah Kiefer

Describe your first interactions with your administrator and/or principals and how did that set up the upcoming school year.

- I started by asking what outcomes they were hoping for- what did they want people to know, do, understand, create, etc.? That conversation helped us get clear about our goals and we could make a plan from there. - Laura Thomas

- Let them know I would not be reporting back to them about teachers, but I'd give them weekly updates on what I've worked on with teachers for them to go observe - Adam Juarez

- As a district coach, I work with five elementary schools, a middle school, and a high school. That first fall, I met with each administrator and simply asked questions: What is going well this fall? What challenges are you seeing? How can I support your team? This opened the door to further conversations, and I jumped at every opportunity I could find to be in buildings. After that initial meeting, administrators invited me into their buildings to meet with their teachers, which led to invitations classrooms as well. – McKenzie Fuller

- I was split between 2 buildings - one where the principal was incredibly open to my being there and one where there was far more hesitation. I didn't force myself on the building - but I did have conversations, and I really listened to what was said. It's amazing how much you can learn about people by paying attention to their body language. I also kept my mouth shut and only shared opinions when I was asked. I learned the climate and culture of the building. This afforded me the time I needed to understand how the building operated and gain the trust of both principals. - Sarah Kiefer

- My Instructional Coach position was created mid-year by a new superintendent. Two of us were hired. As this role was very new to our district We were basically told by our superintendent to "figure out how to best help teachers become better teachers." We were able to purchase a set of six Breakout EDU kits and a class set of virtual reality viewers - Google Expeditions and Breakout were the door opener to many classes! - Cammie Kannekens

Creating Successful Systems

What systems did you create for yourself in your new position? (Website, Digital Forms, Newsletter etc.) Describe one of these systems and how/why you designed it this way. Was it ultimately successful?

- I usually started by asking the teachers what their preferences were and then we built out from there. – Laura Thomas

- Forms and Sites. This system became my Google Innovator project. - Adam Juarez

- I created a one-stop shop spreadsheet for myself. The first tab is my schedule and what campus I'll be on. The next tab is my resource page. I put all links and important information that I need on a daily basis. I have several tabs for documentation. Depending on what work I'm doing with the teacher depends on the tab. I have a tab for working in classrooms, 1:1 with teachers, working with teams, etc. This spreadsheet has helped me track my work and where I need to be and with who. The tabs with documentation help with my end-of-year evaluation as well. I designed it to be my one-stop shop document and it has been so helpful. - Lisa Hockenberry

- One of the first things I did was build a coaching website. I wanted to have a single spot where teachers could find all of the things I was sharing via email, newsletter, and professional development. Over the last four years, it's evolved significantly, and I've had to learn to be okay with that. I've deleted resources, pages, even full sections that are no longer relevant or useful to my teachers. It's sad to see so much hard work disappear, but that's just the reality of a coaching job - especially when you're working with technology! – McKenzie Fuller

- One of the first things I did was schedule "morning PD". I wanted to put myself in front of the staff so they could get to know me but also, they could learn and count the professional development for their own learning plans. I relied on tools that would allow me to show them quick and easy activities to do with their students and quite often, I shared about programs they were already expected to use. It was fairly successful - with a certain group in each building - but I do not do this anymore because of time constraints. I do not regret doing this morning PD - it allowed me to build relationships and get to know part of the staff. - Sarah Kiefer

- Coaches love systems! I created a Coaches website, monthly newsletter, and Google Forms to gather feedback - probably too many Google Forms at the start! - Cammie Kannekens

Building Relationships

Please share a story (or provide a few tips and suggestions) about how you build positive relationships with your peers and administrators.

- I try to make sure to celebrate teachers as much as possible. It's as simple as a little note when you leave their room after doing a learning walk in their room. I also try to ask questions about things happening in their life that I learn from conversations or social media. Those little interactions make big gains. It shows them you are listening and caring. - Lisa Hockenberry

- I asked someone at the district office to send me a list of all the teachers and administrators and their birthdays. I ordered a huge box of cards on Amazon (they're not terribly expensive) and started writing notes to people on their birthdays. It was a little awkward at first - I felt strange sending cards to people I'd never met. It was a great move, though, because it started conversations with SO many people! They would stop me in the hallway to say thanks or send follow-up emails, and I was able to connect fairly quickly with many of them. Birthdays are fun... even if someone doesn't like to celebrate theirs, it's nice to know that someone cares enough to recognize your special day! – McKenzie Fuller

- Be patient. Relationships take time. You can't rush to make them. They have to grow and that takes time. Be reserved. No one likes a loudmouth / know it all. Allow your actions to speak. Be honest, but you don't have to share all of your thoughts. Pay attention. Look for ways you can be of service to your peers and admin. You don't have to build websites or host weekly PDs (Professional Development) (Professional Development) ... you could be the person who takes needs and figures out how to address them. You don't have to have all of the answers, but you can be a person that will help figure out answers. - Sarah Kiefer

- Arrive early and stay late. I'm a district instructional coach, so I travel to schools, and as our district is rural, this can often mean up to an hour or more (one way) to reach a school. Before and after school is when teachers have a few moments to say, "Hey, I've been meaning to email you about....". Or, "I have a question I've been meaning to ask you...". Being available for these conversations has led to coaching cycles and positive relationships.

- Be extra nice to the administrative assistants. Take time to say "hi" and chit-chat with these ladies. Light up when you see them and greet them by name. I travel between 20 schools, so I'm always needing a little help from a secretary such as when I can't get the printing to work from my computer or I need some extra paper or some scissors. Because I take time to greet them and also offer technology help if they need it, they take my emails seriously and even read our coaching newsletters.

- If you make a promise, keep it. If you say you are going to do something, text yourself a reminder, put it in your calendar immediately, or stick a sticky note on your forehead...whatever it takes. Following through when you say you will do something builds trust and strengthens relationships over time. Likewise, making promises and then forgetting about them causes distrust. - Cammie Kannekens

Please share a story about meeting and interacting with a teacher or staff member that might have been reluctant to want to work with you.

- Many hesitant teachers saw me as IT or quasi-admin. Fixing projectors or computers is not my job, nor is covering a class for them to use the restroom, but doing those things once in a while helped build a relationship with those teachers - Adam Juarez
- Maria was a veteran teacher and an excellent one at that. Technology, however, caused a tremendous amount of frustration for her. She'd listen respectfully during PD sessions, and always sent me quick "thank you emails" after I sent out a newsletter, but never really seemed interested in what I was saying. I continued to send information and was intentional about saying hi and finding ways to connect around other topics when we crossed paths. Eventually, she invited me to her classroom to meet. She confessed her frustration around technology, asked for help, and warned me that she'd need slow, step-by-step instructions. I quickly agreed and it became a very mutually beneficial partnership. I taught her (and her students) skills using Chromebooks, and as she became more comfortable, she would model instructional routines around them. I'm fairly confident I learned more from her than she did from me! – McKenzie Fuller
- I was told to work with a teacher to convert a paper test to a Google Form. He was super reluctant. We only had a small bit of time to work before school, so over the few weeks it took to do this, I listened and guided and shared the benefits of a Form over paper or scantron. Ultimately, this led to a multi-year Friday morning scheduled session. His comment, "I'm willing to learn anything ... I just don't want to do it in a big group" caused me to rethink only offering morning PD. At that point, I began seeking out more small group or individual sessions with the staff. - Sarah Kiefer

Incorporating Digital Learning Standards

Please share a story about how you have incorporated the ISTE Standards for Educators into your Coaching or Digital Learning Leader position.

- Shortly after I was hired, a coach from a nearby district reached out and suggested I attend the ISTE Certified Educator Training that fall. She'd never gone before but had heard it would be good. I wasted no time in registering, and a few months later found myself in a room with other aspiring ISTE Certified Educators. We spent two days digging into the Standards for Students and Educators, and then set out to build our portfolios. This was, without a doubt, the most rigorous educational endeavor I've ever achieved, and it made a significant impact on my development as a coach. The Standards for Educators broadened my view of what a teacher leader should look like further than I ever imagined possible. One of the ways the ISTE Standards for Educators have impacted my position as a technology coach involves participation in a global digital community. Social media and networking have never held a tremendous amount of appeal. As a coach in a rural community, though, this has become a vital part of my own professional development. Through PLNs (Professional Learning Network) like the Certified Educator Community and Twitter, I've been able to curate and contribute ideas, form connections with others, and learn from incredible educators outside my immediate community. – McKenzie Fuller

Defining Success

How do you define success in your position at the end of the year?

- I usually set quality criteria with the folks I'm coaching, so we use those to reflect on our progress together. Success looks different for everyone, you know? That being said, if folks feel that they're better teachers (however they define "better") for having worked with me? That's a win. - Laura Thomas

- When I see teachers implementing technology into their day from the work we have done together. When I have teachers reaching out to me to work with me based on work I've done with other teachers. This always feels like a win. – Lisa Hockenberry

- Success is having a full calendar. Success is when teachers or administrators ask, "When are you coming back?" before I have a chance to suggest a next meeting. Success is when teachers want to work with you due to "word of mouth" stories. - Cammie Kannekens

How do you know if you are being successful in your position?

- If folks seek me out for help, send emails or tweets or texts asking questions. - Laura Thomas
- When kids ask me to come to their classes, but most importantly when hesitant teachers seek me out, not just the other way around - Adam Juarez
- I know I am successful as a coach because I have admin and teachers seeking me out to help with projects. At times it is a quick phone call to troubleshoot a Google application, another time it was to build a process of introducing STEAM activities in the classroom, and another time it is the request of a team of teachers to work through an idea for enhancing the learning in their classrooms. - Sarah Kiefer

Please share a success story about your Coaching or Leadership position

- The way I helped lead my staff during the beginning of distance learning. I created a massive crash course to train teachers in all they needed to teach remotely. - Adam Juarez
- I worked at 2 new campuses this year. I worked on building relationships with teachers and students. My success this year is that at both campuses I could walk down the hall and students and teachers would say "Hi Mrs. Hockenberry" This made me feel amazing to be seen and let me know that I was being successful in my building of relationships. - Lisa Hockenberry

Final Thoughts and Friendly Advice

What advice do you have for school districts interested in creating a Digital Learning Strategic Plan?

- Start with ISTE standards. Focus on student outcomes - Adam Juarez
- Get the input of all aspects of your learning community: admin, teachers, students, & parents. All are valuable voices - all have something to contribute. You should never aim to be "cutting edge" ... rather aim to be the support and structure your learning community needs right now with an eye to the next 5 years. Plans will need to be able to evolve and adapt and change every few years in order to best serve your community. Keep your plan focused on goals rather than tools. - Sarah Kiefer

What advice do you have for brand-new Instructional Coaches?

- Listen. You're a learner among learners and your job now is to listen, learn, and offer processes and resources as appropriate AND to connect expertise within the school or district. The wisdom is typically already in the room- it's your job to surface it. - Laura Thomas
- Teachers will be intimidated or skeptical of you. Honor their years of experience and skill set. Focus on those things and build from there. Meet them where they're at. - Adam Juarez
- Focus on learning strategies and structures rather than tools. Seek out those who are willing to collaborate and spotlight these adventures. Take your time and build authentic relationships. Be mindful of your time and abilities - do what you say you are going to do. Be punctual and reliable. Be honest - if you really don't know or have an answer, say that. And be willing to learn from those who do or figure out where you can find the answers. Be patient. Much of coaching will happen naturally if you let it. - Sarah Kiefer

What advice do you have for brand-new Digital Learning Leaders?

- Give student work and teacher successes an authentic audience - Adam Juarez
- Listen, observe, build relationships, and be humble. This job is a service leadership position and thrives on building a repertoire and relationships with teachers. - Lisa Hockenberry

What advice do you have for the readers of this book?

- Reach out to the author and to the folks featured here- they're happy to help you solve problems! – Laura Thomas

- Share your learning from this book for all of us to learn with you - Adam Juarez
- Start small - choose one strategy to implement and commit to doing it well. It's easy to hear about the incredible things that are happening around us and become overwhelmed. We forget that EVERYONE has taken time to grow into their roles. Give yourself grace, and the freedom to learn and grow over time. – McKenzie Fuller
- Learn. Constantly learn. Don't stop learning. It doesn't have to be learning in degrees or certificates; it can be by reading, building a PLN, joining webinars, or networking. Others will be looking at you - watching you - and if they see you constantly learning, they will follow. Think of the teachers who are "done" .... students don't want to be in their class. They won't love learning. Think of teachers who continually learn ... students want to be with them. They follow their lead. They are inspired by this. Understand that at times learning is hard and sometimes it's easy and sometimes it's fun and sometimes it feels stupid but it's ALWAYS worth it. – Sarah Kiefer

Conclusion

Since 2011 I have practically learned everything that I know about educational technology, pedagogy, and how to support teachers and students by having amazing conversations on the podcast, at conferences, and by watching instructional videos created by educators just like you. These conversations and PD sessions not only have supported me in my journey as an Instructional Coach and Digital Learning Leader but have been archived on TeacherCast for all to see and learn from as well.

Conclusion

"Hello, welcome to the TeacherCast Educational Network. My name is Jeff Bradbury. Thank you for joining us today and making TeacherCast your home for professional development."

Since July 2011, I have had the honor of beginning thousands of podcast episodes, instructional videos, and workshop sessions the same way.

Thank you, thank you for taking the time to read this book and for spending time with me today. TeacherCast always has been and always will be "A Place for Teachers to Help other Teachers." I hope that this book and the stories inside have helped you and will be able to help and support your teachers and students.

This book, a 14-year journey is designed to be the pebble that you can use to toss into the water to begin making ripples. It is meant to assist you, the Digital Learning Leader in creating a culture change in your district that combines digital learning and core curricular standards to create a consistent vision for instruction throughout the whole K12 journey.

How do you achieve this?

By preparing your Instructional Coaching department for success and allowing them to collaborate with administrators, certified staff, and non-certified staff to ensure that there is one clear goal that the district reaches at the end of the school year.

When making the decision to take this journey, there will be a constant reminder that the path will not be easy. As district leadership rotates, the vision will need to be adjusted. As new and emerging technologies appear in classrooms the vision will need to be adjusted.

The one thing that should remain constant in your district is the need to have a cohesive vision for what classroom instruction should look like. Once everyone is onboard with that vision, the rest of the process becomes the result of hard work and dedication to your strategic plan.

If you would like more information about where to start or how to take the first step, please feel free to contact me with any questions. I am always excited to work with school districts, digital learning leaders, and instructional coaches.

On behalf of everyone who has supported me in drafting this book and everyone who helped me write, edit, and publish this book ...

Keep up the great work in your classrooms and continue sharing your passions ... with your students.

Jeff Bradbury

Visit the Impact Standards Companion Website

Scan the QR code below to unlock a treasure trove of exclusive resources, including in-depth blog posts, dedicated podcast episodes, and our comprehensive workbook—all designed to help you implement the strategies from Impact Standards in your educational setting.

About the Author

Jeffrey D. Bradbury

Jeff Bradbury is an ISTE Award-winning and globally recognized digital learning strategist, educational broadcaster, public speaker, entrepreneur, and triplet dad. His powerful message has inspired thousands of educators through the TeacherCast Educational Network, where he uses Future Ready skills to promote digital innovation in the classroom with a focus on equity and diversity. Jeff has served the ISTE Community as an ASCD Emerging Leader, ISTE Community Leader and is the current (2025) ISTE Ambassador supporting the ISTE Certified Educator community. In 2025, he was recognized for his service to education through the ISTE+ASCD 20 to Watch Award.

A sought-after professional development presenter and co-founder of Edcamp New Jersey, Jeff has presented at ISTE, FETC, and Podcast Movement conferences. He has delivered keynote addresses for Pearson, Podcast Mid-Atlantic Conference, and Columbia University's Teachers College. Jeff has also won multiple regional, divisional, and district-level speaking competitions from Toastmasters International.

Jeff is a Google for EDU Certified Innovator, Trainer and Certified Coach, Microsoft Innovative Educator Expert, Trainer & Fellow, and TEDx Speaker. In 2012, he was recognized as one of the Top 50 Educators Using Social Media at the inaugural Bammy Awards and received three nominations for Innovator of the Year. EdTech Digest named Jeff one of the Top 30 Educators in Educational Technology in 2019. He proudly serves on the board for ISTE New England is the creator of Google Educator Instructional Coaches, and is an ISTE Community Leader and ISTE Certified Educator.

After several years as a Music Director for orchestras and opera companies in the New York and Philadelphia regions — including a performance at Carnegie Hall, Jeff transitioned from the musical stage to become a Technology Coach in a K12 school district. In this role, he supported the district's digital transformation into a Google for Education-focused learning environment. He also developed “Cardinal University”, a standards-focused professional development program designed to foster innovative instruction in the classroom in the district.

Created as a passion project to assist teachers in understanding educational technology, Jeff recorded the first TeacherCast Podcast in the summer of 2011. Since then, the TeacherCast Educational Network has supported K12 education through it's educational podcasts, video tutorials, professional development sessions, educational blog posts, and newsletters.

In 2018, Jeff created the TeacherCast Instructional Coaches Network and launched the podcast, "Ask the Tech Coach" to support Instructional Coaches working hand in hand with teachers in the classroom. His work with Instructional Coaches and supporting school districts digital transformation has earned him several international global recognitions including the ISTE Instructional Coaches Award.

He has served K12 Education as an Orchestra Teacher, Middle School Broadcasting and Technology Teacher, Instructional Coach, and Director of Digital Learning.

In 2025, Jeff took on a new challenge as an Adjunct Professor at Fort Hays State University, teaching courses that help educators earn their Master's Degree in Instructional Coaching.

For more information about his work, please visit:

- www.JeffreyBradbury.com
- www.TeacherCast.net

"The journey doesn't end with the tool; it begins with the people.

By simplifying the system, we don't just change the classroom—we amplify the impact for every student, every day."

Rewriting the Narrative: From Process to Impact

Building Sustainable Systems for Coaching, Leadership, and Digital Learning

With two decades of experience in the trenches of K-12 education, Jeff Bradbury specializes in simplifying complex educational systems to help leaders amplify their impact. His mission is to move schools beyond the "one-and-done" workshop by designing workflows that prioritize people over tools.

Strategic Support Pillars

Instructional Coaching Systems

- **Design from Scratch**: Build a coaching program anchored in clear vision and measurable standards.
- **Sustainable Workflows**: Create coaching cycles that reduce frustration and increase teacher retention.
- **Coach-to-Coach Mentorship**: Provide the tactical training coaches need to lead with confidence.

Purposeful Digital Integration

- **Workflow Over Apps**: Shift the focus from "using tech" to "solving problems" through strategic tool selection.
- **Eliminate Overwhelm**: Replace fragmented tech training with cohesive digital learning plans.
- **Classroom Resonance**: Ensure technology serves as a natural catalyst for student engagement.

Strategic Leadership & Culture

- **Vision-Driven Planning**: Align administrative goals with achievable, long-term strategic roadmaps.
- **Change Management**: Navigate complex transitions by focusing on the "Mission → Journey → Resonance" framework.
- **Culture Coaching**: Support leaders in building a resilient, innovation-ready school environment.

Why the "Impact" Approach?

Jeff Bradbury is an ISTE+ASCD award-winning educator who understands that true change happens when systems are simplified. He doesn't just offer sessions; he builds partnerships. By blending tactical EdTech expertise with strategic leadership coaching, Jeff ensures that your teachers, coaches, and students don't just survive the journey—they thrive within it.

Ready to take the next step? Visit www.jeffreybradbury.com/contact or use the QR code to connect!

www.ingramcontent.com/pod-product-compliance
Lightning Source LLC
LaVergne TN
LVHW061221100826
845148LV00004B/816
* 9 7 9 8 2 1 8 9 2 7 4 6 2 *